BLESSED JOHN NEUMANN

Blessed
JOHN NEUMANN

Bishop of Philadelphia

by James J. Galvin, C.SS.R.

Foreword by JOHN J. KROL
Archbishop of Philadelphia

HELICON   •   *Baltimore — Dublin*

Helicon Press, Inc.
1120 N. Calvert St.
Baltimore, Maryland 21202

Library of Congress Catalog Card Number 64-14665

Nihil Obstat: Nicolaus Ferraro, S.R.C. Adsessor, *Fidei Sub-Promotor Generalis* Romae, 18 Maii 1963

Imprimi Potest: Gulielmus Gaudreau, C.SS.R., *Sup. Gen. et Rect. Mai.* Romae, 1 Martii, 1963

Nihil Obstat: Eugene M. Sullivan, *Censor Librorum* Philadelphiae, Feb. 28, 1963

Imprimatur: ✠ Joannes J. Krol, *Archiepiscopus Philadelphiensis* Philadelphiae, 5 Martii 1963

PRINTED IN THE UNITED STATES OF AMERICA BY

GARAMOND/PRIDEMARK PRESS, BALTIMORE, MARYLAND

For one who knows Blessed Neumann far better than I: my mother.

FOREWORD

The performance of simple deeds with constancy and perfection in the midst of great difficulties spells heroism in any servant of God. That is why Pope Benedict XV, in proclaiming the heroic degree of the virtues of John N. Neumann, declared: "We cannot . . . call commonplace the life of a Bishop who, while furthering the material prosperity of his flock, wrought much more to root out abuses, to reform morals, to lift to higher planes the flock committed to his care. . . . Precisely because of the simplicity of his works, we find in them a strong argument for saying to the faithful of whatever age, sex or condition: You are all bound to imitate the Ven. Neumann."

Generally, servants of God elevated to the honors of the altar are proposed as models of particular virtues, vocations or apostolates. It is exceptional for one such servant to be proposed as a model for all "faithful of whatever age, sex or condition." The Venerable John N. Neumann is such an exception.

Because of his diligence, application and self-discipline, he is a model for seminarians. The ardent desire to be a missionary in America which constrained him to study foreign languages; to practice self-mortification in preparation for the hardships he would encounter as a missionary; to venture as a penniless immigrant to the land of immigrants, without prior assurance of being accepted for priestly ordination, qualifies him eminently as a model for foreign missionaries.

His tireless work as a secular priest of the Diocese of New York, ministering to the needs of his flock, and giving particular attention to those who because of language or distance barriers required special care, qualifies him as a model for all secular priests engaged in pastoral work.

As a member and superior of the Redemptorist Congregation, his life of humility and obedience, as well as his indefatigable activity, qualifies him as a model for religious. He was the founder of a religious community of women, and was responsible for revitalizing other communities. He was a retreat master, spiritual director, and confessor.

As the Fourth Bishop of the Diocese of Philadelphia, he was confronted with seemingly insurmountable problems. With great patience, charity and decisiveness, he resolved one problem after another. He showed affectionate concern for the young, the poor and for the immigrants. He introduced the Forty-Hours Devotion, and laid a solid foundation for a Catholic school system, which is historically unique, and which draws on his inspiration as it constantly develops and expands. It is to his credit that the Archdiocese of Philadelphia, which today ranks eighth in total Catholic population, ranks next to first in the total number of students in Catholic educational institutions.

As a Bishop, John N. Neumann's energetic activity was typical of the activity which characterizes the ministry of American bishops and priests. He was engrossed in administrative problems, forever trying to provide parochial, educational and charitable facilities for a growing flock. But all such external activity was but a natural fruit of a deep interior spirituality and zeal.

Bishop Neumann was deeply aware of our Lord's words: *I have chosen you and have appointed you that you should go and bear fruit, and that your fruit should remain (Jn 15:16).* He knew that his sanctification, as well as the sanctification and edification of souls entrusted to his care, depended upon the faithful and effective discharge of the divinely appointed duties of his priestly and episcopal ministry. He knew that *Not everyone who says to me, Lord, Lord, shall enter the kingdom of heaven; but he who does the will of my Father in heaven shall enter the kingdom of heaven (Mt 7:21).* He knew that his pastoral responsi-

bilities demanded an outward expression of his interior spirituality
—his life of prayer and meditation.

As an unworthy successor of John Neumann in the See of
Philadelphia, I am pleased to recommend this biography of my
illustrious and saintly predecessor. As his Eminence Cardinal
Cicognani wrote in 1952: "We need John Neumann, his example,
his encouragement and his intercession."

It is my fervent prayer that this book and the inspiring story
of Bishop Neumann's life receive the widest possible circulation,
and serve as a powerful encouragement for all, but especially for
the clergy and religious, to strive for sanctity through the performance of the simple duties of their ministry.

✠ JOHN J. KROL
Archbishop of Philadelphia

May 2, 1963

CONTENTS

1

IV

In journeyings often,
in peril of water,
in peril of robbers,
in peril of my own nation,
in peril of the Gentiles,
in peril in the city,
in peril on the sea,
in peril from false brethren . . .

2 Corinthians 11:26

PROLOGUE

This is Blessed John Neumann, C.SS.R.,
fourth Bishop of Philadelphia.

Not the white-maned Cardinal of England,
This Neumann never knew the bells of Oxford,
the lamps of London Bridge.
English, he learned from books!

Ante-bellum America, not Victorian England
was this John Neumann's battleground.
He knew our Yankee caperings and curios:
mule-bells on the Erie towpath,
the rowdy chanteys of the log rafters
poling down the Allegheny past Pittsburgh in April,
the pink of dogwood in the Poconos,
the port-lamps of China Clippers on the Chesapeake,
the street names of old Philadelphia.

Half his grown years were under the Stars and Stripes.
He was an American citizen.
Andy Jackson was in the White House
when immigrant John Neumann landed in Manhattan.
Abraham Lincoln was rising to national prominence
when Bishop Neumann was laid in his Philadelphia tomb
in 1860, at the age of forty-nine.

I

1. THURSDAY'S CHILD

March the twenty-eighth. A raw mist crept up that morning off the Schuylkill, drifting eastward across Philadelphia. Old Meg Sloane stamped her feet at the corner of Broad Street and Sassafras, rattling an iron ladle in her steaming vessel of soup. Somewhere to the southeast a bell commenced ringing.

"Pepperpot!" shouted old Meg. "Pepperpot! Just the thing to take the chill off your bones."

She banged her ladle on the iron pot to compete with the churchbell.

St. Mary's bell it was, over on Spruce Street, where a man stood in the little sacristy vesting for the Mass of Holy Thursday. Today was a semi-anniversary. Six months ago this morning at Bardstown, Kentucky he, Father Michael Egan, Franciscan, had been consecrated first Bishop of Philadelphia. He had three priests and four churches in his episcopal see that Holy Thursday morning of the year 1811.

A hundred miles or more to the southwest, in the Maryland hills, twenty teen-age boys awoke in a drafty garret, jumped out of bed, knelt on the pinewood floor. There were smiles on their still drowsy faces. No Latin syntax today! No Math! No French conjugations! Saint Mary's Emmitsburg had no school on Holy Thursday, the start of the Easter holidays. The log cabin schoolroom was empty. Father John Dubois could relax for nearly fourteen days, his second Easter as teacher, headmaster, founder —and idol of Emmitsburg. Schoolmastering was at times a trying cross.

Across the seas in the heart of Christendom, the dome of St. Peter's hung white in the Roman sunshine. Too white; and much too quiet. Today there ought to be bells. And *Vivas,* too! But the Holy Father, Pius VII, was not in Rome; had not been for almost two years. As a matter of bitter fact, the aged Pontiff was held at Savona, incommunicado, the captive of Napoleon Bonaparte.

In Ireland, Daniel O'Connell's was a rising name. That morning in Dublin, there had been bells for the *Gloria,* bells to scatter the gulls over Anna Liffey, to ruffle the placid swans! At the moment, children from all over Dublin were gathering for Catechism, as was custom on feast day and Sunday. At Saint Nicholas of Myra's on the gospel side of the church, the ten front benches bobbed with the heads of sixty-three boys and girls, giving answer to the four marks of the true Church, the seven capital sins. Heads and hands were quiet now, as sixty-three little heads gave undivided attention to a young man explaining the next lesson. His name was Frank Kenrick. He was sixteen and tall.

"And now, boys and girls, we'll go over and make a visit to the Blessed Sacrament. And . . . no class this Sunday, being that it's Easter."

Sixty-three heads bobbed agreement. Frank Kenrick smiled.

Emperor Napoleon Bonaparte, master of all Europe, that same March morning of 1811, had for the moment put the conquest of Britain and Russia from mind. He was down on his knees in the palace of the Tuilleries—not because it was Holy Thursday! *Mais non!* He was kneeling on the parquet floor of his wife's apartment, dangling a monogrammed egg-spoon before his little son, on the lap of the Empress Marie Louise. The "King of Rome," as he called him already, was exactly eight days old.

Nineteen-year-old Marie Louise was still a stranger to Paris. There but a year, her heart was homesick for the long green lawns of Schoenbrunn, for all the spires and towers of her Vienna. Notre Dame might be a glory on its island in the Seine, but *"Der alte Stefferl,"* St. Stephen's cathedral on the Danube, was home for young Marie Louise. There in Vienna, at the Italian church of Saint Mary of the Snows that same March morning, a priest sat hearing confessions. His name was Father Clement Hofbauer. He was Vicar General of the Redemptorists, an order still unknown in the Austrian empire; though he had hopes of establishing houses there, or—in America.

Finally, and here begins our story, directly north of Vienna, in the pretty Czech village of Prachatitz, some twelve miles southeast of Budweis, the cry of a new baby was heard. It rang like a tiny bell through the parish church of Saint Jakob, as the chill baptismal water touched his scalp.

The ceremony over, Father John Ledehey removed stole and white surplice, dipped quill in ink and, without asking any data of the beaming father, commenced to write. No need to ask information. He knew Mr. Philip Neumann with his comfortable knitting business. He knew the mother, Agnes Lebis, one of the neighborhood girls. The quill scratched the baby's name into the old Parish register: *John Nepomucene Neumann, born and baptized this twenty-eighth day of March in the year of our Lord 1811.*

"You chose a good patron for the boy, Herr Neumann. May he grow up to be as good a man as his namesake, St. John Nepomucene. He is the first to be annointed with the new chrism, blessed just this morning at Budweis."

The priest smiled.

"Who knows? Some day, he may be a priest."

The tiny red-faced baby squirmed in his blankets.

Philip Neumann smiled like sunrise. The priest blew two careful puffs of breath across the fresh ink, waited a moment and closed the book.

"You know the old saying, Herr Neumann: 'Thursday's child has far to go.' Well, he can be sure of warm stockings for the journey, made on his father's looms."

Herr Neumann beams happiness. He whispers something to the godmother, Frau Macek, the Burgomaster's wife. Frau Macek carries the baby over to the statue of our Lady. The others follow. They kneel and dedicate the newly christened baby to the mother of God.

Out in the vestibule the party pauses. They recall the good

wishes of the priest for their Thursday's child, little suspecting how far from home John Nepomucene Neumann will go. Three times he will cross the Atlantic. He will crisscross the wild forests of western New York, walking, ever walking. He will know almost every mountain and valley of eastern Pennsylvania—still walking, most of the way. He will go on horseback. He will travel by stagecoach, by steam train, by canalboat on an endless errand of love. Ohio will know him, and Delaware, too, and Virginia and Maryland. Half his days he will live on the other side of the world, under the Stars and Stripes, hurrying on his endless errand till the afternoon he dies. This Thursday's child has far to go, far indeed.

A quarter-century from this day in Prachatitz, the Emmitsburg schoolmaster will meet him during his first week in the New World. Cleansed of red ink and chalk dust, the right hand of John Dubois will then twinkle with a bishop's ring, his thumb will glisten with chrism and he will christen John Neumann a second time, ordaining him for the Diocese of New York.

Thirty years from this day in Prachatitz, a letter from America will reach Redemptorist headquarters in Vienna. By then, the saintly Clement Hofbauer will have died. But to his successor as Vicar General, word will come from Pittsburgh, in 1841, that new recruits are joining the Order overseas. They are beginning to take root in the New World.

"Our first Redemptorist novice is a young diocesan priest from Buffalo, Father John Neumann. May he be the first of many more here in the United States."

Dublin's teen-age catechist, Frank Kenrick, will also meet John Neumann, will kneel before him weekly in Baltimore for confession. Precisely forty-one years from this very March morning, Francis Patrick Kenrick, Archbishop of Baltimore, will consecrate John Neumann as his successor to the See of Philadelphia. And eight years later, he will ride up to his old See, to preach a last farewell at John Neumann's casket before interring him among his own. He will see tears in the eyes of many. He will weep himself. He will, perhaps, even hear some old woman refer to the deceased as a "saint" and, silently, he will agree.

Thursday's child has far to go!

But for the moment, the first lap of his journey is a short one, a few minutes trip through the snow from the church door to a house in Upper Lane marked 129. Against the snapping March wind the little group sets out for home.

"Mama, Mama, here they come!"

The noses of two small girls press against an upper window, the baby's older sisters, Catherine and Veronica. Philip Neumann unlatches the door, and steps inside.

"Mother, I've brought him home to you a Christian. The priest hopes he'll be as good as St. John Nepomucene. He said he might someday be a priest!"

Neighbors came dropping in all evening: the tailor, the schoolmaster, the postman, the cobbler and his wife, the baker, the organist, paying their respects and commenting on the *"new man* of the house." The pun was the cobbler's and he clapped the happy father on the shoulder, chuckling at his own wit. Philip Neumann, as though he had never heard so clever a play on words, roared with contagious joy. The cobbler is waiting for a nip of Mother Neumann's homemade peach brandy. But this is Holy Week; Frau Neumann has strict opinions about Lent. There is no peach brandy that day even to celebrate the "new man of the house."

"Did you hear what they're saying, Herr Neumann? Napoleon and his Grand Army are marching into Russia."

Herr Neumann listens politely. He had much more important news. Baby John has spoken his first word!

"Herr Neumann, the mail coach from Budweis just brought word. The little Corporal got his coat tails scorched in Moscow. His army's in tatters and retreating for its life."

Napoleon's retreat seemed unimportant. John Neumann had taken his first step.

For more than a year the new baby basked in the family spotlight, banging his spoon while Papa Neumann said grace, chortling and drooling in the cozy kitchen during evening Rosary. No matter! He was fondled, smiled at, played with, kissed— rights preeminent of all small babies. But let no one titter at his antics during prayers! Papa Neumann ruled his household with such gently firm persuasion that one glance was enough. The spotlight dimmed out soon enough for little Johnny Neumann. By summer of 1812, Joan, his baby sister, had arrived.

Like small boys the whole world over, John crept and then toddled about the house on endless rounds of exploration, poking into nooks and closets, into mother's jars of cooking herbs, her sewing basket, the candlesticks on the family altar, the fire under the copper kettle on the hearth. But what held him especially spellbound was the clack and whirr of the busy looms downstairs. Four workmen managed the noisy shuttles, as the spindles paid out yarn and the knitted goods grew as by magic before his two big eyes.

Sometimes, if he promised to be good, Frau Neumann took him with her to church. She was a devout woman and hardly missed a morning Mass. As soon as he could talk, he learned his prayers; learned to speak with our Lady and the Saints as though they were part of the family, which, in fact, they were. Before bedtime, while Papa Neumann read by the lamp, puffing on his cherrywood pipe, Mother gathered the children about her to tell in her own words some story from the Bible, or from the life of their patron saints. She talked until the town hall clock boomed eight solemn bongs. Then she closed the book; kissed the children Good Night, tucked them in bed and tiptoed back to her work.

Now John had a baby brother. They called him "Wenzl," short for Wenceslaus.

One morning when the peaches hung sweet in the orchards of Prachatitz, Frau Neumann dressed her oldest son in a brand-new suit and packed him off to the village school. John Neumann was six years old.

"See, Mama, I can print an A."

"Look how well I write my name: *John Neumann.* Aren't it good."

"*Isn't,* John; not aren't!"

"Papa, today Father Schmidt told me I can make First Communion soon—I know all my catechism."

Each afternoon he brought some fresh bit of news from

school. "My little book-worm," his mother would call him. He was forever curled up in a corner with a book. Avid for knowledge, he never stopped frowning *whys*.

One spring evening when the moon hung big over the tall old firs of the Boehmerwald, he lay in the quiet house, his chin cupped in his fists, staring thoughtfully up through the garret window.

"Mother!" he called. There was urgency in his cry.

Thinking he must be sick, his mother dropped her darning and flounced quickly up the stairs to his room.

Sober as a little alderman, John turned round from the window.

"Mother, what keeps the moon from falling down?"

Whether Mother knew, or did not know the answer, she put one finger to her lip and said:

"Shh! You'll wake your little brother."

The baffled young scientist snuggled quietly under the cool sheet to ponder on outer space where God held great colored moons cavorting on strings—like that whiskered balloon-man at Kermess.

"Veronica, Mama, Papa—everyone! Father Schmidt asked me if I'd like to be an altar boy. He's going to teach me the prayers."

That was in the fourth grade; John Neumann was ten.

Father Schmidt, one of the young curates at Saint Jakob's, often dropped into the schoolroom for classes in catechism. He noticed in the front bench the quiet round-faced lad with the big serious eyes, hungrily drinking in everything.

After the usual bungling mistakes, John Neumann soon was letter-perfect as an altar boy; and punctual too. He loved sick calls, when you tinkled the bell and held a lighted candle before the priest, bearing viaticum to someone up the road.

On a May morning Father Schmidt took the boys for a hike into the nearby hills, naming all the flowers and trees and weeds they passed, along the way. He plucked one blossom and with the point of his penknife, showed them the different parts of the flower. He showed them the various leaf shapes and barks, the individual contour of each class of tree. Young Neumann was amazed, fascinated. Through the tiniest key-hole he was peering into the mind of God! Thereafter, the natural sciences were his passion, a love he fostered to the end.

But in the classroom one morning the teacher asked a question.

"What are you going to be when you grow up?"

One by one, the boys gave answer. John Neumann blurted out: "A barber."

During his last two years at the village school, twice each week, Neumann went to the rectory for lessons in Latin. That did not mean he was thinking of the priesthood. For any lad who planned to continue his studies, Latin was a basic branch. Since he had outgrown his fancy for barbering, there was medicine, law . . . even theology. Philip Neumann half-hoped his oldest boy would study medicine. Prachatitz could use a good doctor.

But Frau Neumann, in her usual businesslike way, got down on her knees and made a pact with the Patron Saint of Bohemia, St. John Nepomucene. She wanted John to be a priest.

One October morning in 1823, twelve-year-old John Neumann shook his father's hand, kissed his mother, waved to the neighbors, to Father Schmidt at Saint Jakob's, and set out over the hills for Budweis. There, with the Piarist Fathers, he was to begin the gymnasium course.

Thursday's child had far to go.

2. THE LONG WAY 'ROUND

All his life, it seemed, he had been on the way to school. Not that he minded school. John Neumann had a hunger for knowledge. Anyway, school was now at an end for him. These past two years he had spent completing his theology at Prague—*Zlata Praha*, as his mother called it—the golden city on the Moldau where his namesake Saint John Nepomucene had won his martyr's crown. Yesterday, he had come back to his Alma Mater at Budweis to take the final comprehensive examination. For five sweltering hours, he had stood under fire before the seminary faculty. He had weathered the ordeal. Fit for Holy Orders, they had judged him. But it was not quite as simple as that!

Today, a taller, older and a wiser John Neumann set out from Budweis over the hills for home. He had sent his trunk on ahead by stagecoach from Prague. He had written that he was coming. And now, unhampered by baggage, he walked with swinging arms and quick short strides, weighing matters over in his mind.

He knew every lap of these dozen miles by heart. Farms with their snow-white ducks and long-horned oxen. Buttercups, nodding in lush meadows to the chime of cow-bells, as the summer wind blew cool from the Boehmerwald. He knew them all, every haystack and plum tree, every curve and dip of the road. After long months in the stuffy city, these open hills worked like elixir. Up yonder was Nettolitz with its shrine of our Lady on the crest of a hill. Goyau, Skocic, Pfefferschlag, he knew them like the buttons on his coat! Further on he would come to the squat white churchspire of Chrobold. Two hills beyond that, was home. The road would curve gently to the left, sloping down to unfold his favorite panorama, a scene he had painted in oils last summer and given to his sister Catherine as a wedding gift. No matter how often he came to that turn of the road, the view brought a lump to his throat. Cupped in a ring of tiny hills lay Prachatitz, his home-town.

Worth all the months away was the magic of walking down

that country road into town. You could anticipate what would happen. Quietly you unlatch the door, tiptoe into the kitchen. Mother is busy at the hearth. Unobserved, you creep up behind her, blindfold her with your hands and whisper:

"Guess!"

(But no need for guessing! All day she's been awaiting you.) With a start of delight, she turns to clasp you to her heart.

"Welcome, John. Welcome home again."

You could anticipate it all! In a twinkling the girls appear; Veronica, Joan, Louise. Soon teen-age Wenzl comes through the open door at a bound to clasp your hand. And finally Dad comes up from his looms.

"Tell us, John; how was the year?"

The annual ritual begins, everyone talking at once. From his monthly letters home, they already know the answers, but it sounds better to hear him tell it himself. He loved studies, they know: History, Philosophy, Science, Theology. He had most of the New Testament down by heart, and the Old Testament too. Scripture was his passion. His trunk was crammed with commentaries on the Bible. His trunk held all sorts of things: books about Botany and Physics and Astronomy, his labelled collection of leaves, his microscope.

"John, you'd rather have books than britches!" Uncle Tomasek used to say.

"How many languages now, John?"

That was another sure-fire question. He holds up both hands folding the thumbs against his palms.

"One for each finger, mother."

He knows eight languages. German, of course. They speak that at home. Czech, too, his mother's language. After two years in Prague, Czech comes easy now. Then Greek and Latin. Besides, he has enough Spanish to read the letters St. Francis Xavier wrote from the Indies. He has translated many chapters of Blessed Liguori, too, from the Italian. Lastly, there is French and English. He *had* to acquire these, though at home he had never told them why. He needs French and English for America!

With two classmates, John Neumann planned to go overseas

to the wilds of North America as a missionary. One Yankee diocese with the apocalyptic name of Philadelphia was begging for priests who spoke German. Bishop Kenrick had already been informed by letter of three volunteers in Budweis. Neumann was waiting the answer from day to day. The plan was more than just a pipe-dream. Neumann was a practical sort. He had already made application for a passport, had filled out numberless forms and mailed them to Vienna. That would enable the three young missionaries to leave shortly after their first Masses at home.

But something had misfired. Yesterday at Budweis, after passing the examination for Holy Orders, Neumann learned that ordinations were indefinitely postponed. Bishop Rudzicka was not well. Anyway, there were enough priests in Budweis for the needs of the diocese.

These were the things that preoccupied John Neumann's mind that tenth day of July of 1835 as he hiked the dozen miles to Prachatitz. How would he ever break the news, not only that he was leaving home, but that ordinations were cancelled? He might even have to depart without a First Solemn Mass.

At home everything was in readiness, he knew. For months they had been excitedly writing him the details. The whole house scoured clean as a butterchurn. The roof rethatched. Blue gravel on all the walks. At every window, gay red geraniums in pretty green boxes. And a bright-hued Madonna newly frescoed on the house façade.

"And Papa," Louise had written, "Papa went up to Linz two weeks ago, and came back with a new pair of high black boots. He'll look smart as a Guardsman the day of the First Mass—embroidered shirt-cuffs, a new black vest with pink and orange needlepoint and fine white billowy trousers to tuck in his boots. . . ."

John Neumann's heart ached at the thought of their disappointment. His brain went numb as he lifted the latch of his mother's house.

But the household had already been told. Wenzl had been to Budweis the previous day, had run into Adalbert Schmid, John's classmate and friend.

"Poor, poor John," sighed Frau Neumann when she heard. She forgot her own chagrin. At the time, she had no inkling that a First Solemn Mass would never brighten her eyes, that John would leave home for America before the Bishop annointed his hands.

They were gathered at supper some weeks later. John described the wonders of Prague again for his mother, the thousand windows of the Hradcany, the chimes of St. Vitus' cathedral on Sunday morning, the soft golden tint of the city's old bridges and ramparts.

"I must tell you something that happened last winter."

He told of two imperial gentlemen in long fur coats who called at the Clementinum where he lived. They asked for someone who knew French, Spanish and Italian, preferably a young man in the ordination class.

"That's *you*, John," Frau Neumann interrupted pridefully. "What did they want?"

Here was John's chance to break the news that was gnawing his heart.

"They wanted a secretary for some Imperial Embassy, mother. But I wanted no part of *that*."

He toyed with the fork on his plate, praying for the right words.

"No, mother. The Lord has his embassies too. Embassies in far away places—overseas. That's what I really want," he blurted, "to go to America as a missionary!"

The look of the six faces round the table alarmed him. Joan's knuckles were rubbing her eye. Louise burst into tears. The line of his father's mouth drew taut. He sat there stunned. But Wenzl grinned. America!—Indians, fur-traders, gold. "Maybe I can go with you," he whispered. For the moment, Frau Neumann said nothing.

Suddenly John was doing all the talking, talking more than he had ever done in a lifetime. Passports! Red tape! Adalbert Schmid, his classmate who was going too! Sailing ships! The Atlantic! The expected letter from Bishop Kenrick of Philadelphia! Austria's new mission society the Leopoldine Verein that would pay his passage! The wonderful letters from missionaries they published in their *Annale!* Indians near the Great Lakes! Immigrants by the boat-load with no priests to take care of them —John Neumann was talking for dear life lest anyone hobble his heart's desire.

He told how the idea first came in Budweis some two years ago—as he sat in Scripture class listening to Father Koerner explain the second epistle to the Corinthians. The professor, reading St. Paul's account of hardships endured to spread the Gospel, looked up at the class and said:

"There are priests today, in America, who can match those hardships of St. Paul. . . . And some of you may one day join them in the New World."

Just a passing remark, but it kindled a spark and a flame that tormented John Neumann's soul. Ever since, he had been in training for the hardships of North America. That was why he had studied English. On and on he talked while supper grew cold on his plate. His eyes were shining with his dream.

Frau Neumann's eyes were shining too, under a glaze of tears.

"If it's God will to take you away from us," she assured him, "who are we to stand in your way? If God wants it, he will see to it that you get safely to America."

But as the weeks of summer wore on, it almost seemed that God was opposed to his leaving home. Time after time, he was summoned to Budweis. Now it was the cathedral Chapter, demanding written permission from his parents before they would sanction his leaving the diocese. Now it was passport trouble. He had failed to complete the application forms. He needed an affidavit notarized. He must indicate precisely where in America he planned to reside. But he didn't know that. Bishop Kenrick had not answered his letter. Perhaps it was all a sign that God wanted him to be a priest at home. John Neumann prayed all the more.

Father Dichtl, his old friend and adviser in Budweis, had told him to expect obstacles. "When things look dark," he told him, "turn to our Lady." Neumann did. All summer long, when not in Budweis on business, he hiked the countryside on pilgrimage.

Bohemia is dotted with rustic shrines of our Lady; Goyau, its bulbous spire deep in orchards of plums; Podsrp of the Seven Sorrows; Nepomuc, his patron's birthplace. High on a hilltop stood Strakonits, famed for a carved Madonna of Victories. Schwarzbach, Klattau, Pfefferschlag—their steps worn smooth by the knees of saints. One by one, John Neumann went to them, fasting most of the way, hardly stopping to rest his legs, never doffing his coat. He must harden his body for the ordeal of America. He must win our Lady's favor to his plan.

At Chrobold, a few miles from home, came an unexpected token of that favor. The local pastor invited the young cleric to come back in early September to preach on our Lady's birthday. Neumann was overjoyed. At home he breathed his little secret to no one; and at home no one told him that they knew, and planned to attend. John did not notice Veronica and his mother that evening in the crowded church as he preached his first sermon on Mary, the Help of Christians. At its close he quoted a little prayer he had learned as a small boy. He told his listeners to say it often themselves.

> *Mary, assist me in my needs. Intercede for me with God in life and death. Show thy maternal kindness. Present thy children's prayers to God who chose thee for his Mother.*

Tears of joy glittered on Frau Neumann's cheek. It was a prayer she had taught him to say each night before bed.

But even had his mother missed the joy of it, the neighbors would have brought her full report. Outside the church the pilgrims begged John Neumann's prayers, attempting to kiss his hand as though he were an ordained priest. All the way home they clucked approval. But, of course, there were some who must observe that for all his brains, it was a pity he hadn't sense enough to stay home near his mother. She was not growing any younger. He owed her that much at least, the solace of his priestly company in her declining years! Many a local busybody naively said as much to his face. Humbly he heard them out, smiled, tipped his hat and walked on. What the neighbors thought never swayed John Neumann. But it pleased him no end to learn that his mother had been at Chrobold for his sermon. It might well be the only such chance in her life. For, ordained or no, he was leaving for America, come spring.

The frost of Christmas lay on Prachatitz when John encountered a new obstacle to departure. From Budweis his friend Schmid wrote to tell him that the Leopoldine Society refused to defray their passage.

"For any such disbursement of missionary funds, a formal request in writing must come, not from the aspirant missionaries, but from the diocese adopting them."

More red tape! Still more uncertainty. Seven months now and no word from Bishop Kenrick of Philadelphia. Dear good God, what should he do? It was Christmas Eve. Through the snowy streets he trudged to midnight Mass and poured out his heart in prayer before the Crib.

Up in the loft of *Jakobskirche* in Prachatitz a dozen choir boys carolled to the magic of two Bohemian fiddles. The Mass was over. High overhead the church bell tumbled for bliss in a sky of crackling stars.

Vesale Vanoce!

The faithful poured into the street, shouting greetings to the neighbors.

Frohe Weihnachten! Merry Christmas!

John Neumann rose from his knees in the dusty clutter of the sacristy and quietly made for the door.

"Wait, John!" the Dean called out from the ambry, hustling out of his starched linen alb. His heart went out to the sad young man who by all rights ought to be singing Christmas Mass this year himself. Moreover, by clerical grapevine he knew that the Mission Society had curtly refused Neumann's request.

"I have two little chores, John, I'd like you to do tomorrow ... or rather, *today*."

Sober-faced, Neumann waited the pastor's pleasure.

"First," twinkled the Dean, "I want you to go home and eat a good dinner at your mothers. It must be a long time since you've had roast goose, with her special Christmas stuffing, apple, chestnut and raisin!"

The thin mouth puckered with devilment.

"And the second thing:"

He reached out and gripped the young man's shoulder affectionately.

"The second thing: forget about the Leopoldine Society! Cheer up, John, I think we can find a way to get your fare for America. *Vesale Vanoce.*"

Merry Christmas indeed! John Neumann glowed with gratitude. He stepped lightly into the frosty morning and glanced up at the stars. Aldebaran blazed like an emperor's ruby! The lopsided points of Orion hung low at the end of the Upper Lane. He remembered Canon Dichtl's counsel:

"When things look darkest, turn to the Mother of God. She will help."

She had done just that tonight. She had answered his prayer. No wonder in the Litany they called her the "Cause of our Joy!" As he wandered homeward still gazing at the stars, he hummed an old Czech carol half aloud.

"John, have another spoonful of stuffing," coaxed Frau Neumann at dinner.

Promptly he held out his plate. The Canon's orders! He had more plum preserves, too. After all, it was Christmas—the last at home.

After New Year's the snow came in earnest. It piled up on the frozen hills of the Boehmerwald, blowing in long high drifts on the roads. Lent was at hand. It was Shrovetide.

Old Francek Pokorny bundled into his coat that Monday morning, knotted a faded green scarf round his ears, slung the sack on his shoulder and set out on his rounds. His job was a pleasantly sociable one, knocking on door after door with the morning mail. At Shrovetide, every housewife in Prachatitz would have tarts fresh baked and sugary pastries, and maybe a nip of home-made brandy for a poor frozen postman in out of the wind.

"A letter for you, Frau Neumann." Pokorny's russet cheeks blew a white plume of breath at the kitchen door.

"Come inside, Francek. Sit down and have a bite."

On the kitchen table was a mound of powdery *Faschings-kuechle* alongside a pan of cherry-strudel piping hot. Pokorny's eyes brightened as he sat down.

"It's from Budweis, M'am . . . from John. I remember his handwriting."

A week ago, John had slipped off on one of his usual trips to Budweis—or so everyone had thought. He had not come back.

Frau Neumann broke the seal, turned her back to Pokorny and began reading. Yes. John was gone for good! The letter was his formal goodbye.

"It's as hard for me, dearest parents, as for you. But I have no doubt that this is the sacrifice God asks of us all. May his holy will be done."

With the hem of her apron, Frau Neumann dabbed at her eyes.

"Your strudel's delicious, M'am." Porkorny cut himself another sliver of the cake.

Frau Neumann did not answer. As the two sat in the cozy kitchen, the pot boiled noisily on the hearth. The stocking looms hummed in the room below. Far away, John Neumann's coach rattled north toward Linz. He had no companion. At the last moment his two friends had backed down. He had about forty dollars in his pocket, and fifty days of travel before he reached the docks at Havre.

Bohemia was pink and white with apple spray before Pokorny came whistling along the Upper Lane with further news from John. It was almost Ascension Thursday.

"Letter from Paris, M'am."

John mentioned only the happy things of his trip: Munich, his surprise call on cousin Phil Janson, smart in the braid and blue of King Ludwig's palace guard; Nancy, where he met the nuns from Prague; the spires of Chalons at the fork of the Marne; Paris and Notre Dame where he heard Lacordaire; the churchyard of Père Lachaise where he saw the tomb of Abelard. No word of his dwindling funds, his mounting apprehension. He had not the heart to worry his loved ones back home.

"Here I am in Havre, boarding ship at last. The *Europa* it is called. An American three-master bound for the port of New York. Captain Drummond has announced that we sail today with the tide."

The page was dated: Thursday after Low Sunday, April 11, 1836.

Forty days later, on the eve of Trinity Sunday the sailing packet *Europa* dropped anchor in the Narrows within sight of land. Seagulls cried round the masts. Here and there, amid the green fields of Brooklyn, rose spirals of supper smoke. Neumann stood at the rail drinking in the peaceful scene, impatient to be ashore. Forty days without Holy Communion! First off, he must find a church. Then what? He knew no one in the city. He had written to the Bishop of New York when Philadelphia turned him down, cooled his heels in Paris awaiting an answer. No answer came. His funds exhausted, he had determined to board ship and trust in our Blessed Lady. He had the address in his pocket with his rosary and a few coins—about a dollar all told. As he walked down the deck it began to rain.

But suddenly, a few days later, everything was bright. In the little red-brick house at the corner of Crosby and Prince Streets, old Bishop Dubois received John Neumann with open arms.

"Mais oui, monsieur! I most certainly can make use of you. New York could use a dozen young men who speak that many tongues."

The Bishop paused and looked out the window.

"I suppose you've heard of Niagara Falls. Well, I have a place for you up there. I found many German families there on my last visitation. They have no one to care for them."

Within the month, John Neumann would be ordained at the cathedral on Mott Street. He was speechless at the thought. After all these months of doubts and worry, after all these miles of land and water, at long, long last he would say his first Mass.

3. LOW BRIDGE

De Witt Clinton, Governor of New York, was eight years dead, but his grand Erie Canal was very much alive. In 1836 York Staters were inordinately proud of "Clinton's Ditch." There was nothing quite like it in America. It was the largest artificial waterway in the world.

"Ever ride over a river, mister?—I mean, cross it without your keel touching a drop of riverwater from bank to bank?" Erie water crossed the Mohawk, the Genesee, on four magnificent aqueducts.

"Mister, bet you never sailed keel-over-housetops in a counterstern!"—A purely rhetorical question. Long flotillas of freight scows, ballheads, arks, line boats and packets moved across the Irondequoit valley skyline, like fairytale argosies, borne on Erie water along a seventy-foot-high Embankment near Fullom's Basin, a dozen miles this side of Rochester.

A boat trip was fraught with pleasant surprises along the entire three hundred and sixty-three miles of Clinton's Ditch—primeval woods with frontier cabins in the clearings, wild gorges and frothy rapids, neat Dutch farms and hamlets, grist mills, Yankee steeples, orchards red with fruit. The canal wound through regions steeped in the lore of frontier American history. It had eighty-three ingenious stone locks that gently lifted freight and passengers to a height of five hundred and sixty-eight feet, from the tidewaters of the Hudson at Albany to the level of Lake Erie at Buffalo. In young America's book, the Grand Erie Canal was the eighth wonder of the world.

But the canal was more than just a Yankee conversation piece, a tourist attraction en route to Niagara Falls. Erie Canal linked the backwoods with the coastal cities, bringing timber, grain and meat in exchange for a hundred items needed on the frontier: handsaws, window glass, tea, calico bonnets, McGuffey Readers, ploughs, patent medicines and people—people by the tens of thousands.

Erie Canal quickly became the main immigration route not only to the Niagara frontier but, farther west, to Ohio, Michigan, Indiana on the Great Lakes. Canal-travel cost but a tenth of the fare by stage, with few of the discomforts of taking a Conestoga wagon over corduroy roads and haphazard shunpikes. A canalboat could get you to Buffalo in half the time! In 1836 twenty thousand canal boats locked through Erie waters. No trouble finding a captain to put your name on his westward way-bill and, for four cents a mile, carry you as far as you chose to go.

Newly ordained Father Neumann, on the last night of June, left Schenectady on the *Indiana* of the United States Line. He liked the boat on sight. It reminded him something of Noah's Ark in an old Bible history back home in Prachatitz—black hull with a red stripe at the water-line; long squat cabin, clean and white, with gay red curtains blowing out of twenty green-shuttered windows. If the boat held to its schedule of eighty miles per twenty-four hours, Father Neumann should make Rochester for Sunday, July third.

Schnectady, Schnectady . . . is half the way to Utiky . . . A snatch of towpath doggerel jingled teasingly through his head as he stretched in his narrow berth. He dared not turn lest he tumble out on the cabin floor. He hardly dared breathe for fear some lath or canvas stay in the bed-frame might give way—and he land with a thump on the man below. He lay there on his back, elbows on the edge of the mattress, his head and heels just reaching either end.

For everyone else aboard, the beds were too small. For Neumann they were just right. The shipwrights who made the *Indiana* must have had someone of Neumann's build in mind; at least for the sleeping quarters. On either side of the cabin were eight three-decker berths, forty-eight in all. For once, thought Neumann, his short stature was a blessing.

He was blessed on several counts. First, to have a berth at all. Some two dozen men were sleeping on the cabin floor. Also, to be located near one of the little square windows. The cabin air was stifling, reeking of burning sperm oil in two feeble betty-lamps, suspended from the ceiling. They made sputtering sounds all night —like a small boy with a runny nose.

Schnectady, Schnectady . . . is half the way to . . . At last Father Neumann sighed off into sleep. But at almost the same moment the lineboat shook from stem to stern, thumping to a stop with a grating sound. The cabin hissed with the rush of escaping waters. Drowsy growls. Excited whispers. The petulant cry of a small child, in the women's quarters, forward.

"No cause for alarm," snapped someone, an agent for the Holland Land Company. "We're only passing through a lock."

Through the shutters of his little window Father Neumann could see nothing but a blank wall of gray stone blocks scraping against the boatside, as the vessel inched higher and higher in the lock. Outside, he could hear conversation with the Irish lock-tender: the captain telling of ex-President Monroe's death in Manhattan. A horse snorted on the tow path.

"Cleat up." That was the Captain's voice.

"Ready, hoggee." He spoke again.

"Aye, aye, sir." A young voice answered.

Neumann lay awake listening to the peculiar night sounds of Erie water, as the lineboat began moving gently forward on its way. Schoharie Creek, Auriesville, Caughrawaga slipped past in the night. Somewhere in the distance he heard fiddle music and laughter. Waiting for sleep, he began fingering his rosary. Big Nose and Spraker's Basin glided past. They were nearing Canajoharie when Neumann fell asleep. All was still now but for the rhythmic snoring of passengers, the clip-clop of horses along the dusty tow-path, the gentle lap of water against the vessel's bow.

O the E-rye-ee was risin, the Strap was gettin low,
I hardly think we'll get a drink till we get to Buffalo.
America's a dandy place, the people are like brothers;
And when one gets a pumpkin pie, he shares it with the others.
And then on Independence Day (and who's a better right to?)
We eat and dance and sing and play, and have a dance at
night, too . . .

Captain Ariel Quimby glanced down the breakfast table—practically the length of the boat. Over his flowered sarsanet waistcoat he patted a napkin, satisfied that everything was in order: platters of scrambled eggs with sausage and bacon, bowls of boiled green cabbage, spicy pink ham, rough-cut wedges of Herkimer cheese, yellow corn bread, gobs of golden butter, pancakes with ewers of buckwheat honey—maple molasses, too, if you wished. Plenty for all his ninety passengers and five-man crew. More than enough. He sipped at the coffee. Good!

In less than an hour—while the passengers adjourned to the roof-deck—the entire cabin had been transformed into a dining hall. Those three-decker berths ingeniously collapsed under red-cushioned settees along the walls. The partition, cutting the women's quarter from the rest, had been removed. The breakfast table stretched from the crew's cuddy at the prow to the galley at the stern, where Abdenago Blossom, the Negro cook, practiced black magic with his skillet. At the moment it sputtered with a dainty morsel for Captain Quimby's breakfast, a succulent shad caught near Bowman's Flat that very morning before sunrise. Abdenago had caught it himself.

What Neumann had been told in Manhattan about canal-boat breakfasts had been no overstatement; he would never see so much good food again.

Though the ninety passengers did not crowd the vessel, still there was little room to walk about at leisure. One either sat in the cabin or settled among the carpetbags on the roof-deck. At the stern stood Captain Ariel Quimby, his elbow propped on the tiller, an American flag and the name *Indiana* hand-painted on his gray castor hat. From his shoulder there hung, on a bright green cord, a brass-bound telescope and a tarnished bugle, like the weights of a clock. From time to time he blew a *trahn-ahn* with the bugle in salute to east-bound gala-boat or counterstern. He hailed locktenders, pathmasters, peddlers along the towpath. He told stories to the passengers. He announced the names of oncoming villages and towns: Herkimer's, Fulmer's Creek, Morgan's Landing, Ferguson's.

At mention of the German Flats, Neumann glanced up from his prayers, the Office of the Precious Blood. He wondered how many Catholics dwelt in those rich lowlands. Some, no doubt, had lost the Faith long since, for want of a priest who spoke their native tongue.

"*All good Jackson men, bow down!*" cried the bowman.

Father Neumann, coming to the end of the third psalm of None, inclined his head for the *Gloria Patri*—and just in the nick of time! A low occupation-bridge all but knocked the hat from his head. After that, he dutifully bent his body to the waist at the cry of "*Low Bridge*" or "*All good Jackson men, bow down.*"

Once the novelty of riding the canal had worn off, the trip became quite monotonous. One tired of the bugle's endless *trahn-ahn,* the clip-clop of the three horses ahead on the towpath, the interminable delays at the locks. After Utica, on Saturday morning, as the *Indiana* pushed along the "Black Snake"—with no lock to impede passage as far as Syracuse—passengers hardly looked at the flat landscape. They talked of Andy Jackson, of the land boom in Buffalo; they played backgammon and poker to pass the time. Neumann read his Office for the feast of the Visitation, distracted occasionally by the strange Indian place names: Oriskany, Oneida, Canistota, Chittenango. Two spots he would remember: Stony Creek, just west of Rome, and Kirkville. At both these points the clamor of "Breached" had been raised on the towpath. An embankment had crumbled, the water emptying out of the Canal. That cost a good twelve hours, with the *Indiana* mudlarked in the silt of the empty ditch. All hope of getting to Rochester by Sunday was gone.

Church bells summoned to worship as the lineboat rode up the main street of Syracuse. *Trahn-ahn* cried Captain Quimby's bugle, as idlers on the bridges gawked down at the *Indiana*. To see a boat moving up the canal on a Sunday morning was rare. None but fancy line-boats might stir on Erie water on the Day of Rest. Righteous folk objected. Not young Neumann! He was glad to be hastening towards Rochester where Bishop Dubois had requested that he stop awhile. There were many German Catholics settling there who would welcome the visit of a priest who spoke their language.

From Bellisle to Weedsport the lineboat glided in solitary majesty past dugouts, arks, countersterns—all tied up along the berm-side of the canal. Near Canton they passed a gospel-raft where a hand organ ground out music for a Methodist revival meeting. The long raft was crowded with stolid farmer folk in their Sunday best.

By the time they reached Weedsport and Port Byron it was mid-afternoon, and taverns were holding their own "revivals"— with Blackstrap at three cents a mug, and Canajoharie "Scotch" for those who could afford a penny more. Fiddle strings mourned for Killarney, bagpipes for Loch Lomond. The tough canawlers mourned with the music and called for jig-tunes and reels.

Father Neumann wondered if these merrymakers had kept the Faith of their homelands as well as they kept its tunes. His missionary heart ached for his own people scattered in the upland clearings along the way. Who took care of their souls? And those twelve-year-old driver-boys on the towpath? And the bowmen and deckhands that he saw brawling so often with pike and fist for the right-of-way through the locks?

Among the tall reeds of the Montezuma marshes the vessel poked its way in the late afternoon. It was a dismal, brooding sort of place—in keeping with Father Neumann's thoughts at the time. So much to do here in America and so few priests to accomplish it. There were no more than thirty-five Catholic priests in the whole State of New York! People were coming by the thousands; priests, one at a time. And to think that his entire class in the seminary at Budweis had not been ordained that year because the diocese had too many priests!

"Low Bridge!" They were approaching Clyde.

Dutifully Father John Neumann bowed his head.

At Lockpit, shortly after supper, a pair of fiddlers came aboard the *Indiana*. Soon they were joined by an accordion. A sportive holiday air seemed to catch hold of the passengers. Neumann did not quite realize the significance of the night before the Fourth. He would! The fiddlers began tuning their strings. A space in the center of the deck was quickly cleared of stools and baggage. Soon the dancing began. Lyons and Lockville passed by, where grogshops rang with an old canawl chantey about a Mule-called-Sal. Soon the stars were out—and the mosquitoes.

As usual, the canalboat's cabin had been converted into sleeping quarters; but few aboard went down to bed. Father Neumann however, retired around ten, more to escape the merrymakers than to sleep. The ceiling shuddered with the pounding of heels on deck. *Trahn-ahn* went the captain's bugle. Outside a waterfront boardinghouse, the racket of mugs drumming on tables gave tempo to another boatman's refrain—a famous one on the Erie Canal:

O the E-rye-ee was risin, the Strap was gettin low,
I hardly think we'll get a drink till we get to Buffalo.

Drowsily a distant churchbell tolled midnight, when suddenly an earth-rocking *boom* brought Neumann bolt upright in bed. The sputtering sound of fire and flickering light outside the cabin window had all the tokens of catastrophe. Lacing his boots, Neumann sprang down from his upper berth, only to hear the fiddlers still busy. Someone was "belting out" a parody to the tune of Yankee Doodle:

America's a dandy place, the people are like brothers;
And when one gets a pumpkin pie, he shares it with the others.
And then on Independence Day (and who's a better right to?)
We eat and dance and sing and play, and have a dance at
   night, too . . .

The disaster Neumann had imagined was only a cannon proclaiming the sixtieth anniversary of American independence: July Fourth. Along berm and towpath, pine-torches sputtered gaily as far as the eye could see. Boys darted to and fro on the wooden bridges, banging rocks on stolen saucepans. One of the tow-mules hinnied in panic, lost its footing and slipped with a loud splash into the canal. John Neumann in all his five and twenty summers had never witnessed anything like this—not even on the Emperor's birthday. Firecrackers, pistol-shots, a sudden burst of star shells high over Port Gibson. Abdenago Blossom, the *Indiana* cook, shouted "Halleluja," forgot his troll-line with its slab of salt pork, trailing at the stern. He'd catch no shad tonight.

As scheduled, the twenty-one gun national salute commenced

at sunrise, as the *Indiana* pushed along the Grand Embankment, west of Fullom's Basin. Every town with fuse and a keg of powder made patriotic boom; every church with a bell in its spire made merry in the name of Independence. By now Neumann had abandoned all idea of further rest. But there was solace in the knowledge that Rochester was only three hours away.

Eight miles back, at Pittsford, the *Indiana* had made its last change of horses before Rochester, three skittish sorrels in a hurry to be home. Now the lineboat was swinging to the right, past Hill's basin, and Rochester straggled before them on either side of the Canal. Up the east bank of the Genesee they moved; under Court Street bridge.

"Whoa, Johnny, whoa."

Instantly the foam-lathered sorrels stopped dead on the tow-path. The red-vested hoggee glanced up at the bridge in time to spy a pair of towheads drop down out of view. With a burst of unprintable profanity he cut at the horse's rump, wishing it were either of the two boys. The horses started moving. Just ahead, the seven sandstone arches of the Aqueduct glinted red in the sunshine. Beyond, you could see Elbert Scrantom's clattering millwheels, the white rapids of Genesee Falls.

Veering left, the *Indiana* slewed proudly across the Aqueduct towards Exchange Street and the heart of Rochester. Loafer's Bridge bristled with its crop of spectators. Handkerchiefs fluttered welcome everywhere. Even from the upper balcony of Rochester House at water-side, hotel guests leaned out to watch the vessel's arrival. At precisely nine ("Methodist time") the *Indiana* swung into Child's Basin . . . amid a flurry of hackmen, porters, hotel-runners. "Rochester," Captain Ariel Quimby announced. "Rochester." There was no happier passenger on the gangplank that fourth day of July of 1836 than young Father Neumann. At last he could begin.

"Tell me now, my brave spalpeen, what kept you, anyway?" Father Bernard O'Reilly, pastor of St. Patrick's, Rochester, had his altar boy on the carpet. "Haven't they told you that the eight o'clock Mass starts at eight—not ten minutes after?"

Jackie Flaherty looked demurely penitent, knowing all the time that the priest could not be cross, even if he wanted. He knew the mischief Father O'Reilly could mask behind a straight sober look. Half out of his surplice, the boy commenced a description of the Fire Company's dazzling display that morning in front of Kilian van Renselaer's Eagle Tavern. It was part of the celebration of the Fourth. They did gymnastics on ladder rungs, holding leather buckets in their hands. They had a bright red contraption —made right here in Rochester, too—that sucked water from the Genesee and spouted it sky-high over the rooftops. (Obliquely, all this explained why Jackie Flaherty had been ten minutes late.)

Just then two brass cymbals clashed in the distance; a corps of fifes began whistling.

"Jiminy! They must be parading up Fitzhugh Street." Jackie Flaherty undid a dozen black cassock buttons with one expert tug.

"Hurry up—or you'll be as late for the parade as you were for Mass." Father O'Reilly chuckled as the boy went scampering out the door.

Up Frank Street dashed Jackie to the corner of Fitzhugh where, head-first, he lunged into a stranger laden down with a heavy bag.

"Excuse me, sir."

Thus did Father John Neumann discover where Father O'Reilly lived: alongside St. Patrick's, at the corner of Frank Street and Platt.

Word spread fast. A new priest had arrived on the *Indiana*. No. Not an Irishman! Some other sort. He looked German; talked only a few words in English.

When rumor of the newcomer reached the ears of Herr Jakob Twingelstein, pontifically he assured his wife that it was Father Joseph Prost, the Redemptorist, who had passed through Rochester last October! ("He promised to come back and stay.") But when young Seppi Twingelstein came home for dinner, after the Main Street parade, he informed the family that the new priest's name was Neumann. What is more, Seppi said, he liked him! He had given Seppi a stick of licorice. He had also commissioned Seppi to gather the boys and girls for catechism tomorrow in the basement of St. Patrick's.

That evening at Bernard Rupp's tavern at the corner of Fitzhugh and Main Street, there was speculation over the pretzels and Lagerbier. By bed-time, few were the German Catholics in Rochester who had not heard the news, and did not thank God for at last sending them "a priest of our own."

That first week in Rochester, his first in the active ministry, was an exhilaration for Father Neumann. How touchingly grateful everyone seemed for the smallest spiritual favor. And so delighted to meet a priest who spoke German. From little clues in their talk he quickly saw the hardships many of them had borne for want of a priest. The ten-year-old boy, for example, who had accompanied his mother from Rochester all the way to Albany, and then down to Manhattan to have his little sister baptized. Bernard Klemm had done just that, seventeen years back, when Rochester was no more than a hamlet with a single gristmill on the Genesee. Neumann could surmise why everyone was so happy to have him in their midst.

Yet he knew he was but touching the surface. Many, he felt sure, had grown lukewarm, had given up Mass and Sacraments for want of a priest they could deal with in their mother tongue. So many had told him how they went Sundays to St. Patrick's, but yearned for a sermon "like we had back home." The children, poor things, needed schools to learn both German and English, to master the rudiments of the Faith.

On Sunday, the seventh after Pentecost, Father Neumann said Mass for the German Catholics in the "Irish" church—the only Catholic church in the city. He preached on "false prophets who come in the clothing of sheep," the gospel of the day. Being his first sermon after ordination, he was nervous. But the sound of German phrases in St. Patrick's pulpit charmed his listeners. They listened hungrily to every word. He urged them to hold fast to their Faith, to teach it to their little ones and—to pray fervently for a German pastor who could stay with them permanently. If Father was flattered by the fervent gratitude of ever so many, after

Mass—grateful for his German sermon, hopeful that he might stay in Rochester—he was soon deflated by Herr Jakob Twingelstein, the Trustee.

"You're much too new for us here in Rochester, Father Neumann—much too green."

At the moment the young priest had just finished christening little Caroline Koch, daughter of Bernard Koch and Antonia Charles—his first Baptism. The thrill of it dulled the intended sting of Twingelstein's remark. In that one baptism, he felt, all the forty sea-sick days on the Atlantic, the tiresome canal-trip with all its discomforts and embarrassments were repaid. "If I never perform another priestly act," he wrote that afternoon in his diary, "my ordination is vindicated. I have opened heaven to a little one."

Father Bernard O'Reilly, though he understood not a word of German, roundly complimented the young priest on his sermon. He liked young Neumann. He did not miss the zeal with which he had gathered the children each afternoon to teach them catechism. He observed the devout way Neumann prayed. But he could not refrain from his little joke at the expense of the young man.

With owlish gravity that evening at supper, he drew out Father Neumann, inquiring into his studies in Europe, his voyage from Havre to New York, his speedy ordination by Bishop Dubois. Suddenly putting fingers to temples, O'Reilly gasped in seemingly genuine alarm. Father Neumann did not catch the mischievous twinkle in his eye.

"But Father Neumann—maybe I shouldn't be calling you *Father* at all, at all! You may not even be validly ordained. Sure everyone knows, you need an *exeat* from your home-bishop, dismissorial papers from Budweis!" He reached for a book. "Let's see what Blessed Liguori has to say about you." With studious solemnity he thumbed through a battered *Theologia Moralis*.

Poor Neumann spent an uncomfortable hour after supper. His jovial host had no inkling of the havoc he had wrought. Neumann was sure that his priesthood was valid—but *was it licit?* Could he say Mass tomorrow in good faith? and go on to Buffalo with peaceful conscience? He sat there, only picking at his supper. But, fortunately, something happened to restore his peace of soul quickly. Someone knocked at the rectory door.

"*Gruesz Gott,* Father O'Reilly! I'm back again. I have just now by canal-boat come."

The newcomer, chuckling at his brave assault on the English language, set down his carpetbag on a chair. The chuckle was contagious. It seemed to fill the wooden rectory with peace. Neumann liked the man even before introduction. Neumann judged that he must be a few years older than himself, but not many. Also, that *Gruesz Gott* gave him away for a fellow country-man. Somehow, for all his youth, this stranger radiated a calm maturity. He seemed a good man to know.

"Welcome. Welcome, Father Prost." (Obviously, O'Reilly liked the man too.) "And how are your Redemptorists faring out in the wilderness?" O'Reilly did not wait for an answer; he pointed at Father Neumann. "This young man is on his way to Buffalo, his first assignment."

O'Reilly winked at Prost. "He was *validly* ordained last week in New York—or so he says."

Prost quickly saw through O'Reilly's ribbing. He walked over and shook Father Neumann's hand. "Don't let this Irishman catch you off guard."

"Ah! Ah! No secrets now," chuckled O'Reilly. "Remember, I only *sprechen* English."

Prost had spoken to Neumann in German.

It took very little coaxing to induce Father Neumann to stay another day in Rochester, before setting off on Erie waters for the Niagara frontier.

4.   ROCHESTER INTERLUDE

"If you'll kindly excuse me, gentlemen—I must go over to church for a spell."

Father Bernard O'Reilly had the tactful grace to let his two house guests by themselves. They should have much in common, being from the same part of central Europe. Besides, the practical Prost could give young Neumann important hints for living on the Niagara frontier.

"None of your tall stories now, Father Prost!" O'Reilly stopped in the doorway, his eyes atwinkle with mischief. He glanced at Father Neumann. "Watch out Father for this Redemptorist. Faith, I think he must have kissed the Blarney Stone by *actio in distans!*"

Prost wagged a finger at O'Reilly.

"What is a blarneystone?" asked Neumann, toying with the book on his lap.

Prost shrugged. "Oh. Some little joke, I suppose. After a week with him, you should realize how much he enjoys throwing people off balance—and with that innocent face of his. Like this business about your dismissorial papers." Prost shook his head. "You should never have taken him seriously, Father."

"Thanks to Blessed Liguori, here," Neumann tapped the book on his lap, "and to yourself, Father Prost, my mind is now at peace. I'm sending to Budweis for my release in writing from old Bishop Rudzicka."

Prost, slightly nonplused to be coupled in one breath with the prince of moral theologians, turned in his chair. "Thank you, Father Neumann for practically canonizing me. Blessed Alphonsus Liguori is one of the family, you know."

Father Neumann already knew quite a bit about Blessed Liguori. In his luggage he had a manuscript of the *Via della Salute,* half translated from the Italian original. Back in Budweis, as a seminarian, he had read the man's life.

No matter. Prost explained to his young friend how his

Redemptorists had been founded by Blessed Alphonsus de Liguori to preach missions to the abandoned poor. ("That was in Naples in 1732.") Prost touched on Father Clement Hofbauer, who had transplanted the Order beyond the Alps. "It's taken us almost a century to take root outside of Italy. Only sixteen years ago, we finally got imperial permission for a monastery in Vienna. Now we're in Belgium, Holland and . . ." Prost sighed audibly. ". . . and *here.*"

"In a way, Father Prost, I came to America because of a Redemptorist: Simon Saenderl. Back in Budweis we used to read avidly the *Leopoldinen Berichte* with Saenderl's inspiring accounts of work among the Indians of Michigan."

"I spent the past winter with Father Saenderl at Green Bay."

Prost hesitated, debating whether he should discuss with this young priest his Order's grim predicament in America—the thing he had been sent from Vienna to investigate at first hand. For the past four years his Redemptorists had been ranging the American backwoods in hope of locating a permanent foundation where they could settle down to community life. Superiors in Vienna were anxious; to date, the pioneers had had no success.

The fact of the matter was that the missionaries, at the beck of bishops with little notion of the needs of community life, had been stationed pellmell over a radius of a good thousand miles, in the vicinity of the Great Lakes. There was Franz Haetscher in the white solitude of Sault Sainte Marie, driving his dogsled to minister to Chippewas and tough French trappers. And Tschenhens, circuit-riding the Ohio woods, searching out German settlers everywhere. Often, after Mass, he must ride for as much as eight hours without so much as a bite. In a little log house near Peru, Ohio, Brother Aloys kept house for Tschenhens; but with the priest away for weeks at a time, there was little religious companionship.

Brother James, alas, had not been so fortunate. Retained at Cincinnati as cook at the bishop's house, eventually he had abandoned his religious vocation, completely disillusioned. Prost had met him last summer on the streets of Manhattan, earning a livelihood peddling whale-oil from door to door.

Another Brother had returned to Europe, convinced that

community life in America was impossible. Back in Vienna now, he had nothing good to say for life in the United States.

Finally, out in Green Bay, Father Saenderl labored alone among his Ottawa and Menomenee Indians, living from hand to mouth on the occasional gifts of venison and maple sugar the Redmen left at his door.

"A wonderful missionary, Father Saenderl." Turning to Neumann Father Prost mustered a hearty smile.

"He talks the Ottawa language as well as any white man, with the exception, perhaps, of Father Frederick Baraga. The Ottawas love him; call him *Nosse Simon*. You should have seen the welcome they gave him, when I brought him back with me to Green Bay from Detroit."

Prost had a new adventure of Father Saenderl's to relate—one Neumann had not read in the pages of the *Leopoldinen Berichte:*

"Let me tell you, Father, about our trip to Green Bay last November . . ."

Neumann sat up in his chair.

"It was blowing snow in Detroit when we boarded ship, the last ship of the season. Some sixty passengers were aboard, mostly men: pelt traders, land prospectors, lumberjacks, trappers, a doctor bound for Mackinac—Father Saenderl and I."

Father Prost interrupted his story to advise Neumann to buy good warm clothing. ("Winter in Buffalo may not be quite as cold as Green Bay, Wisconsin; but it's colder than anything you knew in Bohemia.") Then back to the story. Prost described the vessel crunching through shell ice, the floes thickening round it, as they neared Mackinac, between Lake Huron and Michigan.

"The trip took almost three weeks. A blizzard came up. The sails crackled, stiff with frozen snow, as the ship nosed past Beaver Island. Everyone was on edge. Men cursed their ill luck; they drank to keep warm."

By now Neumann was trapped by the story.

"Remember the Prophet Jonas?" Prost continued. "Well, Father Saenderl and I came pretty close to a similar fate. No whale, though! All evening a vicious Nor'wester pummeled the vessel, slicing through the sails, rasping at the cabin windows like nightmare. Decks and rigging were coated with ice. We were scared to death. Everyone was. Father Saenderl and I huddled in a corner of the cabin, fidgeting with our beads, too terrified to stir an inch. It was like hell itself: the screaming wind outside, the passengers in the chill cabin, swilling liquor, cursing, damning, blaspheming.

"Then it happened. The ship made a sickening lurch; and shuddering through all its timbers, the prow locked fast in the ice. Panic broke loose. 'There's a Jonah aboard!' shouted one of the crew. 'Someone aboard is bringing bad luck on the trip.' A huge brute of a lumberjack scanned the cabin. 'Not one; two Jonahs!' His eye alighted on the pair of us.

"No sooner had he pointed us out than twenty men rushed us to the cabin door, fully intent on marooning us on the ice. They would have, too, had not the doctor talked sense to them. It was horrible, Father Neumann. I still waken at night in a cold sweat at the memory."

Outside the open window of Saint Patrick's rectory, a mother halooed a boy home for bed. The boy was making noisy protest in a high treble, claiming that all the other kids were still out playing. An old argument, though futile. *Trahn-ahn.* A canalboat signaled hoarsely, a few blocks away. The July air was still and very humid, but, somehow, the thrashing noise of millwheels along the river sounded cool.

Father Neumann leaned forward for the rest of the story.

"We had to abandon ship," said Prost matter-of-factly. "We clambered, all of us, down the side of the vessel and trudged across the frozen bay, two miles to shore. For seven more miles Saenderl and I ported our luggage on our shoulders through the deep snow, through the dense woods, until finally we reached the settlement of Green Bay."

Prost remembered that past winter with a shudder: the huge unfurnished barn of a house that Bishop Resé of Detroit had foisted off on them for a Redemptorist foundation. Against his better judgment Prost had accepted it, chiefly because the good Bishop had paid for it with money allocated for the Redemptorists by the Leopoldine Foundation in Vienna. Without even consulting them, the Bishop had spent the money.

Prost, when he saw what Bishop Resé had bought for them, was sick at heart. Oh, it was big enough for a community—too big. But the location! It stood in lonely grandeur in a wooded No-man's-land. How could a religious community live where a single priest could barely subsist?

It was a miracle that Saenderl and himself had not perished there in the sub-zero weather. They had burned huge hickory logs in the open hearth. But the house was so big; it had been built for an academy. Icy drafts from the lake blew at will through the chinks in the clapboard walls. Snow blew in, making drifts on the puncheon floor. There was no glass in the windows. Oftentimes, the Mass wine froze solid in the cruet.

He would not forget that winter at Green Bay. The hunger and cold, the utter frustration, the irony of it all. What prayers he had made to our Blessed Lady for conformity with God's will, for patience, for light to make the right decision.

In March a half-breed *courrier de bois* came plodding through the snow with a letter from Rochester, New York. The German Catholics had bought a church. Would Father Prost please come back to them to be their pastor, as he had promised. Perhaps Rochester was the answer to his problem: a permanent foundation for the Redemptorists in America. Perhaps!

As soon as the ice had broken on Huron and Erie, Father Joseph Prost had taken the first sailing vessel eastward to Buffalo.

"Father Saenderl must soon be leaving Green Bay . . . for good."

Neumann did not understand; so Prost explained. Green Bay was to be the first Redemptorist foundation in America—a central base of operations, whence they could radiate outwards on mission work through Michigan, Ohio, Wisconsin. But the dream was impossible. Green Bay itself was no more than a small Canadian and Menominee trading post—hardly more than two rows of frame houses with a few saloons and supply stores. Possibly it could support one priest; never, a full community. Father Simon

Saenderl could not live there alone. It was against the Rule on which he had made his Redemptorist vows.

"There's an old monastic adage," said Prost, *"Vae soli.* Woe to the loner! That is why we Redemptorists must live in community. In fact, it's a danger for any missionary priest to live too long by himself."

The words had a telling effect on young Father Neumann.

"I may as well admit, Father," Prost continued, "we Redemptorists have not been too successful in America. I mean, in finding a permanent base of operation. Superiors in Vienna are not at all pleased. Last year, in fact, it was decided to recall our men, but our saintly Vicar General, Father Joseph Passerat, persuaded his consultors to delay the return-order for a while. That's how I happen to be here. Father Passerat sent *me,* of all people, to investigate the situation." Prost laughed at himself.

"Do you know what Passerat told me? (Personally, I think the man's a saint—though others think him a complete misfit for the job of Vicar General.) He said to me: *Father, we shall have a permanent foundation in America the year that Blessed Alphonsus is raised to the altars."*

"When will that be?" Neumann wondered.

"Your guess is as good as mine, Father. Soon, I hope."

"I'm going to tell you a strange thing, Father Neumann." Prost stood up and wheeled towards his listener.

"Seven years ago, instead of the black Redemptorist habit, I wore the white robe of a Premonstratensian monk. I was a novice at the time; and before taking vows, was sent down to Vienna to complete my university studies. An odd thing happened to me, my first day in the imperial city. I was out sight-seeing and . . ."

Father Neumann was all attention, fascinated by the personality of the man.

"Anyway, I happened to be passing the fine old church of Maria Stiegen, with its quaint octagonal spire. I saw a white-haired Redemptorist coming down Salvator Gasse. He did not notice me. He did not look up at all; but turned in to the monastery, next door to the church. I can't explain it . . . but something about him made

me want to join his Order. I wanted to be a Redemptorist like
that man." Prost paused a moment. "The man was Passerat."

"Still talking your heads off!" Father Bernard O'Reilly had
come back from his chores in the church. He turned to Father
Neumann.

"What do you think of him? I hope he's not trying to make
a Redemptorist out of you, Father." O'Reilly once more had that
look of owlish innocence.

Prost saw it. He slapped his thigh, laughing.

But Father Neumann was held by a strange coincidence. Just
an hour ago, when Father Prost came through the doorway and
set down his bag—the same idea had flickered through Neumann's
mind: a vague yearning to join the religious family of this whole-
somely happy countryman. It was only a passing thought.

Prost, still laughing, said: "Father O'Reilly, now that you mention it, I think this young man would make a first-rate Redemptorist."

Neumann was embarrassed no end.

Elliot Spencer saw no point in protest that morning more than
any other, as his wife pinned the flower in his buttonhole. Abigail,
he knew, had set ideas on the matter. If dapper Charles Morton,
bowing guests into Rochester House by canal-side, could sport a
rosebud in his coat, so could her husband, Elliot Spencer. To
Abigail it made small difference that Morton owned one of Rochester's best hotels, whereas her husband made beer-kegs and flour
barrels in his cooper-shop, down near the canal. That summer
morning Abigail had cut a bright orange marigold in her garden
for her man's lapel.

At precisely seven-thirty by the clock of the Methodist steeple,
Elliot Spencer, master-cooper, set out for his shop. Strolling
leisurely across town, he hummed a favorite old Methodist hymn-
tune, being a zealous member of that persuasion. He seldom passed
up a chance to win new converts for the Methodist fold. Though,
truth to tell, his zeal had misfired entirely with the nine apprentice
coopers in his shop on St. Paul Street.

One of them, Malcolm McCandlish, was a dyed-in-the-wool Presbyterian from Portadown in the north of Ireland. With McCandlish he never argued. But the remaining eight were Catholics, and fair game for his zeal—five country cousins from the south of Ireland, and three brothers from Germany: the Kennings from Hanover.

The five Kerry cousins, for all their round-eyed attention to Spencer's biblical arguments, never missed a Sunday morning at Saint Patrick's. They wouldn't be caught dead within bell-shot of the white steeple of the Methodist church! As for the three Kennings, they did more than listen. They met the master cooper on his own ground. They gave him, as it were, his choice of weapons, and beat him at his own game. They could quote the Protestant bible as glibly as any circuit rider.

Louis Kenning had a handbook of Christian apologetics which provided ammunition for all three brothers in their daily skirmishes into Scripture. More than once, Elliot Spencer would have fired them on the spot, only that he needed their skill in his shop. They were craftsmen, all; perhaps the best carpenters in Rochester. So great was their bargaining power, that Elliot Spencer grudgingly agreed to give them time off, whenever they asked it in the name of their Catholic Faith.

Sauntering down towards canal-side that July morning, Elliot Spencer thought of his nine assistants, pounding away since daybreak in his cooper shop. Every flour mill in town needed barrels, and cooper Elliot Spencer, thanks to the Kennings, made Rochester's best.

But something was wrong that morning. Spencer's arrival at the shop caused havoc. The five Kerry cousins glowered blackly at him as though he were the devil himself. Not so much at him, as at the flower in his coat. Bewildered, he fingered the fluted marigold, as a villainous grin spread across the dour face of Malcolm McCandlish. Elliot Spencer frowned. What was wrong? Where were the three Kennings?

Ignoring the question, McCandlish broke out into song: the opening bars of *Boyne Water;* and bedlam broke loose in the cooper shop. Four wooden mallets flew at the singer's face. They missed the mark. Soft at first, then loud and derisive, the man from Portadown was chanting:

> *I'm up to my hips in Kerry blood*
> *Up to my knees in slaughter.*
> *Ten thousand Micks laid down their bricks*
> *At the Battle of Boyne water.*

As he chanted, he pounded on an empty barrel as though it were a Belfast drum.

A fifth mallet hit the target. The singing stopped.

"What's wrong. What did I do?" sputtered Elliot Spencer.

The five Irishmen, too mad for words, stormed out of the shop.

When Malcolm McCandlish came to, he explained to Spencer that the next day, July twelfth, was a peculiar sort of holiday in the north of Ireland: Orangeman's Day. On that day, in 1690, Protestant William of Orange had defeated Catholic King James II at the battle of the River Boyne. It was no day to flaunt the color orange in a Catholic Irishman's face.

As for the three Kennings, McCandlish explained, they would be gone for a fortnight "on a matter of religion"—to help remodel an old Negro meetinghouse on Ely Street for a German Catholic church.

Elliot Spencer kicked full tilt at a brand new barrel, and swore an un-Methodist oath.

"Abigail! with her silly notions."

He ripped the marigold from his coat and ground it under heel.

"Guten Morgen, Pater Neumann."

Over the racket of hammer and saw at Ely Street, Louis Kenning shouted a greeting to the figure in the doorway.

"And Father Prost! So, you've come back to us at last."

All three Kennings hopped down from the scaffolding, followed by a dozen other workmen. They had the old Baptist meeting house almost converted for Catholic worship.

"Father Prost, you'll be able to say Mass for us *here* next

Sunday." They took for granted that he had come to stay. "We're fixing up living quarters downstairs for you, Father."

Proudly the three Kennings took Prost and Neumann on a tour of inspection of the church. It was a good buy for sixteen hundred dollars, Prost admitted. The basement could serve part-time as a school for the children. To which Neumann smilingly agreed. The neighborhood, being close to the canal, was a bit seedy; but it was a beginning. The German Catholics of Rochester soon would have a church of their own.

"Those Kennings are a treasure." Neumann and Prost walked out into the street. "Perhaps I can induce Louis to be schoolmaster. I think he could really teach the Faith and make it stick."

Father Neumann, during the past week, had heard many tales of the daily arguments in Spencer's cooper-shop. He told Prost the incident of the preacher that the cooper had brought in to argue the Kennings down. The True Faith, Louis Kenning told the preacher, has to be eighteen centuries old. "But your Methodism is in existence only a century."

Since Kenning's English was not perfect, the preacher felt superior. Blandly he assured Kenning that times were changing, that even religion had to keep up with the times.

Louis Kenning held up his hand. "Where does it say that in your bible, my friend? Where does it tell you that the world must wait seventeen hundred years for Methodism? No, sir. You won't find that anywhere in your bible; but I think you'll find something about false prophets coming in the latter day."

The story of Louis Kenning and the preacher was known all over town.

"He'd make an excellent schoolmaster," said Neumann, after telling the story. "I hope I can find someone like him out at my own mission field."

Buffalo was on his mind: and as Father Prost could observe, John Neumann was still a babe-in-the-woods.

During the next few hours, as they walked around Rochester, Prost briefed the young missionary on several important points for his apostolate. Things, he felt sure, Neumann had never learned in the dry pastoral theology of Prague and Budweis—but essential for America. Prost could surmise the sort of person Neumann would have to deal with along the Niagara frontier. But how would he tell him?

"Father John," he began, "I hope you are not misled by the generosity you've witnessed this past week at St. Patrick's. The people, the way they contribute to the collection basket. It's an old tradition they brought over from Ireland. Poor as they are, they never forget priest or church."

(Was this the right approach, Prost wondered.)

"Our German Catholics, sad to say, are not blessed with such a tradition." (Prost got right to the point.) "The cold truth is that they are not used to paying weekly towards the support of priest and school and church. Back home, the government took care of all that. Not here, though.

"In the old country the parish church was a landmark, older than the town hall. Not so, in America! Here your church may be a log hut in the woods till you can scrape up means to build the Lord something more respectable. Look at the makeshift I'm going to have down there on Ely Street, till better times."

They were walking along the east bank of the river, up towards Genesee Falls.

"So, Father Neumann, though money may be the farthest thought from your mind" (this was his point!) "though your quest is souls and their salvation, you'll have to educate your parishioners to generosity. You'll have to beg, fume, berate them week after week, till they assist you with pennies and dollars. If you don't— mark my word!—you'll live to regret it."

Prost could see the shocked look in his friend's face at this seemingly unspiritual approach to the ministry.

"Look!" Prost pointed across the river to the turning mill-wheels.

"Those mills are grinding wheat, raised by Yankee farmers. The Yankees are prosperous. They live in white frame houses with tilled fields and red bulging barns. Their German neighbors, still new in this country, are living hand to mouth, breaking their backs at clearing stumps and tilling the stubborn land. They envy the Yankee. They hope, some day, to raise bumper crops too, for the mill. They yearn for prosperity; and they're hoarding every penny, in hopes of one day having a cozy white farmhouse instead of a crude log shanty near the creek. You'll find them the same around Buffalo, Father." Prost was orating, careless of passersby, warming loud to his subject.

"*Thrift,* they call it; but its real name is *Greed.* It hardens the heart. It chokes off all love of God. So, as I say, unless you instill generosity into your people, you'll have lukewarm, half-hearted Catholics."

Neumann now saw the zealous missionary speaking from the heart, as Prost enlarged on the axiom that sacrifice makes for better Catholics.

"Believe me, Father, a man esteems the more, the things he pays for. Let him pay in labor, or time, or his savings towards a church, and you'll find him taking personal pride in it, thereafter. You'll find him more often at Mass and the Sacraments."

Many a time in the next few years John Neumann would think back on the wisdom of those words.

"We'd better turn back," suggested Prost, "if you're planning to leave this evening for Buffalo."

Back to St. Patrick's they strolled for packing and goodbyes.

At Child's Basin a packet was loading for seven o'clock departure. There, while Father O'Reilly made arrangements with the captain for Neumann's passage, Father Prost made a rough sketch of Buffalo so that Neumann could find his way from canalside up to the residence of the Catholic priest, at the corner of Edward and Main Street.

"Father Pax is expecting you. He told me so Saturday, on my way here. The old pastor, Father Mertz, is home in Luxemburg, collecting funds. (Money again!) And Pax is pretty worn out, being the only Catholic priest on the whole Niagara frontier. It's a large territory, Father Neumann, as you'll soon find out." Encouragingly, Prost concluded, "Father Pax is a good man. He'll treat you well."

Dinner chimes hummed along the white verandas of Rochester House. Mr. Charles Morton, a fresh rosebud in his buttonhole, was standing at the main door.

Trahn-ahn. The familiar bugle notes.

"Cleat up." The packet slowly began to move away.

From the rail of Loafer's Bridge, Father Prost leaned down to shout an *Auf wiedersehen,* as the boat slid underneath. Along-side him, Father O'Reilly, still mopping his forehead from the exertion of the walk, shouted a loud "God bless."

Father Neumann waved back.

"He'll have a hard rill to hoe," said Father O'Reilly, who knew the Niagara frontier. For two hard-riding years, it had been part of his Rochester parish.

Prost waved once more, as the packet turned a bend in the canal and passed out of sight.

The first fifteen hours—from Adam's Basin to Gasport—were notoriously monotonous. Flat prosaic countryside, aptly called "the Long Level." Better-class packets purposely departed Rochester at night-fall, since sleep was the best thing to do.

About noon next day, they came to the first bit of interesting diversion: the five double-locks that gave Lockport its name. The town itself sat on a crag overlooking the canal. And overlooking the town, a monster advertisement—huge white letter on a brick wall—read *Priestcraft Unmasked.* That was the printing office of a stridently anti-Catholic weekly. Its subscribers would hardly welcome Father John Neumann. It had many subscribers along the Niagara frontier.

From Lockport on, primeval forests crowded either side of the canal. Houses were few—mostly log cabins, each with its little clearing; then, the thick dark woods again. But every six miles, the impenetrable wall of leaves was cleft by a straight clean swath of cleared timber, the work of Ellicott's axemen, when they surveyed the Holland Land Purchase in 1800. The whole of Niagara Country was crisscrossed with such swaths, making squares, six miles to a side. The squares, in turn, were subdivided into lots of three hundred and sixty acres, for easy purchase by the pioneers.

Pendleton and Brockway slipped past as the canal curved north and then west in an easy half circle.

Father Neumann was beating the bounds of his mission territory, as the packet nosed southward towards Tonawanda and Black Rock, making, at long last, for Buffalo, with the sun at its stern.

5.   BOOM TOWN: BUFFALO

Buffalo, in the mid-eighteen-thirties, had a pocketful of dreams. It held the gate to the Great Lakes, the whole west. Soon, through its harbor docks western crops, western ore, western live-stock must funnel eastward to the coast. The staidest city alder-men were starry-eyed. In no time at all, their lakeport would be a second Manhattan!

Buffalo, scarcely four years chartered as a city, already had more than sixteen thousand on its census. Every day Concords and broad wheels brought freight and passengers from Albany; the grand Erie Canal brought crowded lineboats and packets. New faces appeared at the rate of a thousand a morning: tourists and transients for the most part; still, while they remained, they kept Buffalo shopkeepers busy. Waterfront storekeepers did a brisk trade in such pioneer items as bear-traps, ploughs, bibles, Seneca oil, Bowie knives, apple seeds, spinning wheels—almost anything from a coonskin cap to a Conestoga wheel.

For merchants and hostlers business had never been better—and for the building trades, too. Buffalo's growth had all America talking. As cities go, it was midway between a rugged frontier town and a clean-cut prosperous metropolis. Buffalo, in 1836, was like a farmboy outgrowing his denims; but soon to be wear-ing tailor-cut cassimeres—if one man had his way: Mr. Benjamin Rathbun.

Rathbun, a short, self-effacing, quiet-spoken fellow with a

fancy for black broadcloth suits and white cravat, was often mistaken for a clergyman. Few knew him intimately. But in July of 1836 he was "Mr. Buffalo." Single-handed, he had conjured up a dream on the shores of Lake Erie.

In less than fifteen months Ben Rathbun had reared some hundred and forty-seven buildings within the city limits: a new jail on Batavia Street; on Main, at the corner of Eagle, a spacious theatre; a block of stores for Joy & Webster near the canal. He built Gothic Hall. He built stores of all dimensions, dwelling houses all over town. For Colonel Alanson Palmer he built the five-story American Hotel: "an establishment," so read the ads, "with features only to be found in certain royal palaces of Europe." Rathbun told the city fathers that the wheel-rutted muck of lower Main Street was an eye-sore: it gave a poor impression of Buffalo to the packet-trade. His quiet logic goaded them into paving the slope with bluestone flags from canal-side to the terrace. No matter where one turned in Buffalo, some far-sighted project of Benjamin Rathbun was under way.

Quarries, brickyards, sawmills hustled feverishly to supply Mr. Rathbun's carpenters and stonemasons. Two thousand five hundred men were on his weekly payroll—almost a quarter of the population! Coachmen on the Albany stagelines, shipwrights along the canal, store clerks, cabinet makers, waterboys, mattock- and sledge-wielders, accountants, longshoremen and out-of-town buyers of land, all were in his employ. Any random Saturday you would find his employees with their wives, milling through his company stores on the east side of Main Street, redeeming scrip for a week's provisions. Benjamin Rathbun paid wages mostly in groceries, furniture, drug goods from his own shops. All Rathbun's ready cash was tied up in a dozen civic projects. He borrowed from local banks and businessmen—and from moneylenders at three percent a month. His name was his bond. The signature of Benjamin Rathbun on any slip of paper in the year 1836 was as good as gold.

As scaffold and building crane mounted skyward at Mohawk and Tupper and Chippewa Streets, so did neighborhood spirits. So did the price of real estate. Lots, bought for a song, rapidly mounted in value. Not just on Main Street; everywhere, even far beyond the city boundaries. Midas-touch Ben Rathbun had purchased a huge tract, ten miles away, near the Falls; platted it out in neat squares for his projected Niagara City; and put it up for auction. Posters along Main Street from Long Wharf to the Broadwheel Tavern announced to passersby that on Monday, August 3, 1836, there would be a grand sale of lots at Niagara Falls.

"He'll make a pretty penny on this deal," said the friends of Benjamin Rathbun.

Rumors of quick wealth buzzed like June bugs wherever people gathered—on canal-packets moving up and down Erie waters, in noisy smoke-filled grog shops near the docks, at Eagle Tavern, the Mansion House, and over farmers' kitchen tables— everywhere along the Niagara frontier.

"Heard about John Sage? He's closing his barber shop near the Eagle Playhouse. Retiring for life! They say he made a small fortune on a land deal with some fellow from Watervliet."

Everyone had a story.

Land! People talked of nothing else. Every Tom, Dick and Harry had suddenly become an amateur surveyor, scratching out maps—of canal-side acres and corner lots—on the earthen sidewalks with whip-butt or the heel of a boot. Two German farmers up at the Plough Inn, their heads long locked in confidential whispers, left the tabletop scarred with triangles, made with a dinner fork. Every man was his own real estate agent. Buffalo was land-mad to a man.

Up in the small wooden church of St. Louis, near the end of Main Street, the Catholic priest berated the foolhardy greed of his flock: selling their hard-won clearings for a handful of wildcat notes. So loud did he thunder that old Judge Ebenezer Walden could plainly hear him through the open window of his Edward Street home on Sunday mornings.

"*Pax* is his name," snapped Judge Walden. "In Latin it means Peace; but he shouts more like War."

Father Alexander Pax shouted Sunday after Sunday, and on

week days in his rounds of the countryside. Some paid heed and held their acres. Others sold out. He stopped one afternoon at Gould's carriage shop to ask an apprentice about repairing a harness.

"But, Father," said the lad, "haven't you heard? I've given up that sort of thing. I've bought *land*."

By July of 1836 the biggest land boom in American history was at its peak. Not only in Buffalo, everywhere. Vast tracts purchased by the Government from the Indians—in Michigan, Indiana, Ohio, Missouri—were now up for sale. Speculators borrowed paper money from local banks for use on the frontier. They purchased large parcels of wilderness from Government land offices at the fixed price of $1.25 an acre, and used the land as security for further loans.

In Philadelphia Nicholas Biddle had enlarged his bank loans to the tune of two and a half million dollars a year. By the start of 1836 he had one hundred and eight million dollars in banknotes in circulation. Inflation was ballooning at astronomical speed. Local banks, eager for business, were issuing paper far beyond their resources. Every mother's son with a pennyworth of credit borrowed banknotes to purchase land. Nobody seemed to worry. Prosperity hung like a golden apple above the twenty-four United States.

Up in the southeast corner of the White House, in Washington, a lamp glowed in the President's office. But Andy Jackson was not there. Cane in hand, he had gone out in his shirtsleeves into the sultry night. He was in a glowering bad temper, what with the humid weather and the state of the country at the moment. Old Hickory, as they called him, could curse like forked lightning when provoked. It brought quick action. Tonight, however, being all alone, he merely talked to himself, muttering like summer thunder.

A mouse scurried across the Presidential stables. Andy Jackson leaned on the gate of the paddock, patting the long nose of Truxton, his favorite horse.

"I'll show them who's boss," he growled.

Somewhere a locust gave vent to a dry raspy screech. It was close on midnight.

For some months the President had been disturbed by the country's aimless spending. Was Nick Biddle behind it, he wondered, manipulating the entire inflationary spree, somehow, to embarrass the President for dethroning Philadelphia's United States Bank? Last March, Roger Taney had reported that the United States Treasury was glutted with worthless local banknotes, accepted in payment for Government lands. Congressman Benton of Missouri had ardently described the national predicament before the assembled senators. He had introduced a proposal to compel buyers of the public lands to pay in silver or gold. The Senate politely listened. They had tabled the proposal. That was two weeks ago. Now Congress had disbanded for the summer recess: Clay to his julep and jockey country of Kentucky; Dan Webster to his white New England wells and village greens. Nothing had been done about inflation.

This very afternoon Jackson had summoned his cabinet and laid the case before them. On his own authority he proposed to issue a circular ordering all land commissioners, after a certain date, to accept only specie-hard cash in payment for Government lands. The Cabinet had advised against overriding Congress. Old Hickory had listened sullenly, and dismissed them.

"I'll show them," he growled.

Truxton hinneyed approbation.

Patting the thoroughbred, Jackson stomped out of the stable, straight across the south terrace, and up to his office.

"Donelson," he barked, rapping at his nephew's room.

Major Donelson, his private secretary, sleepily came to the door.

"Come into my office at once. We have work to do."

So the famous Specie Circular came into being, over the bold signature of Andrew Jackson, President of the United States. It was dated July 11, 1836.

It would take some days before the land offices at Batavia and Buffalo got word. Weeks, perhaps, before it reached the west. Congress would brand it autocratic effrontery. State banks would smart at the inbuilt insult to their solvency. Popular confidence in all paper money would falter.

A depression was in the offing, one without parallel in the history of the United States.

Father John Neumann knew nothing of inflation or the Specie Circular, the afternoon of July twelfth, as he hoisted his luggage under arm, and stepped off the packet at Long Wharf. So this was Buffalo! Somehow it had a slapdash look—busier than Rochester, bigger than the settlements and towns along Erie towpath, though not quite as seasoned. He remembered Prost's map, with the X at the foot of Main Street. "Look for the National Hotel." Prost had been picturesquely practical in his directions for locating the Catholic church and Father Alexander Pax, the pastor.

The slope of Main Street was a bedlam of carts, coaches, wagons. Runners for the hotels besieged the new arrivals. Seneca peddlers, in blue leggings and bright red jackets, held out baskets of dusty raspberries, bouquets of pond lilies, bunches of sassafras and wintergreen. Silver rings flashed in their earlobes. Neumann had never before seen live Indians. He hardly expected to meet them, selling herbs and flowers.

Unexpectedly, at the corner of Exchange, a whiff of spearmint—or was it honeysuckle?—surprised his nostrils. No wonder. On his right, facing the old Mansion House, stood the comfortable brick residence of old Louis Lecouteulx, with fruit trees and gardens covering an entire block. Close by the iron fence lay a fragrant herb garden—sage, lavender, mint, boneset, marjoram. Blood red ramblers, lemon colored hollyhocks, and the waxy cones of lilies made the garden gay, but there was one spike of blue that Neumann could not identify! What was it, he wondered.

"You're not thinking of buying my place too, Ben?"

A hand touched his shoulder. Startled, Neumann turned round.

"Beg pardon, sir. I thought you were an old acquaintance of mine." It was Mr. Louis Lecouteulx.

Further on, Hayden, the bookseller, bowed deferentially as Neumann passed. Hequembourg, the jeweller, bade him a cheery good afternoon, as though he'd known Neumann all his life. Between Seneca and Swann Streets Mr. Philip Dorsheimer grew solicitous.

"You shouldn't be carrying that heavy bag, sir."

But on second glance, he apologized. "Excuse, please. I thought you were someone else."

Across Main Street, a long queue stood waiting at the door of the United States Bank. On his own side of the street, a heated argument was in progress . . . coming to a boil, as Neumann approached.

"I tell you, its dome is going to be three hundred feet high."

The speaker noticed Neumann walking towards him.

"Ask Rathbun. (Sure it's him. Bet that bag he's lugging is loaded with banknotes, too.) Ask him. Go ahead."

But as Neumann came abreast of the group, they burst out laughing, slapping and ribbing one another.

"He's sure a dead ringer for him, anyway!"

Many of the streets bore Indian names: Mohawk, Genesee, Huron, Chippewa. Neumann shifted his bag. His clothing prickled uncomfortably in the afternoon heat. Now he had come to the end of the pavement—at Genesee Street. Here, the brick sidewalks ended too—another of Prost's landmarks! Four more streets before the church, and he should pass two inn yards. There they were, just ahead: Plough Inn and Broadwheel Tavern.

"Can you tell me, sir: is that the Catholic church?"

"Yes, sir. That's it." The man scratched his poll and grinned. "Say, Mister. Has anyone told you: you're the dead spit of Mr. Benjamin Rathbun."

Early next morning a Yankee farmboy in dusty blue denims came whistling up the plank road from the Village of Williamsville, driving three pigs to the market in Buffalo. Ichabod Smith had his heart set that Wednesday morning on finding a honey tree —a hollow sycamore in the woods where a bee swarm had built their hive. Scanning the treetops on either side of the road, Ichabod all but stumbled into an oncoming horse and wagon.

"Whoah!" The driver tugged at the reins.

Startled at sight of two clergymen riding a rickety buck-board, Ichabod grinned apology and hurried after his porkers.

"He's not one of ours," said Father Alexander Pax. "You'll meet his guardian one of these days. A good man, Oziel Smith! He's a big name in Williamsville: owns two mills, the tannery at the creek, the Eagle House on Main Street."

Pax was feeding Father Neumann necessary information for his territory, north and east of Buffalo. "By the way, Father. It was this Oziel Smith who gave the land for your parish church."

Father Pax had given young Neumann his choice last evening—the city or the country.

"I'm a sturdy son of the Boehmerwald," Neumann had smiled. "I was ordained in New York for work on the American Mission."

What he meant was that he thought it only proper to take the rougher portion of the Niagara frontier. Pax had been ordained in Europe for the diocese of Metz. He was thirteen years Neumann's senior in ordination. Besides, he looked on the brink of physical crackup. And no wonder, trying to take care of the whole territory singlehanded: from Eden and Hamburg in the south, to Batavia and Niagara Falls. His poor little log-house rectory on Edwards Street had hardly more than a bed, a book shelf and a few chairs.

A chipmunk scurried in front of the horse, darting into the woods. Crows cawed hoarsely in the distance.

"You'll laugh, Father Neumann, when I tell you how Oziel Smith came to give us the land." Pax was filling in more background for Williamsville.

In belief, Smith was a Universalist, he explained, but it galled him that only one church, the Methodist, had received gratis from the Holland land agent, a sixty-acre "gospel plot." Now they had sold part of this free gift for a tidy sum; they were planning to build a white meeting house with spire and clock, like they had back in Vermont! So Oziel Smith, for the sum of thirty dollars, gave a generous lot of ground on Williamsville's Main Street to the Catholics for a church—on one condition: it must be built of stone, and the biggest church in the village!

"So, Father Neumann, you will have the only Catholic church, that is not built of wood, between Rochester and Cincinnati!"

Pax reminded him that this stone church at Williamsville was still without roof or floor. There was no glass in the windows. It had not been at all easy getting the few Catholic families to give their time and labor, stone and money, for so large an edifice. But with Father Neumann residing there, things should speed up!

"That's what we call the Guide Board Road." They had come to a fork. The horse kept to the right branch, as Pax pointed left. "You'll find that a convenient way to get to the chapel of St. John on North Bush, Father."

As Neumann turned his head to look back over his shoulder, the main road suddenly jingled with bells. In a cloud of rising dust and a thunder of bouncing planks, three mammoth wagons of limestone clattered past them for Buffalo.

"This is the main route between Batavia and Buffalo," explained Pax. "It passes straight through Williamsville. So you'll have no difficulty hailing a stage coach any time you have some problem you want to discuss with another priest."

The details confused Neumann: North Bush, six miles in this direction; Cayuga Creek, six miles that way. Roads. Landmarks. Names of prominent people. Neumann decided to make a map for himself with all the roads and landmarks clearly marked in his sprawling parish. He had about three hundred German families and some hundred more French and Irish in his care. But no two of them lived within a mile of one another! Some were as much as fifty miles apart. Most had purchased land and were, year by year, clearing the forest for farmland. Some were squatters, living in lean-tos along the creeks. Few were exactly prosperous—as yet!

"But in ten years' time," said Father Pax, "once their lands are cleared of stumps and rocks and taproots, so they can sow and reap the crops they choose, they'll be every bit as well off as any country-born Yankee. That dream sweetens all their sweat."

To John Neumann those words sounded like Father Prost at Rochester all over again.

The Perrywinkel, at Williamsville, was a newcomer as taverns went in the eighteen-thirties. It was not in a class with Asa Ransom's place at Clarence Hollow, four miles away on the road to Batavia; nor Eagle House in Williamsville itself. The Perrywinkel sold nothing stronger than good German beer from Rudolf Baer's brewery at Cold Springs. It was not the only tavern in the village. But the proprietor, Mr. Phil Wirtz, was the soul of affability and Elizabeth, his wife, was a cook without equal this side of home.

Teamsters and waggoners en route to Buffalo often stopped at the Perrywinkel. An infallible sign of good food! Stages stopped, too. When business became almost too much for the Wirtz couple, like an answer to prayer came a letter from Luetzelstein in Alsace. Anton Wimmer wanted to send his teenage daughter to America—that is, if his old friend and townsman, Phil Wirtz, could provide lodging, and keep a fatherly eye on her. That was in the spring of 1835. That same summer sixteen-year-old Trilby Wimmer came to the Perrywinkel at Williamsville. She would earn her keep, waiting on customers, keeping the place neat—until Anton and the rest of the family came over from Alsace.

A year had passed since then. Anton was still in Europe. Trilby had learned a smattering of English from the coach trade who stopped for a bite to eat. She was a pretty thing with her braided blond hair, her lace apron, her gay Alsatian frock. Frau Wirtz insisted on that. The Perrywinkel must be Alsace in miniature. Lisa Wirtz wore the old country costume, too, as did her husband, while waiting on guests.

But the place must not be "foreign"; it must be American, too. With a touch of the businessman, the diplomat, she named the place *winkel,* the German word for a cozy nook. The "Perry" was for the dapper naval hero of Lake Erie. So neat and clean was the Perrywinkel, thanks to Trilby and Lisa, that Lance Palmer, Buffalo financier, had once declared that her floor and tables were whiter than the holystoned deck of the *Julia,* his luxury yacht. Well they might be: Trilby scoured them each morning with sand and water from Ellicott Creek.

But this particular morning Trilby, along with her other tasks, had to scrub and tidy the extra room in the garret. Frau Wirtz wanted every copper pot sparkling. She needed a bouquet of columbines and white daisies for the table. She wanted wild strawberries, if there were any. So many extra things. Desperately, Trilby hoped to finish her chores, and be dressed in Sunday best, in time to meet the new boarder, Father Neumann, when he arrived. He would make the Perrywinkel his headquarters for the present.

But nothing went right that morning. Frau Wirtz forgot the Sauerfleisch on the hearth; and the place reeked of smoking vinegar. Phil Wirtz found two buttons missing from his best jacket. Down at creekside the soot stuck fast to the copper kettle, though Trilby rubbed it with grit till her hands were raw. She came running up through the woods with the kettle scoured at last, only to be stung by a hornet on the tip of her nose. Her braids streaked with blackpot, her nose red with pain, she was ready to scream when, straight ahead, at the door of the Perrywinkel, she saw Father Pax' horse and trap. Herr Wirtz was welcoming the new priest.

"Trilby, come here," beckoned Wirtz.

Everything went wrong.

That afternoon Father Neumann wrote a few lines in his little day-book. *"Williamsville, July 14, 1836*—Lord Jesus, my earthly desires are almost all fulfilled. Here I am in America, a priest and a missionary. Now I have a flock of my own." And as an afterthought, he wrote, "Father Alexander Pax is a man after my own heart."

II

6. MASS AT WILLIAMSVILLE

Indians knew, that summer morning, that the trout would be running along the eleven miles of Ellicott Creek. Young Tuscarora braves, up before dawn, straddled boulders in midstream. With drawn bows in hand, they watched the fish flick through the chuckling waters. Squaws, less sportsmanlike, scooped the silvery creatures pellmell out of the creek with dripping home-made seines. By cockcrow, Yankee farmer boys would longingly eye the creek, their minds only half on their chores. They would remember, too, with chagrin that, being the Sabbath, they could not go fishing; not till after meeting, at least. By that time, shucks, it would be too late.

The new priest at Williamsville noticed the fish in Ellicott Creek that morning, too. He saw them darting among the cool green stems of jewel weed and arum lilies, when he went down in the gray hours to wash the sleep from his eyes. But to tell the truth, it was the flowers that took his attention. He noticed something else—an abnormal quiet in the whole neighborhood. With mild shock he realized that the mill wheels were idle along the banks of the creek. Somehow, he did not expect money-mad Yankees to stop work on the Lord's day! But the silence was a delight. No whine of buzz-saw, chewing through green maple and cedarwood. No chug-alug gristmill, stomping corn into yellow meal. No fog of limedust, either, from kiln or quarry up the creek beyond the mills. Even the tannery, this side of Main Street

61

bridge, was idle, though the acrid stench of cowhides, steeping in the vats, still rose nauseous as on weekdays.

Before Herr Wirtz of the Perrywinkel was astir that July morning, before Trilby had kindled fire in the hearth, the new boarder, Father Neumann, had tiptoed downstairs and out of the little inn. He had washed his face in the creek, shaved, recited Lauds for the tenth Sunday after Pentecost. He had gathered up vestments, chalice, a book of the Gospels, and set out along Main Street towards the unfinished stone church of St. Peter and St. Paul.

Mentally, as he walked up the street, he rehearsed his sermon for the morning: on the gospel, "My house is a house of prayer." Should he weave in something about the unfinished church—hardly a house of prayer with no roof and windows? How would he impress the people? Would they think him "still too young and *green*," as the fellow had told him last Sunday in Rochester? The whole street was still quiet. The morning stage from Batavia was not due in Williamsville until eight, on its rollicking way to Buffalo. Only then would the village come to life.

Inside his rootless church he opened the creased manuscript of his sermon, written last evening in the garret of the Perrywinkel. Up and down the uneven floor he walked, with quick short steps, repeating it half aloud.

"Good Lord, help me to keep it all in my head . . . and to deliver it well," he prayed.

The date was July seventeenth.

"Mother of God, today we shall solemnize your Carmel feast of yesterday. Help me, good Mother, to drive home my point. Help me, and I promise to establish your confraternity in the parish. Help me to instill in them a love for you and your divine Son."

Before the wooden altar, he knelt down to recollect himself.

Robins skittered on the walls. A pair of bluejays dove in and out through the glassless window frames. A goat strayed in through the front door.

Where had he put the altar cloth that Frau Wirtz had laundered for him? Locating it, he spread it on the *mensa*. He set the little brass crucifix in place between the candlesticks, brought all the way from Budweis, the gift of his friend, Father Dichtl.

"Lord, I'm busy about so many things," he apologized, kneeling once more to his meditations.

Except for one on the new fire engine, purchased that spring, there was no bell in the village. So, Williamsville slept till the stage coach arrived. The stage served as a horse-drawn alarm clock between Batavia and Buffalo, a galloping timepiece by which the Niagara frontier knew when to get up on a Sunday morning.

This morning it came bowling whip-a-crackle along Main Street, trace-links and harness bells atinkle, drumming loud on the plank bridge over Ellicott Creek, with a rousing ti-ra-la of bugle notes, and all the dogs of Williamsville yapping in its wake. If that did not arouse the place, thought Neumann, nothing would.

Not that it actually mattered to Father Neumann. Of the forty families comprising the village, less than half-a-dozen would be at Mass. The rest were either stern-lipped Methodists, Unitarians from New England, or German Mennonites from Pennsylvania. Mr. Glezen Fillmore, the popular Methodist circuit rider, was holding a prayer meeting that morning, two miles to the west, in old Tim Hopkins' barn.

Mennonites, Bible in hand, would be out *en masse* in their Sabbath black. Just beyond town, on the Buffalo road, they had a good stone meeting house. There, newly called John Reist, the deacon, would raise his hands (and his voice) over bowed black hats and bonnets—all twenty-one of them. All in all, Williamsville was a pretty godly place on a Sabbath morning.

By ten o'clock that day, Williamsville carts, buckboards, buggies, would all be moving westwards along Main Street, bound for places of worship. The pious Yankee gentry—Drakes, Vanettas, Colvins, Rogers, Ayres—hands folded, backs straight, eyes downcast, would move in their thin-spoked carriages over the wooden bridge at Ellicott Creek, past Oziel Smith's new Eagle House, on past Wirtz' Perrywinkel, past Hoffmann's and Juba Storr's establishments, past the little post office, past the line of unpainted frame houses on the south side of Main Street—and then (for the briefest moment) the heads in every vehicle would swivel right, for a glimpse through the doorless gap in the stone façade of the Catholic church.

To their sincere way of thinking, St. Peter and St. Paul's was Main Street's one unconscionable eyesore. Poisonously, it pricked at their souls like a long-nailed finger—the hand of the great *Whore of Rome!* What black magic had old priest Mertz of Buffalo employed on Oziel Smith, to make him surrender a plot of good Yankee ground for a popish mass-hall—and on Main Street, too!

For almost seven months, now, the church's limestone shell crouched by the side of Main Street, its eyeless windows mocking the passersby like sockets in a death's hand. With a fearsome fascination, the eyes of Williamsville were drawn to it on the way to Sunday meeting. When would the foul Thing coil to strike with all its superstitious abominations, its medieval mumbo-jumbo of sacraments and mass?

As far back as memory these Yankees had heard nothing good of papists and their church. Now, Catholics were infiltrating the entire Niagara frontier: ragged Irish, beer-swilling Germans, shifty-eye French Canadians. They were swarming in from overseas like flies . . . like . . . like malaria. Buying up the woods in the north of Amherst township and clearing farms. In Clarence, too, and Tonawanda, and Cheektowaga. Buffalo crawled with them. Benjamin Rathbun had several hundred in his employ. The Government ought step in—before good upright citizens took the law into their own hands!

Now they were building Mass-halls. Didn't they have one up in Buffalo at the north edge of town?—or was it two? And a shantyhouse chapel of St. Michael down Cayuga Creek way? And one at North Bush, hidden in the woods, a mile or so in from the Guide Board road? But now *this,* built of solid stone, native Onandagua limestone—bold as brass, on the main road to Buffalo, right in the heart of Williamsville!

"Next thing, they'll have the pope here in person, baptizing the countryside with water from Niagara Falls!"

"Mark it, Caleb. The day isn't far off when Yankee Williamsville has a live papist priest walking its streets!"

On one point they were agreed to a man: Methodist, Presbyterian, Mennonite, Universalist—Catholics were a menace to be feared!

Williamsville was not quite aware that a "live papist priest" was already living in its midst. That very morning before the Batavia stage had wakened the Calebs and Judiths and Joels, hours before they hitched horse to cart for Meeting, Father John Neumann, his morning meditation completed, was waiting the arrival of the first parishioners in the stone shell that was St. Peter and St. Paul's.

Ruefully, the priest gazed at the bare altar, wishing he had flowers for our Lady of Mount Carmel. Some thoughtful soul might bring some from home, perhaps.

Someone did.

Frau Irma Bachmann soon arrived, with an armful of snow white peonies.

"Pfingstrosen for the altar," she smiled, introducing herself.

On hearing the name "Bachmann," Father Neumann remarked that he had already met her husband.

But to no avail! Irma proceeded to fill the new priest in on all the details of the Bachmann family. Paul, her Mann, was from Alsace, a watchmaker by trade. He travelled on business extensively. He knew the Niagara frontier like the palm of your hand. If Father Neumann needed a guide on any of his sick calls, her Mann, Paul Bachmann, would be only too glad. . . .

"Of course, Father . . . Paul is one of the trustees. He did his share, too, in collecting funds for this new church."

Father Neumann had tried to tell her that he knew all about her husband; had met him yesterday.

"I hope you like your room at the Perrywinkel." Irma had changed tack suddenly. The Bachmanns would have liked to boast that the priest was boarding with them; but Father Pax had placed him at the Perrywinkel.

"Father Neumann, anytime you'd fancy a good meal—homemade Knockwurst or Knoedel mit Erbsenbrei," she smiled, patting the sleeve of his cassock, "you're welcome at the Bachmann place. Anytime at all. It's just a step from here, right behind the church . . . near the creek."

Beyond Irma's ample shoulders, Neumann observed the steady arrival of buggies and farmcarts. Others were coming up Main Street on foot.

"I'll see that each Sunday you have flowers for the altar, too."

Neumann nodded appreciation. Patiently he shifted his weight to the other foot. Wasn't that Phil Wirtz over there near the chestnut tree?

"And Father . . ." Irma transfixed the priest with her eye, "if there is any other way I can be of help: training first communicants, singing solos . . ."

Neumann's eye had wandered off again. This time he distinctly saw Phil Wirtz staring at him, as much as to say that he was being monopolized by the watchmaker's Frau, at the expense of his other parishioners.

By Mass-time Neumann had been introduced to most of them: Leslers, Schmidts, Demmers, Lunds, Jeanrois, Fessards, Bittermanns, Muellers, Hallorans, Kellys. Too many to keep apart. He confused Max Schneider, the local schoolmaster, with Sam Herberger of Transit. Neither party minded the error. But when he inadvertently called Phil Bachmann "Herr Hoffmann," sparks almost flew. Jolly Phil Hoffmann and the watchmaker-trustee hardly bade one another the time of day.

Jacques Poutier, retired trapper, was tickled to hear Neumann drop a few words in French. Mrs. Mike DeCourcy and Mary Holloran stopped to bless their stars aloud, that God had sent a priest who talked their language, too. . . .

"Not an easy thing to know what he's saying! But God bless him," they agreed, "he has a fine big head! He'll be talking English we can understand in no time at all."

Some thirty-seven families came that Sunday: most had spoken a word or two to the young priest. There were promises of timber for the roof, boards for the floor. Carpenters promised free labor. And there were promises of clothing, food, even money as need arose. Clearly everyone was delighted at a resident priest.

An old grandmother could not get to Mass that morning. The Besch family, who lived a few miles from her in Tonawanda, deep in the woods, a few miles from the canal—they were telling Father Neumann about her: how she had a bad case of undulant fever, "the shakes." Being old, she might be dead in a few days.

"I'll go visit her this afternoon, if you'll show me the way," said Father Neumann.

Just then an imperious tapping sound laid silence on everyone.

Startled, Neumann looked up to see Melchior Pfau, the trustee, rapping a block of limestone with the point of his cane, gesturing everyone inside. The sun flashed on the gold buttons of his Sunday frock, lighting his florid, sunburnt face, so that he looked more like some court chamberlain at imperial Schoenbrunn than a work-a-day tiller of Cheektowaga farmland.

"Time for Mass, Father. Everyone's here."

For the fraction of a minute, Neumann clenched his fist tight; then, meekly, he went into the roofless church with the rest. Up at a table near the altar, he commenced vesting for Mass.

"These are the announcements." It was Melchior Pfau again. His tone was polite, but more like a gentleman talking to his valet.

Neumann glanced at the sheet of paper.

"Thank you."

He knotted the cincture round his linen alb.

Herr Melchior Pfau, red face, brass buttons and all, walked out of the sacristy, followed by Herr Paul Bachmann—a very solemn procession of two. Did not this young Bohunk greenhorn realize that they were his trustees? Had he no respect for their function? Down to the back of the church strode the pair, standing near the open gap that was the main door. Father Neumann started Mass.

He expected distractions. What else, with no roof, windows, doors! Rubberneck squirrels darted along the walls. Redwings and a catbird unlimbered their repertoire in a stand of ash behind the church. John Schmidt's horse broke loose from the rustic hitching-post, causing commotion among the other animals. Several men had to leave. A baby commenced crying—and in the midst of the bedlam, Irma Bachmann, seeking to be helpful, struck up a hymn.

Es blueht der Blumen eine. . . . In a shrill quaver she waded into the opening bars, awaiting the encouragement of accompanying voices. But the melody soared too uncertainly for pursuit. Bavarians had a variation in the words. The Jeanrois had never heard the melody before. Ella Shanley knew English words for the tune—"It is the name of Mary . . ." But all left Frau Bachmann to her solo.

The sermon was well received. Young Trilby Wimmer listened as though Father Neumann were Bourdeloue in Paris, quite heedless of the sidelong glances of sixteen-year-old Martin Pfau, admiring her golden braids. Jacques Poutier cuffed at a bottlefly that buzzed before his black moustache. Even Katy Carrol looked attentive, though the priest knew that Katy didn't understand a word of German. Herr Melchior Pfau, at the rear of the church, listened chiefly to be sure that Neumann read his announcements. He smirked contentedly at the adroit way the priest had woven them into his sermon. (He took full credit both sermon and announcements: that a House of Prayer needs windows and floor and roof; that the sooner people set to finishing the remainder of the church, the quicker it will become a worthy house of worship.)

The altar boy had no bell; but by the time of the Elevation Frau Irma Bachmann had subsided into silence. Heads everywhere bowed low. Conrad Thee, as Father Neumann elevated the Host, struck his chest a resounding thump. All else was solemnly quiet.

Kneeling on one knee at the rear of the church, Paul Bachmann saw from the corner of his eye, shadows moving in the gap of the doorway. Before he could turn to investigate, a shower of pebbles, cowdung and corncobs hurtled down on the bent heads of the congregation. A roudy guffaw ripped the silence; several buggies sped suspiciously fast along Main Street.

In the shock and excitement, the faithful did not notice a

rock, lobbed over the church wall, almost strike the chalice in Father Neumann's hand, as he whispered the words of consecration. But Max Schneider, the schoolmaster, who was near one of the windows, traced the rock's trajectory to the horsechestnut, where he spied three of his scholars, Mennonite rascals. Mentally, he put several stout birch rods in pickle for the morrow. He did not have the nickname "Schneider the Hider" for nothing.

Meanwhile, Father Neumann quietly finished the Mass; and was escorted from the altar by the two altar boys.

The catechism lesson that morning was brief, it being the first. But from the outset the children took to the new priest. Before class was over, he could call most of them by name; and he knew where they lived. He had small Willi Hoffmann repeat, in his own words, the story read in the morning's gospel: about the Lord casting the merchants from the temple. He arranged to give several of the older boys lessons in Latin, so they could answer the Mass prayers.

"We'll have twenty altar boys," he told them, "with red cassocks for processions; but you'll have to behave like gentlemen, and always be here on time."

He promised also to teach them to sing: boys and girls.

With a blessing, he sent them racing off to their parents, waiting outside.

It was three that afternoon when he reached the house of the old grandmother in Tonawanda, bringing Viaticum. It was five before he started back for home—on foot. He remembered, in reverse, the route by which Franz Besch had brought him in his farm-cart: the Guide Board road, Rudolf Baer's tavern at Cold Spring, then left on to Main Street and straight to Williamsville and the Perrywinkel.

The stars were out by the time he came to Cold Spring. Rudolf Baer, seated in his doorway after a prosperous day, saluted the passerby—in German. Anyone with that sort of boot had to be from the old country! Neumann returned the greeting, telling Baer who he was and where he was bound for. As an afterthought, he remarked:

"Did you know, sir, you have a namesake up there in the sky?" Neumann pointed to a cluster of stars. "It's called *Ursa Minor*, which is Latin for *Baer*."

All the way home to the Perrywinkel poor John Neumann reproached himself for his petty display of learning. How could he expect God's blessing on his work, if he succumbed to such silly vanity? When would he detach himself from worldly standards? *Ursa Minor,* indeed! As penance for his sins, he resolved to go supperless to bed.

But the remark made a deep impression on the tavern-keeper. Baer reported it to anyone who dropped in for a beer.

"That new priest up in Williamsville is a smart man. Why, Gott in Himmel! he told me there's a batch of stars named after me, right over my brewery."

One afternoon old Tim Hopkins heard the story of Father Neumann's star-lore. His boy, seventeen-year-old Nelson, heard it too. Young Nel had his heart set on entering Union College over in Schenectady, but he lacked foundation in the natural sciences, Nel Hopkins went up next day to the Perrywinkel.

So Father Neumann, in exchange for his knowledge of astronomy, acquired a young instructor in English.

7. SAM PATCH

The date, August 2, 1836, would be circled in gold on the calendar of Buffalo's Eagle Theatre. Dean and McKinney, the owners, were giddy with success. Their first-night audience had roared applause at Danforth Marble's rib-tickling parody of the Yankee peddler—glib, pack-laden, canny *Sam Patch*. The performance made an instantaneous hit. It would run for weeks; months, perhaps.

Dan Marble, a down-at-heel actor a week ago, was suddenly the toast of Buffalo. That very evening he found, on his dressing-room door, an engraved invitation, signed by millionaire, Lance Palmer—a request for his presence aboard his luxury yacht, *Julia,* moored off Buffalo Light, for a dinner party after the show. He winked at his likeness in the cracked wall mirror, tapped the new Panama on his head and sallied out into the summer night. At the corner of Eagle and Main, Lance Palmer sat waiting in his two-horse phaeton.

"Good evening, *Sam Patch.*"

As the carriage moved off towards Long Wharf, the bell of St. Paul's struck eleven. Lance Palmer glanced over his shoulder, up at the lighted second-floor window of Benjamin Rathbun's fine brick residence at the corner of North Division Street. He could see the silhouette of "Mr. Buffalo" moving to and fro in the lighted window, walking the floor.

"My friend, Ben Rathbun, must be cooking up some new scheme."

"His auction at Niagara is tomorrow."

The bell of St. Paul's struck one, struck two, struck three— and the lamp still burned in the red brick mansion at the corner of Main and North Division. Mr. Rathbun still paced his study. He was worried. Something told him that his luck had run out.

Earlier that evening, on the steps of the Eagle Theatre, a distinguished looking gentleman had saluted him by name; asked how business was. Innocuously, the stranger chatted about a trip to Philadelphia, a luncheon with banker Nicholas Biddle. Suddenly he changed tack.

"I don't believe I've introduced myself. Evans is the name: Mr. David Evans of the Bank of Erie, Pennsylvania."

The man's face was cordiality itself. Still, in the low pitch of his words, there was something that gave Ben Rathbun to suspect that David Evans knew.

"I'd be honored," smiled Evans, "to invest good money in any new project of the great Benjamin Rathbun. How would a note—say, for seventy-five thousand—sound to you?"

Before Rathbun could recover, Evans had tipped his hat.

"I'll be seeing you tomorrow—at the Falls."

Small wonder Rathbun paced his study at three in the morning. Strapped for quick capital, two months ago he had forged the name of David Evans, Esq. to a promissory note for $75,000, exactly. He would eventually reimburse Evans, of course; but meanwhile, Evans had found out.

Money—the root of all evil! Desperately, Benjamin Rathbun ran his fingers through his hair.

Six miles away, at Williamsville, Father Neumann was having money problems of his own. From the moment he pitched into the job of roofing the church, the curse of greed bedevilled him. (How true were the words of Father Prost!) Money, for nine-tenths of his parish, was the only yardstick. On weekly trips to Buffalo, when his farmers stopped at Jabez Goodell's Broadwheel for a stein of beer, talk turned automatically to the topic of *How much*. Possessively, they bragged of their *Landsmann* Phil Dorsheimer, who owned the Mansion House on Main Street, and Rudolf Baer, with his Cold Spring brewery and tavern.

Old Tim Hopkins of Williamsville was notable to Neumann's flock, not for having fought as a brigadier general in the War of 1812, or for being the best read gentleman in the township, self-educated, too—but because he owned so much land. By the same token, Oziel Smith was a riddle. With mills and taverns and plenty of Williamsville real estate a few years back, he now seemed to be almost giving it away. The land for their own church on Main Street was a good example.

Money was the measure of everyone, everything. How much was it worth? How much would it bring? How much did it cost? Before moving a finger, these German farmers stopped first to estimate how much they would lose—or make—by a transaction. This, Father Neumann learned when he called for volunteers to put a roof on his church.

After Sunday Mass, two dozen had agreed to haul timber next morning from their farms to the sawmill at Ellicott Creek. The rest begrudged the time they would lose in the cornfield. "Time is money," they drily explained.

Many of the German settlers had learned trades in the old country—masons, master cabinetmakers, carpenters. When Neumann had suggested that they donate their skills toward the new roof, the majority begged off. Previous commitments: permanent employment with Benjamin Rathbun in Buffalo. Good wages, too!

Sixteen volunteers were on hand that first Monday morning of August. Under the guidance of young Ottony, the carpenter, they made good progress, too. He showed the unskilled how to rive shingles with mallet and froe, twenty at a time, from short-cut pine logs. The mill could take care of cutting trees for joists and timbers. But the rest must be made by hand on the premises —shingles, trunnels, clapboards, and pointed hardwood pegs.

As general overseer of construction, Neumann appointed Phil Hoffmann, a genial and efficient Bavarian with a knack for borrowing the necessary tools from the local Yankees, and for keeping the workmen contented. That arranged, Neumann sat himself down on a log near the church, and set to whittling oaken pegs for the shingles of his new roof. Pegs were cheaper than nails, lasted longer anyway.

A heap of new-made shingles lay ready by one o'clock, when young Trilby Wimmer raced over from the Perrywinkel to call the men to their lunch. Her bright yellow hair hung in two long braids, her scrubbed face shone with good health; and though barefoot, she was wearing her gay Alsatian dress and apron.

Before you could count *eins-zwei-drei,* the sixteen workmen had followed her back across Main Street.

"Father Neumann."

A small boy rushed into the Perrywinkel, where the men were finishing lunch.

"It's old Granny Schaentzlein—down the road toward Cayuga Creek—She's having one of her spells. The ague. She's asking for the priest." The boy was panting for breath.

"And, I don't think I know all my addition tables, either!"

Once Neumann had learned of the savage whippings dealt out by "Schneider the Hider," he dismissed the schoolmaster and assumed the task of conducting school each afternoon himself. That way, he could be sure the children were well instructed— and in the bargain, save the schoolmaster's salary. He must save every penny to make ends meet.

Trilby shooed the boy away from the table.

"Out! Out with you. Go study your addition tables under the trees. School begins in half an hour."

It was an uncomfortable afternoon, insufferably hot under the garret rafters of the Perrywinkel, where school was now conducted. Father Neumann had a hard time keeping young heads concentrated on spelling and arithmetic. Class was dismissed a half hour earlier than usual. Granny Schantzlein was waiting for the priest.

Despite the heat, Father Neumann wore his long black coat, his high leather boots. To see him made one feel warmer. He set off along Main Street, crossed the bridge over the creek and turned south along the Garrison Road in the general direction of Cayuga Creek.

The heat of the last few weeks had turned the roads to yellow powder. If the hot spell continued, many more of the poor along the shallow creeks and swamps would be abed with ague and swamp fever.

On the road, a young Irishman met Neumann. His wife was in poor condition, would Neumann mind if . . .

Over at the Eagle Theatre in Buffalo, *Sam Patch* was reaping a second round of bravos . . . before Father Neumann, his visits made, set out again for home. With the heat and the dust and the thistle burrs, he could have passed for Sam Patch himself! Fortunately, the moon rose early that evening, lighting his way.

But the moon also brought farmers' dogs out, snarling and baying at the short dark figure hastening back to his room in Williamsville. When one dog wearied, another started up—from one farm to another, from one clearing to the next.

Overhead the sky was a rich summer purple. There were many stars. Directly in front of him, Neumann recognized the pulsing golden light of Capella in the constellation of Auriga, the charioteer. Higher up the sky, he traced the five stars of Cassiopeia's Chair. High overhead hung Deneb, in the Northern Cross. Deneb, he reminded himself, was fifteen hundred miles from the earth. Was young Nel Hopkins, his "English professor," watching Deneb, he wondered. Neumann had loaned the boy his brass telescope, that he and Anton Laad had used so often in Budweis.

Budweis! A year ago, little did he surmise that being a missionary in America would entail such unpriestly chores as foreman, paymaster, carpenter's handyman, truant officer, pharmacist and—for all he knew—steeplejack, before his church was under roof. And this was just the start. Some sort of schoolhouse was needed in Williamsville, something better than a tavern-garret for the twenty children now coming to class. Cayuga Creek needed a more respectable church. And North Bush, too, could use a schoolhouse.

One thing, however, was sure: Neumann couldn't go on like this. Roofing churches was one thing, and necessary. But he dare not leave his soul roofless for all the tempests of the world. For his own protection, for his soul's safety, he must frame a Rule of Life for himself, and abide by it.

Hiking up the stumpy East Transit line in the moonlight, Neumann sorted ideas for an order of the day. He would rise at sun-up; recite Lauds, make morning meditation, and say Prime before Mass. After making his thanksgiving, he would say Tierce. Then each weekday morning, from nine to eleven, school. After that he would work on next Sunday's sermon, and at mid-day say Sext and None. He would read the Bible after lunch until school began, at two. At four he would dismiss the children. He must find time to study English better himself, to instruct the children. And he must write letters to Prachatitz, to friends in Prague, in Vienna, in Budweis. There ought be a set time for that, too. At all events, at six o'clock he would go over to the church to recite Vespers and Compline before it got too dark. He had the evening then for study, and before going to bed, he would anticipate Matins of the next day.

The thrash of millwheels intruded on his thoughts—Ellicott Creek. The smell of fresh sawdust, the stench of hides tanning, told him that Williamsville was close by. The village was in darkness as he crossed the wooden bridge and hurried down Main Street to the Perrywinkel, and up the creaky ladder to his room in the loft.

He still had part of his Office to read. He had not eaten since lunch. His feet throbbed with the heat and tightness of his boots.

Lighting the tallow stump on his table, he yawned, took up his breviary. Compline done, he closed the book; then, opened it again. Better start his new Rule of Life at once. He anticipated Matins for St. Peter in Chains before at last going to bed.

During lunch next day, a stage from Buffalo pulled up at the Perrywinkel.

"Did you hear about Benjamin Rathbun? He's been jailed."

Excitedly, the passengers told of the big land auction at the Falls. The arrival of two U.S. marshals; and Mr. Rathbun, in his sober black suit, politely greeting them, then walking arm in arm with them over to the waiting coach.

"And now he's in Buffalo, lodged in his own jail!"

With Rathbun's arrest, his numerous civic projects came to a standstill. Two thousand workmen were suddenly without work, without means of livelihood. Drovers, masons, carpenters, quarrymen, all clamored for back pay; but the paymaster, Lyman Rathbun, was nowhere to be found. His brother Benjamin's forgeries, it was rumored, had exceeded over a million dollars! It would take all the assets of Rathbun's estate to liquidate his debts, and even then, his workmen could expect no more than fifty cents on the dollar. People were in an ugly mood in Buffalo. A lynching party even tried to storm the jail on Batavia Street, and Benjamin Rathbun, inside, trembled in his black coat.

The price of property dropped to practically nothing as the summer and fall wore on. Land that had sold for forty dollars a foot now brought scarcely that an acre. Respectable firms went bankrupt in Buffalo. Prosperous citizens became paupers overnight. Some blew out their brains. Lance Palmer's curly brown hair turned gray. His Tupper Street mansion, his coaches and thoroughbred geldings, his American Hotel, his luxury yacht were sold to the highest bidder. He tramped Main Street in a stupor; had hardly a friend to call him by name. Buffalo's dream of easy money turned into a nightmare of misery.

But it's an ill wind that blows no good.

Father Neumann now had a dozen more journeymen carpenters shingling his roof—men deprived of jobs by Rathbun's arrest. Some considered their sudden loss of livelihood in Buffalo a chastisment from God for refusing to help the priest. Anyway, the church at Williamsville was finished before the first snow.

All over Niagara frontier the pinch of the Depression had left its mark. Paper banknotes were worthless. Many a German farmer who had sold land for paper money lived to regret his folly in not listening to Father Pax. Cash became scarce. In a week of Sunday mornings, Father Neumann seldom found a dozen coins in the collection. But in lieu of coin, some brought farm produce to church: potatoes, a smoked sausage, corn meal, a few heads of red cabbage, a hatful of eggs.

Those with farms could at least barter produce for cloth, for utensils, and in emergency, for medicine. But not everyone had farmland of their own. Neumann often met such families in his hikes through the swampy woods—children with hunger-pinched faces, with large insolent eyes. Often he crammed his knapsack with food from his own lean larder, and took it to the destitute.

Undernourishment made them easy prey to all manner of ailment. Many died without candle or priest, but only because their call for Neumann failed to reach Williamsville on time. Sick calls multiplied by the week. Father Neumann's short sturdy legs crisscrossed the Niagara frontier—walking sometimes forty miles in a day—down to Eden or Java; out towards Black Rock, Tonawanda and the Falls, sometimes eastward to Clarence and Batavia, or the shanty towns along the canal.

There were whole weeks when Father Neumann could keep no order of the day at all. He accused himself of not keeping to his resolutions but his confessor, Father Pax in Buffalo, assured him that, in emergencies, souls came before personal prayer and private resolutions. *Sacramenta propter homines*, he reminded. It was more important to bring Viaticum to the dying.

"If you should die on such an errand of mercy, Father Neumann, the good Lord will not call you to task."

Those words of his confessor gave peace to Father Neumann's soul. He often called them to mind as he walked alone through the solitary forests on frosty nights that fall.

After school, one afternoon in mid-September, he went across the street to the church. One of blacksmith Job Bestow's apprentices—Mike Deasey—was making two iron hinges for the main door.

"Father Neumann, I hate to trouble you. My wife is down with shaking ague. I wonder, could you get down at all to see her?"

The Deaseys lived down in Plumb Hollow on the far side of Cayuga Creek. Neumann had passed their little shack in the swampy lowlands several times. There were four small children, all boys.

"If you like, Father, I can get you a horse. One of Riley Monger's geldings is over at the shop, new shod. I'll have to take it down to Cayuga Creek, anyway."

"Thank you, Mike, I think I can make it quicker on foot." The priest was a notoriously poor horseman.

The afternoon was glorious, with the leaves just beginning to turn, a touch of chill in the air. How his old friends, Adalbert Schmidt and Anton Laad of Budweis days, would marvel at the colors of American trees.

Into his knapsack he had packed a few potatoes and a small chunk of sausage, and for the Deasey boys, a handful of molasses and peppermint bullseyes; also, in the event that he might have to stay the night at Cayuga Creek, he packed altar stone, vestments, chalice, some wine and a host for Mass. Off he went, the knapsack strapped to his back, the holy oils in his coat pocket, the Blessed Sacrament in a golden pyx near his heart.

"Hey, there goes Sam Patch."

Two farmboys saw Neumann going down Garrison Road and into the woods. With the pack on his back, he did look like some Yankee peddler making the last trip before winter, with a cargo of bone buttons, ribbons, scissors, nutmeg and clocks. He walked rapidly. The days were getting shorter and he hoped to reach Plumb Bottom before dark.

The smell of wild grapes was in the air. Sunlight filtered through the turning aspens and maples, giving a golden aura to the air. To Neumann, it seemed like a private Corpus Christi procession, with Viaticum for Nora Deasey near his heart. The time sped by. It was still daylight when he reached Cayuga Creek.

Mike Deasey, in a hurry to get home to his ailing wife, took the horse, a lively pinto, down the same route Neumann had fol-lowed towards Cayuga Creek. The twilight was a long, golden one. On either side the woods stood thick, with the road cut straight for miles.

Far ahead, in the gathering dark, he noticed three sputtering flames, like torches. He grew cautious, fearing highwaymen who might kill him for the pinto gelding. He slowed the horse to a canter.

"Halloo!" he shouted into the dark down the road.

No answer.

There was no sign of torches; but as he moved forward, he heard a moan as of someone in pain.

At the side of the road was a body, trussed hand and foot. Mike Deasey lit a pine torch to investigate.

"God Almighty, Father Neumann! What happened? Who did this?"

Around the priest's neck was a loose rope, that looped up-wards to the limb of an oak tree. Someone had tried to lynch Father Neumann!

"I'm glad you came along, Mike." Neumann's voice was weak.

"I saw your wife; gave her Viaticum . . . and a bit of medi-cine. I think she'll be all right by morning."

Who the masked men were, or why they had waylaid him, Neumann was not quite sure. They seemed at first to have mis-taken him for Benjamin Rathbun. They spoke angrily of his cheap disguise as *Sam Patch!* His knapsack was packed with gold, they supposed! They talked of his escaping jail. Yet, when they rifled his knapsack, and found the Catholic vestments and the small chalice, they still went on with the business of trying to hang him.

As he hurried homeward towards the Perrywinkel, the advice of Father Pax came back to him—about meeting death on an errand of mercy. But, Thank God, he was still alive! He still had his prayers to say for today, and Matins for tomorrow, the Exaltation of the Holy Cross.

Across the Atlantic, in the Czech village of Kotoum, the young curate, Father Anton Laad, sat up in bed in the middle of the night. He lit a candle and jotted down a few lines in a book:

> This night I had a peculiar dream. I was in a strange house
> in some foreign land. At the end of a dim-lit garret I found
> a poor bed of straw. Beside it, I saw my old seminary-friend,
> John Neumann, taking off his high boots after a long trip.
> He knelt down to say his prayers. I saw his face. It looked
> so very young and happy. His head seemed aglow with a
> heavenly light. I, Anton Laad, dreamed this dream Septem-
> ber 13, 1836.

Next morning at the Perrywinkel, young Trilby Wilmer observed that Father Neumann's bed had not been slept in.

"That's odd," she said.

8.   RUMORS OF SPRING

It caused no little stir in Williamsville when Father Neumann
packed up and left the Perrywinkel. It happened in mid-Lent
of 1837, on a windy March afternoon.

Mike Deasey was shoeing a horse for Bachmann, the watchmaker, over at Job Bestow's smithy on Main Street, when he
noticed His Reverence setting an armful of books in a farm-cart
near the tavern door. At the moment he paid scant attention,
since Bachmann was spinning one of his yarns from a recent trip
into Canada; but when Phil Wirtz lugged out a leather coffer and
hoisted it up on the cart, along with two chairs and a table,
"Blessed God!" exclaimed Mike Deasey, "Is the priest leaving us,
or what?"

"Guess you don't go much to Buffalo, Mike?"

Bachmann's face crinkled in a lewd grin. Cupping his pudgy
fist to his mouth, he whispered something in the blacksmith's ear.

But Mike Deasey did not grin at all. He caught up the heavy sledge like a drumstick and banged it down on the anvil.

"A damn lie . . . so it is."

Mike Deasey was mad.

As the farmcart with Neumann's belongings joggled over the rutted snow and out of town, comment varied along Main Street.

"The little priest must have had a falling out with old Wirtz."

"Could he be moving in with Bachmann, the trustee, down near the creek, I wonder?"

"They say he's been giving science lessons to young Nel Hopkins. Maybe he's going to stay at Sam's place."

But old Sam Hopkins was not a Catholic. That possibility was quickly ruled out.

The postmaster, who had been listening to the varied comments, finally added: "If you want the facts, the priest is moving over to Schmitt's at North Bush. He told me so this morning."

This last bit of information caused even more comment.

"Schmitt! Why, all Schmitt has is a clearing in the woods! A two-room blockhouse with swamp on all sides. Another blizzard like last Tuesday's, and the priest'll be snow-bound for a week. What's he leaving a convenient lodging, a stone's throw from his church, for?"

Williamsville shook its head.

It did seem folly at first blink. But there were reasons that, fortunately for Father Neumann, were not too widely known in Williamsville proper. A nasty little rumor had been going the rounds of the Buffalo taverns, where the German farmers gathered on market days. It was a devilish bit of righteous innuendo: it did not seem quite proper, that a Catholic priest, a young one, should be living in a tavern! Not just that, but a tavern like the Perrywinkel, with a pretty blond wench, like Trilby Wilmer, forever flitting about! The rest was left unsaid.

On a Saturday evening the five pompous trustees of St. Peter and St. Paul's, at Williamsville, convened before the fireplace of Phil Wirtz' Perrywinkel, to probe the truth of the rumor. They cross-examined Wirtz at some length:

"Was it true that the priest and Trilby slept in adjacent rooms upstairs?"

"At what hour did Father Neumann usually get home?"

"Was he in at the moment?" (He had been away most of the afternoon, on a sick call at Transit, said Wirtz.)

"Well, in that case, could they inspect the location of the rooms in the garret?"

The line of their questions clearly implied what the trustees were thinking.

When they came down from the garret, Paul Bachmann announced that "one of the two must clear out: Neumann or young Trilby."

Outside, the March wind howled cold. The door blew open, tossing fresh snow into the cozy room. Bachmann looked up.

"Welcome, Father Neumann. We were just talking about you."

Stamping snow from his boots, Neumann blew softly on his chilblained hands, and stepped across the room to the fire.

Paul Bachmann mentioned the rumor; bluntly he told the priest their decision.

Neumann said nothing.

Melchior Pfau tried to soften matters by further explanation; but the more he talked, the more vile he felt inside.

Father Neumann remained by the fireplace, the ice on his boots making small puddles on the puncheon floor. He stood there, looking squarely at his accusers, smiling ever so faintly.

"Good evening, gentlemen." Quietly picking up his coat, he trudged upstairs to his room.

He had not eaten since early morning. Nor said the half of his Breviary. And there was his sermon for tomorrow, Passion Sunday. It was not an easy matter to focus his mind.

Typically, he did not blame the five righteous trustees. Nor the tale-bearing farmers in Buffalo. He blamed himself. For any lapse among his parishioners—slander, avarice, backbiting— Father Neumann felt personally responsible. The cause was simple: because he was not the pastor God wanted him to be! Were he only more zealous, more mortified, holier, it would redound to his flock. Ever since his coming to Williamsville, this had been his unending battle: to make himself a more worthy instrument of God's grace.

"God must not be satisfied with me."—he wrote that evening in his spiritual diary. "Things are just as bad with my little flock. Only now my faults seem to have made what was bad even worse. . . ."

To preclude further gossip, Father Neumann decided that he must quit the Perrywinkel, though to move would have obvious disadvantages. Williamsville was central, so handily located on the main road between Buffalo and the east! Not only that. There was the matter of the new school, finished just before Christmas. When he had broached the subject of a better place for the children, the trustees had given only a frosty disapproval. The Perrywinkel garret, they declared, was quite adequate for a few hours of school! So, with his own few dollars, and the brawn of several young farmers, he had built a log school himself. Only a fortnight ago, he had bought a stove in Buffalo, bought it out of his own slim funds—to keep the children comfortable during school hours. Now, if he moved too far away, what would the children do?

Enough! He had opened his book to None. There was still his sermon for Passion Sunday. He did not miss the ironic propriety of the Gospel: Christ asking his accusers: *Which of you shall convict me of sin?* He let it pass.

Like an answer to prayer, next morning a young farmer came into the sacristy after Mass. John Schmitt was embarrassed.

"Father, I don't know how to put this, but if you ever want to move, . . . well, I haven't much to offer, but you'll be welcome at my place."

Neumann was overjoyed. Then and there it was agreed: he would move that week from the Perrywinkel to Schmitt's.

Schmitt packed his family into one room of their little block house. On Wednesday, the priest arrived at his new home in the snow-clogged woods of North Bush.

Board? Schmitt wouldn't hear of it.

"Say a prayer for us once in a while, Father Neumann. That will be payment enough."

He was welcome to whatever they had on the table—salt pork, as a rule, with a hard paste of cormeal and water, baked in a skillet under the ashes. (Money was scarce. The great Depression had the Niagara frontier in its grasp. But the farmers at least could eat what they raised.) Schmitt raised his own corn; so, they had cornmeal. Wheat, he couldn't grow yet, their clearing was but five years hacked from virgin forests. They never had white bread. (How could they bake it, anyway, without an oven? An open fire on a fieldstone hearth was all they could afford.)

Living in Schmitt's little log house would be far from luxury, but Father John Neumann did not mind at all.

No longer was morning Mass a mere matter of crossing Main Street to the stone church. At North Bush the log chapel of St. John the Baptist was a half hour's hike through a maze of crooked trails and corduroy cartways in the dense primeval forest. It was still winter, and though the swampy earth was frozen hard, those stout Boehmerwald highboots were a blessing, for often the snow drifted deep over gnarled oak roots and chipmunk holes. One must ever pick one's way with caution, or sprain a leg.

Call it what you will, that daily tramp of a mile and a half to church was hardly a pleasure jaunt. And yet, to an eye as alert as John Neumann's to the world of nature, that walk had its compensations. Maybe the dainty prints of deer in fresh snow. The tracks of scampering rabbits. Sometimes, the lumbering pawmarks of a bear. And always, there was the endless variety of American trees—so different from his Bohemian homeland, where one met a thin patch of spruce, a grove of birch or oak. But here trees grew in prodigal pellmell: ash, balsam, beech, alder, shagbark hickory, butterwood—trees too varied to enumerate! One March morning he counted forty-three varieties between Schmitt's place and St. John's.

Tock! Now he wakened mornings to the swack of axes, as neighboring farmers methodically widened their clearings. John Schmitt was already up and about, as Neumann left, in the faint streaks of day. *Tock!* The axe of a neighbor, a half mile away, bit into a sturdy sourgum. The steady axe-strokes grew louder, as the priest trudged on. Silence for a moment. Then, a crashing of many branches as the great tree toppled with a padded thump in the snow. *Tock! Tock-tock!* All through Mass. Clearing the wood round the cabins was an endless job for the pioneer. Wistfully, Father Neumann wondered when the bush near his log chapel would be cleared, and the timber trimmed, for that promised rectory! His German flock at North Bush had bought him five acres of land round St. John's.

One thing, Father Neumann noticed: no matter how many trees were felled, the wise farmer left one species standing. In cornfield, in pigsty, in potato patch, in clearings still sown with the first crop of grass—the sugar maple remained untouched by the axe. Neumann knew why. He had watched the farmer bore its bark, plug in spiles of hollow sumach, to let the clear, sweet sap tinkle all day into oaken pails. So simple a chore it was, even children could take care of it. The Schmitt boys spent all March replacing brimming buckets. They poured the sap into steaming vats; kept the wood fires smoking all day. In March the sticky fragrance of boiling maple sap filled the woods, filled the whole Niagara frontier. By mid-afternoon, it had thickened to a tacky golden syrup. Boil it still more; set it out to cool in the snow; by morning it was a hard bronze.

The making of maple sugar—the secret handed down through generations of Iroquois to the sweet-toothed pioneers—fascinated John Neumann. He had read about it but never, till now, had he watched the day-long process—from water-clear sap in the pail to the blond chunks of crumbly sweetness.

He wrote home about it to his father; even enclosed a few maple leaves in the letter, for Prachatitz to smell and admire.

All his letters home he filled with observations on his new surroundings. He mentioned Niagara Falls. After all, it was part of his "parish"—though in fifteen months, somehow, he had not gotten to see it at close range. From Schmitt's blockhouse at North Bush, on a quiet night he could hear it, he wrote, "like an endless hailstorm."

But on a quiet night in early May, as he knelt beside an open book in his little room, Father Neumann cocked his head and listened to something new: a noise like the boom of cannon. It came from the northwest. Erie ice was breaking. That, the farmers told him, was a sure sign of spring—surer even than pussy willows; surer, at least in Niagara country, than the belling of peepers in marshes; surer, by a long shot, than the honking of north-bound swans. Once the ice on Erie and Ontario started breaking—that was it! The Niagara spring had come to stay.

The witchery of the American spring played havoc with Father Neumann. Botany was in his blood, botany and bird-lore and astronomy. His eye, his ear—all his senses were trained to "draw the bolt of Nature's secrecies." Every growing thing was a challenge to his probing mind; and here, everything was new. Here were brown wrens, purple-coated grackles, green vireos, warblers like winged daffodils. The whole woods echoed with *coo* and *tweet* and *jug-a-jug*: tinkled with a hundred bird-calls. Hiking to Williamsville for school, he would stop in his tracks to watch a great cloud of wild pigeons, thousands of them, come thrumming up the sky from Cayuga Creek, darkening the curve of Main Street as they thundered off toward Canada in the direction of the canal.

Now the frost was gone. The trails through the woods squished under foot. Here, along the roadside, were clumps of unfurling fiddleheads. Here was blood root, that the Indians used for war-paint—bloodroot with blossoms white as Baptism. Here were yellow spicebush, adder's tongue, dog-tooth violet, purple wakerobin —though Father Neumann tagged them with sonorous Latin names. In the swamp one afternoon, not far from Schmitt's, he came upon a clump of *Caltha palustris* (or so he called it)—heart-shaped leaf like a violet, blossoms like king-size buttercups, each lacquered petal big as a golden *Kreuzer*. Marsh marigold! Immediately he brought it home for his botanical collection.

Spring was an endless enchantment. At night, on the way back from a distant sick call, he had to crane his neck to find the Dipper, so high it hung in the northern skies. Was that Andromeda? It couldn't be! It was only a "constellation" of fireflies, shimmering in a clump of horsechestnut to his left.

Back in his little room, as he finished Compline by candlelight, a cricket set up a din in the calking of the wall. Ladybugs skittered across his open book. A mosquito whined in his ear. And far away, against the drumming boom of the Falls, came the three-note fifing of whipporwills, all through the night.

Often, writing in his private journal, he would chide himself for this avid interest in nature, when he ought be absorbed in God! But Father Neumann was young, ordained not quite a year, and bent so earnestly on loving God for Himself, that he trembled lest the Niagara spring distract his heart. It was all such a series of incessant surprises that, well, it seemed almost wrong to be so fond of it.

But spring was not all blossoms and flickering wings. Spring had its sterner side. With the cracking of the ice, the packet captains blew their lonesome bugles again, and the traffic stirred on the grand Erie Canal. Up from the landings along Erie water: from Lockport, Pendleton, Tonawanda, Black Rock, came the traveling chapmen with stocks of new wares. *Sam Patch* was back! The Yankee peddlers were a canny lot. From farm to farm, clearing to clearing, they went along the entire Niagara frontier.

"What will it be, lady?—needles, a swatch of gay ribbon, thimbles, nutmeg, a jewsharp."

Sam Patch had them all.

"Perhaps milady fancies this bright blue chintz, this fine gingham for a dress—it's the rage just now in New York."

The peddler holds up the cloth for the housewife's inspection; he produces another item.

"Maybe this fine Connecticut wall-clock, made by the great Eli Terry!" The peddler pauses pensively. "I tell you what: I'll hang it up on your wall . . . call for it on the way back—next month."

It took superhuman will power to withstand the peddler's glib palaver, once he had his toe inside the door.

"Money scarce? Think nothing of it." *Sam Patch* was only too glad to barter his trinkets for anything in sight: beeswax, pelts, salt pork, maple sugar.

"What about that eiderdown tick from Lorraine?" "That Delft jug over the hearth? . . . and I tell you what I'll do. . . ."

With each purchase, *Sam Patch* gave the farmwife a few books as a gift.

It was the last item, books, that worried Father Neumann, that

sent him down on his knees in long prayers at night. Each afternoon he recited the rosary in church, recited it aloud—for the
preservation of the Catholic Faith among his scattered parishioners. He wrote to friends overseas, begging supplies of Catholic
books to counteract *Sam Patch's* premiums. In his rounds, in the
wake of the Yankee peddler, Father Neumann often found these
gifts in the cabins of his German farmers: bibles slyly slanted
toward the tenets of some evangelical sect, tracts announcing the
imminent crack of doom, lurid attacks on the Pope, the confessional, the Mass. Often, Neumann pitched these books and pamphlets into the farmer's hearthfire. With these writings in mind,
he prepared his Sunday sermons more carefully than ever, giving
clear explanations of Catholic belief. Several whom he knew
were weakening in the Faith because of *Sam Patch's* books.

Spring, too, brought revivals and camp meetings all over western New York. The circuit riders cantered up the coduroy shun-
pikes through the woods, their saddlebags bulging with bibles, the
fires of Apocalypse burning their hollow eyes. Often as not, they
were unlettered back-woodsmen, chosen because of their flair for
colorful homespun language, a native knack for taking a man's
heart and tearing it to shreds. In those days emotionalism was
supreme.

When the Methodist exhorter mounted a tree-stump in some
farmer's meadow, the summer evening crackled with his message
of salvation. Hungrily the crowds jostled about him in the firelight, hundreds, sometimes thousands of men and women from
miles around. "Glory!" they shouted, punctuating his loud tirade.
He soared up to strident frenzy. "Halleluja!" cried an exalted
farmer. The exhorter's loud leathery voice snaked out over his
restless listeners' heads, like a bullwhip, tormenting their inmost
souls. Groans erupted here and there in the crowd; sobs, com-
mingled with sudden high-strung cackles of laughter—enough to
make one's blood run cold. *"That old time religion . . . give us
that old time religion,"* the people chanted. They stamped their
feet. They clapped their hands. They wagged their heads from
side to side, in rhythm with the hymn—praying for a token of
personal salvation, an outward sign.

When it came, it was terrifying to behold. A wave of mass hysteria broke across the gathering. Father Neumann described these revivals in letters to Budweis and Prague. "If you pass a Methodist camp meeting," he wrote, "it brings to mind the biblical times of Elias and the priests of Baal, such howls of prayer! such repulsive antics! Thus, they claim, does the Holy Spirit come upon them. . . ."

But revivals, as such, were little temptation for Neumann's flock.

"At sight of what goes on," he wrote, "our Catholics are mightily strengthened in the Faith, for they plainly see before them the lesson learned in the catechism: that only the Catholic Church is one, holy, Catholic and apostolic."

With their own eyes, Neumann's people saw the sharp contrast between their own unity of belief and the jigsaw smattering of half-truths held by various sects. They saw with a new touch of pride that no matter what land a Catholic hailed from—Normandy, Bavaria, Ireland, Lorraine—he prayed the same Creed as they. He was quite at ease and at home in the rough log chapel of St. John at North Bush, at the shanty church of St. Michael the Archangel at Cayuga Creek, at the stone church of the Apostles at Williamsville—quite at home, as Father Neumann began the familiar ritual of the Mass.

Catholics might bicker over a dozen non-essentials, and often did. But on the important things of the Faith, they were agreed; and among those important things was the unique position among them of the priest. If German trustees—because they paid Father Neumann his salary—were prone to think of the priest as a sort of hired hand whom they could order about, still they did not fail to note how Irish bargemen and locktenders tipped their hats to Father Neumann on the road, how burly French lumbermen stooped to kiss his hand, how children danced with excitement at sight of him anywhere. He was a person set apart, this squat little man in the high boots and long black coat, who christened their babies and anointed their sick. In clear-cut contrast with deacons, elders, circuit-riders, exhorters, Father John Neumann was different. He was *the priest,* their personal reminder of something more ultimate than clearing stumps, sowing corn, raising homes. He was their assurance that Christ still walked the world, walked even the marshy shunpikes of the Niagara woods.

But one June morning someone in Buffalo dropped a casual remark; and everything changed.

Up at Jabez Goodell's place on Main Street, the Broadwheel Tavern, the usual group of cattle drovers and Conestoga waggoners lounged at their beer, talking shop. All but Hans Fleischer, who drowsed in a groggy stupor, his face on the sleeve of his red flannel shirt. It was always the same. Early each market day, as he drove the cattle in from Cheektowaga, Cayuga Creek, he cracked his whip like the very Fourth of July. He laughed a "good morning" to everyone, even to Father Pax on Main Street— and though Hans Fleischer had not been in church in a fortnight of Easter mornings, Father Pax waved in return. On market day, when still bright and sober, Hans Fleischer was a gentleman; but once business was dispatched, he draped his muscular hulk at a table in the Broadwheel Tavern and called for Lager bier. After that, let nothing cross Hans Fleischer for the rest of the day.

In the tavern that morning, Puncher Bowen was showing the boys his new watch.

"Got it for three dollars," he announced, "from Bachmann down in Williamsville." He held the watch to his ear, listening. Mention of Bachmann brought something else to mind.

"Say, did you hear about that little priest at North Bush? Bachmann tells me he's joined up with the Mennonites! Says he saw this Father Neumann walking arm in arm with Deacon Reist into the meeting house in Williamsville."

Puncher Bowen was not loud but, somehow, Hans Fleischer caught the essence of the story. He stirred in his cups.

"Pious little Bohunk!" he mumbled, indignation mounting, as he raised himself on his elbows.

"Dirty, little, yellow turncoat! I'll fix him," he roared. "I'll fix him good."

Between the rows of hunching teamsters he staggered out into the daylight of the street, the coiled bullwhip dangling from his shoulder, the quirt-lash trailing the sawdust on the floor.

Not all who heard Puncher Bowen's story believed it; but those who did were indignant—though not quite as violently as Fleischer, the cattle drover. Out of Buffalo he lurched, and down the plank road for home. Three hours later, crossing the wooden bridge over Cayuga Creek, he spied the short squat figure of Father Neumann, knapsack on his back, some few hundred yards ahead, making for the little makeshift chapel of St. Michael, on the village fringe.

"Stop!" roared Hans Fleischer. "Stop! you sawed-off parson!" He fumbled for the bull-whip on his shoulder.

"Do you hear me?" Bystanders, who heard his drunken bellow, crowded quickly out of view.

"Parson, I call you, not priest: do you hear? Turn, and face me like a man." With the crackling quirt of the bullwhip, Hans Fleischer chopped the buckle from Neumann's leather knapsack.

Father Neumann did not turn back, proceeding at an even gait down the middle of the now empty street.

"Yellow-bellied hypocrite! Tell us what Reist paid you to join his Mennonites." Fleischer flung his bullwhip to the side and jerked a Colt from his belt. He brandished it over his head, uncertainly; shot twice into the air.

"Little priest, you'd better turn around and answer my question, or that's the last step you ever take."

Neumann did not slow his pace. If he must die, he reasoned, what better way than on an errand of mercy: bringing Viaticum to old Granny Schaentzlein. She had the fevers again.

The Colt did not go off.

Fleischer had tripped on a rotted plank on the road, and stumbled on his face. In moments he had fallen asleep.

When the rumor of Father Neumann's defection—for rumor is all it actually was—reached the Catholic rectory in Buffalo that afternoon, Father Alexander Pax threw back his head and laughed.

"Neumann, turned heretic!" Tears of mirth twinkled in his eyes. Only yesterday he had had a note from Neumann, telling him the real story. In fact, Pax had ridden out to North Bush to consult with Neumann.

Paul Bachmann had not lied. Neumann had actually gone to

the meetings house with Deacon John Reist. That much was true. Once inside, the zealous Mennonite brethren had done their best to convince the "little priest" of the folly of his Catholic way. He had politely listened. They quoted the Scriptures at some length; Neumann heard them out. Finally, Father Neumann began asking seemingly innocent questions, probing under the roots of their belief. Suddenly the whole meeting was in uproar. The "little priest" was more canny than he seemed. How should they know that this Romish priest had the Bible so well, whole chapters of it by heart? After all, they were just simple farmers; they had not the book learning to cope with such obvious guile. Would the "little priest" be willing, they wheedled, to meet some of their elders in public debate? Neumann had accepted.

That was why he had written Father Pax in Buffalo. He had accepted on condition that an impartial judge, agreeable to both parties, be appointed. The date for the debate had been set for Thursday, in the back room of old Jonathan Eggert's home on Main Street, between the hamlet of Snyder and Elysville. Eggert, a retired lawyer, a gentleman of no particular persuasion, would act as arbiter of the debate.

Father Pax, after reading Neumann's note, hitched up his horse and trap and set out for North Bush. After all, a public debate could be dangerous. Would it not be safer if the two of them joined forces? But John Neumann at North Bush was now quite a different man from the person who weekly knelt before Pax for confession. There was no smallest hint of hesitancy now.

"With the help of our Blessed Lady, who crushes all heresy, I'll manage this battle single-handed, Father Pax."

There was such certainty in Father Neumann's face that Pax went back home, thoroughly assured. His sudden visit to North Bush and his amicable departure had assured the Catholics of the neighborhood about Father Neumann, too.

News of the debate spread fast. Even Hans Fleischer heard it the next morning, at Cayuga Creek. More than the expected handful of Mennonites came to Eggert's that Thursday afternoon. The back room hummed impatience, awaiting the arrival of the "little priest." But at the moment, Father Neumann was a half hour away —kneeling in Martin Demmer's farm kitchen with a group of the neighbors, reciting the rosary for the usual intention: "the preservation of the Faith in his parish."

Meanwhile, a gaunt exhorter tied his gelding to a cottonwood sapling behind Eggert's red barn. Bible in hand, he knocked on the door and stepped into the back room. Almost on his heels came two bearded circuit riders who, as they explained to Eggert, just happened to be passing, saw the crowd, and decided to drop in.

All told, there were some forty people in the crowded room and as many more in the yard outside when Father Neumann, with an escort of four parishioners, ambled through the picket gate. Originally, he had intended to come alone, but John Schmitt at North Bush made loud objection.

"You may need protection, Father Neumann, if this friendly debate gets out of hand."

With Phil Hoffmann of Williamsville, Marty Demmer and blacksmith Mike Deasey, John Schmitt accompanied Neumann to the house. The four might not have book learning to argue the fine points of doctrine; but each of them could fell a tree and, if needs be, a man.

No sooner had Eggert called the gathering to order when one of the Mennonite elders took the floor, launching into a sharp attack on the Romish Church: its superstitions, its idolatries, its despotic hold on free men in a free country. The crowd buzzed approval. Ominously, Mike Deasey shifted in a corner, held back by Demmer and Schmitt.

Now the "little priest" rose to his feet, bowed to Jonathan Eggert, smiled at the gathering. Rapidly, he gave a brief account of his visit to the Mennonite meeting house.

"Gentlemen, I said it last Sunday and I repeat it now. I am open to honest conviction. I will join your church—if you can prove to the judicial satisfaction of Mr. Eggert here that your creed is worthy of belief."

Phil Hoffmann's eyes fairly popped from their sockets. But the priest knew what he was about. He had so set the stage that the burden of proof now rested squarely on the Mennonite divines. It would be up to them to adduce convincing evidence of what they believed and taught.

When they had finished, Neumann stood up again and began to cross-examine.

"May I invite you to tell on what authority you believe what you hold to be true?"

"On the authority of the Word of God." Mr. Enoch Long held up his dog-eared bible.

"You believe, then, that God is author of the Bible?"

"Yes: God, the Holy Spirit."

"Did God write the Bible in English as well as German?"

"Of course. He is its Author in every language and edition."

"Very well." Neumann's voice rang clear and confident through the stuffy back room. "Since the Bible has God, the Holy Spirit, for Author, what he says in your bible, he must likewise say in each and every bible in this room. God cannot contradict himself."

Neumann invited the gathering to open their books to a certain chapter, a certain verse. He invited Mr. Enoch Long to read the passage aloud. He had the Baptist exhorter read the same verses from his own bible. Then, the circuit rider.

Old Jonathan Eggert, cupping palm to ear, leaned forward. He put on his spectacles, asked for the three books. One by one, he read the chapter and verse; read them again. He shook his head. One version plainly contradicted the other.

"If your neighbor's version does not agree with your own," asked Father Neumann, "how can you be so certain that God is the author? How do you know that your bible is right?"

Quietly, the priest sat down.

In the rear of the room, Mike Deasey proudly folded two massive arms on his bottle-green shirt, grinning from ear to ear.

But elder Enoch Long had an answer.

"The mere printed word is not so important. What matters is that one have the Holy Spirit to guide his eye as he reads, to point out the true meaning of Scripture, and show what one must believe."

Father Neumann again stood up. "You are personally guided by the Holy Spirit?"

"His light and his truth are ever within us."

Beards bobbed full agreement.

"Is there some way you can prove that for me: that you have the Holy Spirit as your personal guide?" asked Neumann. "After all, I am open to conviction; but you must furnish proof."

"Why, sir, my whole life is proof!" The elder drew himself up tall, looked round the gathering for approval.

"There was a time, some fifteen years ago, when I was a sinner. I stole my neighbor's cattle. I short-weighted grain at the mill. I cheated in many ways. But down at Batavia, one summer's night, I attended a revival and was converted. I fell to the ground and for seven hours did not stir a limb, so powerful was the entry of the Holy Spirit in me. I've been a changed man ever since."

Mischief twinkled in Neumann's eye.

"You have just heard your elder admit to several transgressions. Openly he admits to cheating and theft. I wonder did he give back what he robbed, or its value, to the rightful owners."

"No," came a chorus of voices. "He never did."

"So you could hardly call his conversion genuine?"

"No," roared a voice from the yard, a vaguely familiar voice. "He's the same two-faced rogue he ever was."

Filling the open window, there stood Hans Fleischer, the cattle drover.

Elder Long glared at the window. Mike Deasey slapped his neighbor's shoulder, rocking the room with an impolite guffaw.

Abruptly, the debate was over.

If the gathering had brought no wholesale conversions to the Catholic Church, it at least put a stop to Catholic leakage in Father Neumann's parish. Catholic farmers were no longer nagged by zealots peddling unwanted tracts and free bibles at the cabin doors.

At Cayuga Creek the following Sunday morning, there was much nudging, much turning around. In the rear of the little church, knelt a certain cattle drover, cold sober, in a clean shirt.

It was the first time he had been seen at Mass, in the memory of the oldest trustee.

9. DREAM HOUSE

Bishop John Dubois of New York was almost seventy-three that June. He had little appetite for food. The mists of the East River harried his bones with the creaky aches of age. But that could not dissuade him from his plan, to visit the western fringes of the diocese that summer, as he had done every other year. He must see the new settlements in the primeval woods, bordering Clinton's famous Ditch.

"But, Your Excellency, out there they talk mostly German!"

Dubois flashed Gallic impatience at his consultors.

"Sacre bleu! I can at least let them see their Bishop in cope and mitre at Confirmation! At least I can smile, to let them know I have their interests at heart."

He toyed with his ring in momentary thought.

"Anyway," he brightened, "I can have little Father What's-his-name . . . Father Neumann, speak a few words for me."

Father Neumann, as it turned out, was not needed. At Rochester the Redemptorist, Father Prost, boarded the canal-boat and accompanied the Bishop as German interpreter, to Buffalo and on for the rest of the pastoral visitation. By the time they reached Father Neumann at North Bush, Prost was well in command of the situation. In the name of Bishop Dubois, he catechized the little candidates for Confirmation—and, so quick were the answers, even to one who knew no German, it was obvious that they had been well drilled in the rudiments of the Faith. And how beautifully they sang!

Bishop Dubois was all smiles and whispers. What was that

log-building on the other side of the road? A school-house!
Magnifique! But could one get a schoolmaster to live out here
in the woods? Father Neumann did all the teaching. *Incroyable!*
And those men on horseback, standing in the stirrups, waving
their hats? Parishioners of Father Neumann's.

Everything the Bishop observed spoke well for the young
man he had ordained last year in New York. He was more than
satisfied. He was delighted. He said as much to Father Neumann,
inside the little log hut of Mr. John Schmitt, as the three sat down
to a feast the like of which had been unknown in North Bush
since . . . since the Bishop was last here on visitation.

"But, Father Neumann, you really should have a little rectory of your own. A priest needs privacy."

"I expect to have one very soon. These good people have
already purchased five acres of timberland for me, near the
church."

Prost, reaching for a second helping of Frau Schmitt's delicious Wienerschnitzel, frowned to himself, but made no comment.
However, when Father Neumann and the Bishop had seated themselves in the open carriage, ready to move on to Williamsville—
as the thirty-horse escort swung up into the saddle—Father Prost
climbed into the driver's perch, held up both hands for attention
and boomed out a command that shook even the most stolid of
the trustees.

"One moment, please!"

He spoke a brief word of thanks to Mr. John Schmitt for the
hospitality of his humble house; for his exemplary kindness, too,
in boarding the young priest in his crowded log cabin.

"I speak for Bishop Dubois. While we sat at table, His
Excellency expressed surprise that your pastor had no house of
his own. But Father Neumann quickly came to your defense. You
had purchased land for him six months ago, he said. Excellent!"

The thirty horsemen settled complacently in their saddles.

"But, gentlemen," roared Father Prost, "now that you have
purchased five acres of woods, do you have to wait for Father
Neumann to shoulder an axe himself to clear it? Do you expect
him to abandon your sick and dying, let your children go without

schooling, in order to build his own rectory? Gentlemen, it's a disgrace. It's an injustice to Mr. John Schmitt here, making him board Father Neumann, when he needs the room for his own growing family."

Prost paused dramatically to let his words take full effect.

"If we didn't have Confirmation this afternoon at Williamsville and, then, at Cayuga Creek, I'd have the thirty of you out in shirtsleeves, felling timber right away. I think it that important! Thirty able axemen could fell and trim the logs; and have the rectory half finished by sundown. I know. I have seen it done."

Abruptly, he stopped; dismounted from his perch and got into the carriage with a bewildered Bishop Dubois and a very embarrassed Father Neumann.

Still, it might have been more embarrassing, had not Father Prost stopped when he did. He already knew far more about North Bush and Williamsville than he admitted. The thirty horsemen, that had so impressed Bishop Dubois, were, many of them, Father Neumann's chief tormentors—conceited, cock-of-the-walk trustees. Prost knew their type from his dealings in Rochester. They could break a man's heart. Neumann was much too meek to handle them in the way they deserved: humbly suffering their insolence, only to be trampled on the more. Father Prost had ammunition for a broadside tirade, but he thought better of it.

Hardly had he arrived from Buffalo that morning with the Bishop than people came plucking at his sleeve: men from Plumb Bottom, Rock Dam, Elysville, Ebenezer. Each felt bound to apprise him of parochial affairs. To Prost it was a familiar tune, familiar as a national anthem. Lorrainers denounced Alsatians. Alsatians accused Bavarians. Rhinelanders told in whispers the flagrant villainies of Badenfolk. And the pastor, Father Neumann, was usually in between!

Did Father Prost see that blockhouse, hidden in the woods, across from the church? A tavern, that's what it was! and run by *one of our own!*

"He peddles Red Eye and rum after church; never goes to Mass himself—and our priest lets his boy sing in the choir!"

Did Father Prost know that the Irish from up along the canal were coming to our German church, crowding us out of doors? "And Father Neumann is even taking their children into his school now."

The litany went on and on.

Had Father Prost heard how the "little priest" had brazenly accepted a horse from some French Canadian?

"Why, if he needed a horse, didn't he mention the matter to our trustees?"

And what did Father Prost think of a Catholic priest who ignored the civil salutation of a duly elected trustee?

"I said *Gelobt sei Jesus Christus;* and Father Neumann did not even reply."

That last complaint overstrained even Father Prost's forbearance. He told the righteous gentleman just what he thought for, earlier, he had heard the other side of the story. This devout parishioner, loading a wagon with limestone up at the Williamsville quarry, had spied Father Neumann gingerly riding Snowball, his new white horse, along Main Street in the direction of Clarence Hollow. The man bided his time. Without warning, he uptilted the cartload of stone into the path of horse and rider. Snowball bolted in panic, tipping the priest out of the saddle into the road. The man made no move to help. Instead, he doffed his cap and spoke the Old World greeting: *Gelobt sei Jesus Christus*. Obviously, it was uttered in mischief, and Neumann did not dignify it with a reply. Picking himself up, he led Snowball by the bridle up the road.

Father Prost told the righteous gentleman just what he thought of a "Catholic priest who ignored the salutation: *Gelobt sei Jesus Christus*."

He had learned about Bachmann, the watchmaker, too: his vile calumny against Trilby Wimmer and Father Neumann. He heard of the public debate at Eggert's; and the aftermath—how, one evening in the woods just west of here, a gang of masked men had, a second time, waylaid and almost lynched the "little priest." "He'd have been dead for sure," they told him, "had not a party of Tonawanda bucks come by in the nick of time!" The

Indians had recognized the Blackrobe, cut his pinons, loosened the noose on his neck and released him.

Unsolicited, Father Prost had been given a pretty accurate picture of Father Neumann's everyday trials on the Niagara frontier. But he heard others bless their good fortune in having little Father Neumann among them.

"The beautiful things he tells our youngsters in school! He's taught them to write and read and to add sums. He's wonderful."

They spoke of his tender way with the sick, walking twenty miles, sometimes, through the snowdrifts with Viaticum tight in his frozen hand.

"And, Father Prost, if you ever saw him say Mass!"

From his observations of the little room where Neumann lived, Father Prost could clearly see the sort of man the pastor was. A man's living quarters can be a good index of himself. There were, of course, the usual paraphernalia of the frontier missionary: saddlebags, water-bottle, knapsack packed with Mass-gear, heavy winter coat, each item hanging from a wooden peg on the wall.

But show me what a man reads, and I'll tell you the sort he is. Here was an open leather coffer, crammed with books: Greek Testament, Hebrew bible, a Spanish *Vida de Santa Teresa,* a blue-bound William Shakespeare, Liguori's *Via della Salute,* his *Theologia Moralis,* dictionaries, sermon books, textbooks of mathematics, botany, astronomy. There was a *Summa* of Aquinas, a whole library of ascetical literature. The Spanish mystics were there, and St. Francis de Sales, Lacordaire in the French original, Chrysostom in the original, too. Alongside the leather coffer, on the earthern floor, lay a collection of neatly pressed leaves and flowers, each tagged with its scientific name. And bundles of neatly written manuscript in Father Neumann's hand. The only things that he had brought to America, it seemed, were books!

Gazing about the little room, Prost wondered what had ever made this bookish little fellow volunteer for America. What violence he must have done to all his natural inclinations, to face the uncertainty, the hardships, the loneliness of the American backwoods. He ought to be ensconced behind a desk in some quiet book-lined study in Budweis; in the seminary, perhaps, where life would be regular, where he could alternate prayer with study, each at allotted times. Or, even better, in some monastery, living among confreres of a similar bent. John Neumann's whole makeup cried out against the rough, haphazard life of America; and yet, Father Prost knew, John Neumann had come because he wanted this.

Prost was a prudent man; he would say nothing to unsettle this gentle scholar's soul. Climbing into the carriage, he glanced at the pastor, grinned at Bishop Dubois.

"Father Neumann, *zelus domus tuae comedit me.*"

Neumann smiled politely. The Bishop twinkled at the biblical witticism (Zeal for your house has eaten me.)

Prost himself rocked at his own joke.

All of June had been unseasonably hot. On the day Bishop Dubois left for home, it grew suddenly cool. Cool and damp and cloudy. For half of July it teemed rain. New spawned mosquitoes rose up in whining clouds from the marshy woods, from between the rotted logs of the corduroy roads. Fevers and malaria returned early to the Niagara frontier. People had no stamina, it seemed. No resistance at all. The bitter winter of the Depression; meager diet; thin clothing; and now the abnormal rains—all took their toll.

Each morning Father Neumann found wider gaps in his North Bush classroom. Tots who braved the rain often came with news of an older brother, a mother, sick at home with the "shaking ague." The priest was on constant call; much too occupied to give thought to his rectory.

It was time for the haying. But, for the time being, the rains postponed that job. The German farmers hunched near their cabin-fires, grumbling at the overcast skies.

One of them remembered Father Joseph Prost. He shouldered his axe and set off in the rain, in the direction of the church of St. John. *Tock! Tock-tock!* His axe bit into the bark of a hickory. More farmers followed. The woods of North Bush rang with the rhythm of their strokes. *Tock! Tock-tock!* By late forenoon twenty-four broadaxes were at work, all swinging in unison, toppling and trimming poplar and maple and beech. Yokes of oxen went slogging through the muck, skidding the trimmed logs into place near the little church in the woods.

Earlier that morning Father Neumann had ridden off, in the general direction of Aurora, to several fever victims along the east branch of Cazenove Creek. A long trip for a wet day! In a way, John Schmitt had tricked him into using Snowball, his new white horse. He had the animal, all saddled and waiting, when Neumann stepped out the door. Snowball had a slight anticlerical strain in his pedigree. Call it a touch of the trustee! At any rate, if Neumann had the choice, he usually walked. He was not much of a horseman.

Docilely, Neumann accepted the horse. He listened to Schmitt's parting instructions. But, impatient to be off (Schmitt did not notice this!), he set his left shoe in the right stirrup. Suddenly Snowball was off, hurling Neumann up into the saddle, his back to the reins, his face to the horse's croup! Luckily Schmitt was agile. Leaping, he caught at the bridle in the nick of time and brought Snowball to a halt. It was a bad moment for poor John Schmitt. Neumann was unperturbed.

In after years, whenever Schmitt related that story, he would add that Father was a zealous and a holy priest, and a smart man too. "He knew the word for *horse* in Czech and Greek and Hebrew! He could point out Pegasus on a summer night— Pegasus, the Horse, a twinkling quadrangle of stars climbing over the Amherst woods to the northeast! But give him a live bit of horseflesh like Snowball. . . ." Schmitt could never complete that sentence. He simply shook his head.

Patiently, Schmitt had tried to instruct Father Neumann in the knack of riding. So had Mike Deasey, up in Williamsville. And Sepp Batt, down Cheektowaga way. None had made any headway. They agreed that he was not made for a saddle. For one thing, his toes never quite reached the stirrups. For another, he held the reins too slack. He favored some progressive school of horsemanship: using gentle words to wheedle the horse instead of spur, whip, or a tight rein. It never worked. Snowball did as he pleased.

On the other side of Pine Hill, and not far from Scajacuada Creek, stood the new stable and blacksmith shop of Sepp Batt, a newcomer to the Niagara frontier. By the time Father Neumann had jogged the six miles from Schmitt's to Cheektowaga, he had made up his mind to leave Snowball at Batt's place.

"I'll go the rest of the way on foot," he said.

"But, Father," protested Batt, "you have a twenty-mile trip ahead of you, if you're going to Aurora and then to the Senecas on Buffalo Creek."

Protest was useless. Neumann had made up his mind. "I can make better time on my own two shoes," he contended.

Seppi Batt, half believing him, changed the subject. "On your way back, Father, if it's not too late, I'd like you to bless my house."

"I'll be back before dark," said Father Neumann, shouldering his saddlebag and setting off toward Ebenezer and the west. "Lucky man," he thought to himself. "Four months in the country and already he has a log cabin." A few days before the Bishop came, Batt's Cheektowaga neighbors had gathered for a cabin-raising, completing the house in two days flat. Batt insisted, however, that he would not live under its roof until Father Neumann had blessed it with holy water and the sign of the cross.

Batt on his way from Alsace had escaped shipwreck in a fierce Atlantic storm. He had escaped, he claimed, by a miracle of the Mother of God. Once he had money enough, he vowed to build a chapel to our Lady, Help of Christians, on a piece of his Cheektowaga farm. He told his miraculous story to Mennonite, Methodist, Catholic, indiscriminately. Father Neumann had heard it, too.

It drizzled most of the day. But true to his promise, Neumann was back at Cheektowaga before nightfall. Burdock clung in prickly clusters to his clothes. His boots were caked with muck. His black coat sopped rain. His stomach burned—whether from fever or lack of food, he was not sure. But what alarmed Joseph Batt, at sight of him, was the unhealthy flush that lit his face.

He would not hear of Neumann's blessing the house—not until he had first dried his clothes at the hearth and had a bite of supper. Neumann, too weak to make protest, slumped into a chair, his head aswim with pain.

"May God prosper all who live under this rooftree," said Neumann, after blessing the new house. He turned to Joseph Batt. "And may the day come quickly when you can keep your vow to our Lady." (Neumann would not remain long enough on the Niagara frontier to see that vow fulfilled. Neither he nor Sepp Batt could foresee that, in years to come, the votive chapel of our Lady, Help of Christians, would be a place of summer pilgrimage for all of Western New York—and that in 1959 a beautiful new church of golden brick with deep blue windows would mark the spot where they both were standing.)

"Don't forget to invite me, Father, to your own cabin raising." Sepp Batt chuckled mischievously as Neumann prepared to leave. He told him of the four and twenty axemen toiling all day in his five acres of woods. "That friend of yours, Father Prost, is a firebrand! You can thank him for getting action. By now there must be a fine pile of logs all trimmed and ready. In a matter of days," Sepp Batt predicted, "you'll have a house of your own."

Father Neumann grinned delight at the wonderful prospect. It seemed too good to be true. But that night, when he sank into exhausted sleep at North Bush, he saw the finished rectory in his dreams—exactly as he wanted. He had privacy at last. Now he could keep the resolutions he had broken so often. And read Liguori and Teresa of Avila. And brew herbs for folk medicine, without disturbing a soul. There was a little truck garden at the back of the house where he grew lettuce, potatoes, turnips, for his table. And in one corner he cultivated flowers for the altar. But best of all, he now had three fellow priests living under the same roof with him. He had discussed the project with Bishop Dubois, with Canon Dichtl in Budweis, and had gotten their warm approbation—a training school for European priests and seminarians, to prepare them on the spot for mission work along the Niagara frontier. They were to take over his established parishes, while he would develop new ones himself. It was all too good to be true! A loud clatter of thunder roused him from slumber, breaking the spell. He was still in the cramped little room at John Schmitt's.

But a dream, once kindled, does not easily die. It battens on everything. It flickers like a taper in the most sacred business, only to become a nagging distraction. Strangely, the Latin word *domus* kept cropping up in the Office! It harped on the word "house," reminding Neumann of his own. Proverbs told of Wisdom building one for itself! The first book of Kings asked an ironic question: "Why hath ye not builded me a house?" "Be patient," Neumann told himself. "They will!"

Once he saw the lumber cut and ready, the thought of the rectory haunted all his plans, intruded on his prayers. Returning to North Bush from any sick call, from any week-long mission trip, he hoped to be surprised at the turn of the trail through the forest, surprised by the log-house rectory, all completed. Maybe when I get back from Rochester! Maybe after the fortnight journey to Lewiston and Lower Canada in mid-October! Maybe . . . for Christmas morning they'll have it ready!

Over a year had passed at North Bush—and not a single entry in his spiritual diary. Neumann took himself to task: where was his old-time quest for perfection? His entire schedule of study and prayer had broken down. In the cramped quarters at Schmitt's, with children all around, serious reading was out of the question. There was no privacy of any sort. But that was no excuse.

To Neumann's way of thinking it was no excuse either that he had been busy repairing the church of St. Michael at Cayuga Creek; that he was building a new one at Swormville to St. John Nepomucene; that he now had a school at North Bush where he taught on alternate days with Williamsville. His endless sick calls were no excuse either. No. He was plainly becoming a lukewarm priest.

A phrase uttered by the Redemptorist, Father Prost, the first time they had met in Rochester, came back to Neumann's mind— "Woe to the priest by himself!—*Vae soli!*" How true was the old monastic epigram.

But then he thought of the stacked logs that soon would be his rectory. Any week now they would hold the cabin raising!

Then things would right themselves. In his own house, with peace and quiet, he could keep his good resolves and begin anew to advance in the love of God.

Winter thawed into spring. Bindweed crept over the log-pile. Frisky squirrels skittered up and down its sides. It became a playground for small children while their elders chatted before Sunday Mass. It stood up like a taunt before Neumann's eyes every time he entered the church. But there was nothing he could do. (John Schmitt was heroic in his hospitality. He never complained.) The farmers of North Bush had a hundred and one chores at home more urgent than the house for the priest.

On a Sunday morning in mid-October of 1838, a Yankee convert came into the sacristy of St. John's at North Bush. One of the farmhands up near Pendleton had lost his footing on the towpath, plunged into the canal and broken his hip. "He's in great pain, Father. May even die."

The Mass was over. Father Neumann was in the sacristy doling out sweets to the altar boys. "I'll go at once," he told the man, tossing the whole bag of rock candy in the air. He placed a Host in the Communion pyx, packed his knapsack, tucked up the cuffs of his trousers, ready to hike toward the canal.

"Father, I have a buckboard here. It will get you there quicker."

Without another word Neumann climbed aboard and they were off. A touch of frost was in the air. The woods blazed with color—a gorgeous autumnal day.

"When are they going to build that house for you, Father?"

The Yankee, a lock-tender on the canal, was unable, except in the off-season, to get down to Mass. "It's a shame," he went on, trying to make a bit of conversation on the long trip home. "Why, I can remember—it must be two years ago—when they cut down the trees. All the talk they had about your rectory."

Neumann said nothing.

"Oh! Excuse me, Father. I forgot you had Holy Communion with you."

Bare-headed, Neumann sat in quiet converse of his own. For the whole three hours of the journey he hardly spoke a word.

But when they arrived at the Canal Settlement, it was too late. The young farmhand had died.

Many Irish lived near this stretch of the canal—good people with meager chance for Mass. It was getting late in the day. Thunderheads were piling up to the southwest in the direction of Niagara Falls. By all good sense he ought to stay for the night—but some nameless impulse urged him to be off again for home, the knapsack strapped on his back, his hand on the pyx at his breast.

Soon the rain came peppering through the leaves, slashing down through the forest—a torrential autumn downpour. Then darkness; the trail blurred out; he was lost in the swampy woods.

"Star of the Sea, protect me," whispered Neumann. Panic knotted his vitals—panic and hunger mixed. There were no stars to go by; and the rain was pelting against his face.

"Thank you, Lord," he murmured, touching the pyx. A short distance off he spied, in the darkness, a thin glimmer of light. Groping forward, he found a low cabin of sods, and knocked at the door. He knocked again.

"We do not open to strangers." The voice was that of a child.

"But I'm lost, child, and it rains much."

Inside the hut there was a mumble of voices. The child spoke again.

"Are you the priest, sir?"

"Yes. Father Neumann from North Bush."

At once the door was flung open. "Welcome, Father, welcome." Little Maura Loughlin held a lighted candle high to guide him in. With a start Neumann noticed that the child was blind.

"My Daddy is sick, Father," she said. Her mother and two older brothers had died the previous fortnight. Now her father.

Old Jerry Loughlin had helped dig Clinton's Ditch in 1828. He was more than sick. He was at death's door. He lay on a thin carpet of dry moss over against the wall of sods. He could barely lift the broken beads in his gnarled hands. His breath came quick and raspy. He had not the strength to speak. The candle in little Maura's hand was the only light in the place.

Quickly Neumann unstrapped his knapsack, fumbling through its contents for the Mass wine. He tilted the little bottle to the Irishman's lips. He waited and fed him another sip. The old man gasped a "Thank you, Father"; and opened his eyes.

"May I go to confession, Father," begged the old Irishman.

"And receive Holy Viaticum, too," replied Neumann, indicating the pyx. Plainly, the Lord had led him through rain and swamp and darkness to this poor man's door.

Half the night, the rain continued. By daybreak the skies had cleared. Old Jerry Loughlin was up and about, much improved. He stood at the doorway, little Maura beside him, as the priest prepared to leave.

"God and his Blessed Mother have been very good to you," said Neumann. In the depths of his coat pocket, he found a cheap medal of Mary Immaculate, with a few bits of the rock candy from yesterday. He put them all in Maura's little hand. Cautiously she tested the rough crystal on her tongue. Frowned. Then puckered with pleasure. Neumann chuckled. He waved to the old man and was on his way.

Minutes later a shrill cry rent the woods. "Papa, Papa! I can see the sky!"

By that time Father Neumann was well out of sight.

Six days later the "husky Bohemian mountain-lad," as Neumann called himself, was still too ill to get out of bed. Hunger, exposure, exhaustion had taken their toll. "How did I get here?" he asked John Schmitt. He had no memory of what had happened to him. A party of Tonawanda bucks had found him face-down on the forest floor. They had carried him on an elk skin, home to North Bush. He was a sick man. It was almost a fortnight before he had the strength to walk the half mile to church.

"Here he comes," someone whispered.

The path through the forest was covered with trampled snow. At the turn of the narrow trail, Father Neumann saw the familiar log structure—the church of St. John the Baptist. But the log pile had vanished. In its stead stood a new block-house—his rectory. Touched with remorse at their pastor's grave condition, the farmers of North Bush and the surrounding woods united for a mammoth cabin-raising. They had completed the house in almost a single day.

Neumann stood in the snow, staring in disbelief. There it really was. And no dream! Just as he planned it on paper! A four-room house of beech logs with small square windows, one to a room; a fieldstone hearth with a cat-and-clay chimney built outside.

For a one-day rush job it was expertly made. Beech logs, hand-hewn on two sides, fitted one upon the next for draught-tight walls. What chinks there were had been sealed with moss. Even the notched and saddled logs, that made the corners, were compact as the strakes of a ship. It even had a puncheon floor—logs of black walnut, rived in halves, tenoned to fit roundside-up, into the four mortised ash logs that were the foundation of the house. Not a nail showed anywhere. Nails on the Niagara frontier were still an extravagance. Not a scrap of iron was used for hook or hinge or lock bolt. The puncheon door of yellow poplar swung open on green hickory hinges, with an ashwood bolt to lock it, on the inside. The door was rather narrow and so low that only John Neumann could walk through without bending his head. "What wonderful, wonderful people!" he murmured to himself.

On November 4, 1838, a snappy, snow-blown morning, Father Neumann moved his belongings from Schmitt's, up the half-mile to his own house. It was a wonderful feeling. *"Ego dixi nunc coepi,"* he told himself. "Now I shall begin in earnest to advance in the love of God." After twenty-eight months he had his rectory at last.

10. PHYSICIAN, HEAL THYSELF

Until that Trinity Sunday in 1839, there had not been a new saint in the calendar in over thirty years. It was glorious weather for the occasion. Bells tumbled in a hundred belfries, making the May morning hum. Intermittently, the Tiber boomed with the cannon of Sant' Angelo. Pilgrims in holiday mood, pilgrims from all Europe, thronged the cobbled streets, inching towards the white dome, the columns and fountains of the vast piazza. St. Peter's was packed. Already some thirty thousand were inside the bronze doors.

King Louis of Bavaria was there, his robin-egg tunic agleam with medals and gold galoon. In the royal tribune, beside him, sat Frederick, king of Naples. Maria Cristina of Sardinia looked austerely regal in black Valencia lace, a pendant of matched emeralds at her throat. Frostily, the foreign diplomats absorbed the stares of the curious among the crowds. The crowds continued their gaping, none the less.

High in the apse, candleflames fluttered in cut glass chandeliers. They shed a pulsing glow round the *glorieta,* above the altar, making the painting of the five Beati look almost alive. One of the Beati was the founder of the Redemptorists, Blessed Alphonsus de Liguori. Because of political upheaval, his solemn canonization had been nine years delayed.

Viva! White handkerchiefs fluttered like pigeon wings over the heads of the crowd. *Viva il Papa!* Up in the dome trumpets brayed the papal march. *Viva!* Slowly, on the shoulders of the six Noble Guards, the *sedia gestatoria* swayed, paused, moved on toward the main altar, bearing the seventy-five-year-old Pope Gregory XVI.

The pomp and glitter, the untrammelled demonstration for the Vicar of Christ, was a brand new experience for white-haired Father Joseph Passerat, down from Vienna with four of his religious brethren for the solemn canonization. It was his first time in Rome. Passerat was Vicar General of the transalpine Redemptorists, including that homeless handful in America, led by Father Joseph Prost.

Caught up in the joyous tumult, with a hundred Italian confreres around him, Passerat hardly recalled, just then, what he had said some years before, about their tentative foundation in America: that only when Blessed Alphonsus was raised to sainthood, would the Redemptorists take firm root in the New World.

But in America, Father Prost remembered. Though sick abed with fever in Pittsburgh, that May morning of 1939, Prost knew that the words of Passerat were on their way to coming true. Negotiations were underway at the moment for their first real foundation in the United States—at St. Philomena's in Bayardstown, two blocks from the Allegheny. Soon Father Prost would summon his scattered subjects to Pittsburgh, happy to live, at long last, as their Redemptorist Rule prescribed.

Beyond the open door of the blockhouse rectory at North Bush that May morning, a black-tailed goldfinch perched on a fence rail, and sang for the sheer joy of spring. Azaleas made pink clumps of color at the edge of the swamp. Dogwood was in bloom all through the woods. In the little patch of garden, near Father Neumann's door, young cabbage plants made four brave drills of green; and overnight, the beans had pushed up through the soil. It was a beautiful Sunday morning. But Father Neumann's mind was more on the coming Thursday. Thursday would be Corpus Christi Day.

After Mass that morning at St. John's he held a final practice for the choir. "No school on Thursday!" he told the delighted children. "But be sure to remind them at home that I expect everyone here for the Procession of the Blessed Sacrament. Nobody works on Corpus Christi Day! We all have too much to thank God for: we don't want to forget that. Tell them to think back on what they had here four or five years ago: an empty chapel with only the rosary on Sunday morning! No priest. No Mass. No Sacrament of the Altar."

The children went shouting for home, off through the woods. And for the hundredth time Father Neumann wished that he had a monstrance. If he had some of the skill of his Bavarian cousins, he thought, perhaps he could carve one! Any of the satiny woods of the American forest could make a beautiful throne for the Sacred Host. Of course, a monstrance of silver or gold would be better—like one he had seen at St. Patrick's on one of his trips to Rochester. But it was hardly worth the hundred Yankee dollars Father Bernard O'Reilly had paid for it. Anyway, where would Neumann get a hundred Yankee dollars—or even half that sum!

If he had only gotten an answer from Prague, there might be some hope. A year ago he had written to Dr. Anton Rost at the Seminary, hoping that his friends might be inspired to take up a collection for their old classmate and his mission near Niagara Falls, in the wilds of America. He had mentioned his need of a monstrance. But Dr. Anton Rost's answer, like so many other letters from Bohemia, had gone astray. In three years Neumann had not once heard from home.

Hopefully, he thought of his Redemptorist friend, Father Prost. Maybe the mail coach along Main Street or one of the canal-packets might bring something before Thursday. Many months ago Prost had promised, in his travels round the country, to keep an eye open for a good but inexpensive monstrance for North Bush. Few stores in America dealt in such things. (Barclay Street was mainly residential in the year 1839.) But Catholic families often had chalices and the like as heirlooms. Prost might come across someone who had what Neumann needed—or so Neumann day-dreamed for the hundredth time. If not, on Corpus Christi Day he would have to carry the Blessed Sacrament round the church in his Communion pyx.

Outside the rectory, he paused a moment, contemplating the sprouting beans, the four rows of cabbage plants.

"I'll have to transplant my lettuce one of these days," he thought, and went into the house.

Not far from St. John's stood the log house of Mr. Rudy Elfenbein. It was something more than a house. Better to call it a store—one of those parasitic things that thrived on church-goers. But it was more than a store. Its chief attraction, at least to the male patrons, was the half keg of Utica Blackstrap that stood on the counter. A free drink with any purchase over a dollar! If the customer wanted another, ten cents bought a three-finger slug.

Places like Elfenbein's were the bane of Father Neumann. They sprang up wherever he said Mass. He had no sooner laid the foundations for St. John Nepomucene's at Swormville than two such taverns mushroomed overnight—like the two thieves, one on either side of the church! They were a thorn in Neumann's heart. As a rule, the owners were so-called Catholics, though Neumann never saw them in church—they were too busy to spare the time.

Rudy Elfenbein was what the Germans call a *Schlaumeier*—a foxy rogue, if there ever was. He laid long-range plans. For every dime he gave, he expected a dollar. He seldom lost out in a business deal. For some months, just such a deal had been simmering in his busy mind. It struck him, one winter evening, how the patronal feast of North Bush and that of Williamsville both fell in June: John the Baptist on the twenty-fourth, and SS. Peter and Paul on the twenty-ninth. If he could somehow contrive to have one celebration for the two parishes, it might lengthen out to a week-long holiday.

He could see it now—games for the children in the forenoon, a picnic-lunch, games of strength and skill for the young men in the afternoon; later a dance . . . and, of course, plenty of Cold Spring beer and Utica Blackstrap to lubricate the festive heart. What a goldmine that could be for Elfenbein's log-cabin tavern if it lasted for seven days! It required meticulous diplomacy. One false move, and the project would collapse.

Accordingly, one morning back in March, he had engaged Father Neumann in conversation.

"My good wife and I have been observing your chimney of late, Father. We never see a wisp of smoke. We were wondering if you might accept a warm meal once a day? It would be no trouble, Father."

That first winter in the new rectory, there had been entire weeks when Neumann subsisted on nothing but cheese and dry bread: whatever his kind parishioners might bring. Meager though it was, he never went hungry. As he gave ear to Elfenbein, a sixth sense warned him to "beware of the Greeks bearing gifts."

Neumann's sixth sense had developed remarkably over the past year. He had found his own way of coping with bothersome people—mainly the gossip and the trustee. With the trustee he practiced a vigilant silence, for he had painfully learned how readily a man's words can be wrested out of context. Neumann would listen gravely whenever a trustee engaged him, but he seldom spoke. This prudent reserve exasperated the man, who hoped for a hot argument; he branded it cold insolence on Neumann's part. But it was Neumann's only weapon of self defense—silence.

With someone prone to gossip, he had another technique.

"Father, there's something I must tell you. . . ."

Before Frau Longtongue drew another breath, Father Neumann was suggesting that she first help him with the rosary in church.

"I make it a practice to recite it in public every day for the conversion of sinners and the preservation of the Faith. You're the only one here right now; would you mind?"

Frau Longtongue was trapped. By the time the priest had finished all his prayers, the woman's knees were stiff. The story she had intended to tell had skipped her mind.

Rudy, the tavernkeeper, was different again. Not a trustee, interfering with the running of the parish; nor a gossip—whatever he had in mind, Neumann grasped the chance to call him to task on another score.

"It's good of you, Rudy, to worry over my health; but I've been worrying about your own. Your soul, I mean. Your good wife comes to church every Sunday; but I never see you there. And they tell me that you're still peddling rum to the men after church. You ought to turn over a new leaf, Rudy Elfenbein, and start thinking about your soul for a change."

Neumann ended by thanking him for offering to send a warm supper, but honestly, he had a very small appetite. Rudy was glad to escape; but Neumann never saw him in church, not even on Easter.

"Father Neumann." Rudy's wife was standing at the rectory door on the afternoon of Trinity Sunday. "There is something I must tell you."

At Mass that morning she had heard about the Corpus Christi procession. And now if ever was the time to tell the priest that Rudy had a beautiful monstrance locked up in a trunk in the back room. It had come from Munich last year expressly for the church; sent by her elder brother who was a priest. But Rudy would not part with it. He had something special in mind, he said.

Before she could tell this to Neumann, he had escorted her over to church to accompany him in the Stations of the Cross. For once, his sixth sense had misfired. By the end of the Stations, Rudy was calling her home. It was too late to speak!

Knowing what she did, it wrung her heart that Thursday afternoon to see Father Neumann walking in the procession with the Sacred Host in his little Communion pyx. The choir sang beautifully. Neumann was very happy. But he would have been happier if more of the farmers had come to church.

June was a busy month. The trustees of the two parishes had agreed on the week-long celebration for their patronal feast. Rudy Elfenbein had a dozen axemen splitting logs for an open-air dance floor alongside his house. At his own expense he had cleared a patch of woods for the children's games. He had begun stocking his store with food and liquor. He was happy as an oriole, whistling about his business in the tavern, day after day.

On the Sunday mornings of June, Father Neumann made mention of the coming Patronal feast at North Bush and Williamsville. No one had mentioned to him their idea of a week-long celebration. It was none of his concern, anyway—said the trustees! But Neumann made it his business to explain to all that children's games were in order; even sporting events and a picnic for the grownups.

"But there is to be no drinking; no dancing . . . or I shall pack up and leave North Bush."

On St. John's Day, Father Neumann almost kept his word, only that North Bush had speedily repented. The Blackstrap was merrily flowing at Elfenbein's. Fiddlers were tuning their strings, when someone noticed the wagon at the rectory door, and all Father Neumann's books and belongings aboard it. Consternation struck the merrymakers. They surrounded the little rectory. They pleaded, cajoled, apologized. They promised to disband at once.

"I will remain here," said Neumann. "But go home and pray, lest God punish you for desecrating the feastday of his saints."

Late that evening, Rudy Elfenbein listened uneasily in his bed to a crackling sound like a brush fire. There was no odor of burning, no heat. The sound grew more strident, spreading through the whole neighborhood: a terrifying ear-splitting rasp, that made children whimper, made mothers cross themselves in fear. Rudy lit a match, only to find a few grasshoppers crawling down his chimney into the hearth. More came . . . and more.

A plague of locusts had descended on North Bush, nibbling everything green: new corn, the fresh shoots of potato plants, wheat and lettuce, the uncut hay in the fields. By morning, they had picked the neighborhood clean as a fishbone.

In Father Neumann's garden patch not a plant remained. But the local farmers overlooked that. To them, it was a token of God's evident displeasure. They had missed the procession on Corpus Christi! They had tried to hold a dance on the feast of St. John! And what seemed to lend weight to this conviction was the fact that Black Rock and Cayuga Creek and Tonawanda—even Williamsville—had not been ravaged by the locusts. Only North Bush!

Even the trustees were a bit shaken, and came to terms. Father Neumann smiled at the ways of God. The following week he was out replanting his garden with new seeds from Buffalo. The summer was still young. There still were three good months.

But the months were not good for Rudy Elfenbein. What with the failure of the week-long festival and the plague of locusts, business went from bad to worse. He decided to close down and move away.

The day of his departure he called at the rectory, a large black box under his arm.

"Father Neumann, I have something to give you, but on condition that you change the name of the church from St. John's to St. Rudolph. I have great devotion to my patron."

Much as Neumann needed the monstrance, he could not accept it under any such condition. It must be an outright gift to the church, with no strings attached—or nothing.

Rudy Elfenbein's departure from the neighborhood was a very welcome surprise.

A better surprise awaited Neumann that fall. On the afternoon of September twenty-sixth, Wenzl, his younger brother, arrived unannounced at North Bush. There were so many things to talk about: mother, his father, the girls. As Wenzl doled out scraps of local interest, a wisp of homesickness drifted into John Neumann's heart. Would he ever see the dear old hills of Prachatitz again, he wondered: the crooked streets and the tower of Sankt Jakob's, the storybook city-gate, with the Rosenberg knight in full armor, painted on the wall? But there was so much work here in America.

Wenzl, a devout young man of twenty-four, had but one interest in coming to America: to work for God, helping his brother.

"Your letters home, John—we used to read them over and over. When you mentioned that you could use me, I packed at once. . . ."

It made John Neumann happy that his letters had reached home. Up till then, he had never been sure.

"I hope," said Wenzl, "I can do something around here."

Neumann laughed. He pointed to the gray ash on the hearth, to the church across the clearing, to the little schoolhouse nearby.

"Anything you can do? First, I hereby appoint you sexton and housekeeper. And do you see that log house over in the woods? That's my school. Starting tomorrow, that will be your job."

"Teach! but, John, I'm no scholar. I'd be afraid."

"You can read, Wenzl. You can write. You can add and subtract. Teach them that. Teach them the catechism—and their prayers."

To Father Neumann, Wenzl was a godsend. He did more than teach school. He swept the church, decorated the altar for Sundays. He chopped firewood, dipped candles. When Neumann was away at another mission, Wenzl led the rosary at St. John's.

Each evening, he sent up a brave banner of smoke from the rectory chimney. He was a tolerably good cook, considering the meager appetite of his brother, the priest. (Before spring, he would prove a good nursemaid, too!) In a dozen ways he more than earned his keep at North Bush. But the morning in mid-October that Wenzl took to general housecleaning, Neumann, for a distracted moment, wished that his younger brother had never left Prachatitz at all.

Wenzl liked an orderly house; no twigs and dried leaves all over the fireplace. With a sweep of the broom he cleared the chimney bare.

Neumann noticed the fireplace as soon as he entered.

"Wenzl, I forgot to tell you! I hope you didn't burn those roots and leaves?"

Fortunately, Wenzl, in his methodical way, had thrown them all in one spot.

"It's taken most of a year to gather them all over the woods," explained Neumann.

"Do you know what they are?" He picked them up one by one.

"They are the makings of health for the poor of my parish. Out here on the frontier, doctors are scarce; I've learned to brew herb remedies against fever and coughing and ague. I know a lot about trees and flowers from home; so, in lieu of doctors, I'm putting my knowledge to practical use."

One by one, he set them down on the table: cranesbill, sassa-frass, ipecac, bayberry; bark of tulip and magnolia; packets of withered violets, dried foxglove and chamomile. One by one, he named them, telling Wenzl what each was good for.

"They call this elecampane." Neumann held up a bulbous root toward his brother's nostrils.

"It smells like camphor. Grind it fine; mix it with a powder of comfrey and *Ulmus flava* (that's slippery elm); blend it all with honey, and we have a syrup to cure any kind of cough or sore throat."

In his forty months in western New York, he had learned remedies from the Indians down along Buffalo Creek, and from the pioneers. From them, he learned how the new-peeled bark of slippery elm will heal an open cut; how the root of *polygala senega* dulls the throb of snakebite. And for fevers, the autumnal scourge of the swampy Niagara territory—doctors prescribed Peruvian bark, an expensive rarity in Buffalo—the Tuscaroras had as good a remedy, found cheap in the woods. Take the bark of dogwood and the tulip tree, steep it with winterberry in boiling water. Drink it like tea. Dogwood, *cornus florida* to Neumann, was as good a cure as quinine for malaria.

Father John Neumann was aware that the practice of medicine was prohibited to a priest; but supplying a poor farmer's wife with a cough medicine for her children, a poultice for a running sore, a syrup for a bad cough, was hardly "practicing medicine." This was sheer necessity, in a wilderness where there were no doctors. For Neumann it would be a lack of charity to the poor, if he did not put his botanical knowledge to good use.

Many a person in the Niagara woods owed his life to Father Neumann's careful skill with herbs.

But his own health, Father Neumann glibly ignored. He used a mite too often that "sturdy-son-of-the-Boehmerwald" excuse for breaking all the rules of common sense. Imperceptibly, the raw Niagara winters, the marsh fogs, the mosquitoes, the long stumpy trails through the forests, took their toll. He was no longer "sturdy." More often than he cared to admit, his head spun with a reeling nausea; neck and shoulder muscles screamed with muscular tics. Sudden sweating in mid-winter; needles of hunger in his vitals; and always, that hacking cough he could never quite shake off.

Naively, Wenzl suggested that he take some of the slippery elm and honey concoction.

"Physician, heal thyself," said Neumann with a smile.

With Wenzl about, Neumann had wider scope for his tireless apostolate. He saddled Snowball late in October, riding up the Niagara River toward Lewiston, east along the south shore of Ontario, and down to Batavia, searching out German-speaking Catholics who had no chance to receive the Sacraments—Frenchmen and Irishmen, too . . . anyone.

The Germans of Rochester implored him to visit them. They had been without a German-speaking priest now, for almost a year. Trustee trouble. The Redemptorist would not brook their incessant meddling, and left.

Early in December, Neumann took the Main Street stage for Rochester; stayed there a week, in Father Prost's quarters in the basement of the Ely Street church. But it was too much. On the trip home, his teeth chattered with cold. Fellow passengers passed a jug from lip to lip, the only way to keep warm in the rocketing stage. Neumann passed it by, untouched. By the time he reached North Bush, he had to take to his bed.

Intermittently, all through winter and spring, he was sick: fevers, a splitting headache.

Wenzl fussed over him, piling blanket and bearskin on his bed. He made strong broths, spoon-fed him like a mother, a sick child. Betweenwhiles, Wenzl prayed aloud with him, too. What would he ever do without Wenzl?

Woe to the man by himself!

"Vae soli!" Those words of Father Prost, spoken his first night in Rochester, four years ago, often came to mind.

When God chooses to call a man to a new way of life, he has at his beck an infinity of ways. To the man, it may seem like a chain of casual incident and remark. Even so, there is no peace of mind until the man responds. In Father Neumann's case, this call took the shape of a vague discontent that harried his heart with a dull ache. That, coupled with the luxury of time to think, after a bout with fever; and finally, the arrival of a crate of mission goods from Prague.

For one thing, Neumann was in deadly earnest about holiness. His prayer, on the morning of ordination, had been: "Lord, give me but holiness"; and he meant it.

Unless a priest has holiness, Neumann believed, his flock will not respond to grace. As he lay abed, recuperating in the winter months, he had long hours to assess the forty-four months of his ministry as a priest. His only explanation was that he had not been holy enough. All he saw were the broken shards of fervent resolutions: books unread, prayers left unsaid till the end of day, longer and longer gaps in his spiritual diary. And for that, now that he was living in his own rectory, there was no excuse. *Vae soli!* He could almost hear Father Prost, warning him in that hale, paternal way.

Father Neumann considered his flock, lukewarm, cantankerous, critical, mean, demanding. But the fault was his—not theirs. It was clear evidence of his own lack of holiness!

How stunningly different, by comparison, were the good people of St. Joseph's in Rochester, where, all told, the Redemptorists had labored little more than a year. Still, one could see their influence in the devout silence at Mass, the large numbers at Communion, the respectful attention to the Word of God, the way they prayed aloud. The Redemptorists, Neumann argued, had the spirit of their saintly Alphonsus de Liguori—and their people absorbed it. Neumann had been with his own flock four times longer than the Redemptorists were in Rochester; yet how different the results.

Round the cabin corner, the March wind blew noisily from the north. Down the chimney, it whined, drawing flame from the logs on the hearth. When a man lies helpless abed, everything plays on his fancy.

"Woe! . . . *Vae!*" the wind seemed to bray. *"Vae soli!"*

Imagination, of course. Still, if he were a religious, living in community, he would not be alone. That had been Father Prost's meaning. In community, he would have brother priests to consult, to rely upon. He would have a rule of life that could even make him a saint.

Gradually, the thought became an inescapable obsession, an urgent matter of conscience for Father Neumann. It was no passing whim. He must leave this place, this lonely life . . . or else! As he saw it, it was a matter of his soul's salvation.

Spring came back. The ice had vanished from the canal. Now the packet-bugles blew their two-note calls in the distance. *Trahn-ahn!* Or were they, too, crying *Vae soli*—"alone, you're all alone"?

Neumann, since he knew Father Prost so well, pondered joining his order. But how could the Redemptorists accept him when, as yet, they had no permanent monastery in America? Would they run the financial risk of sending him to Austria for his novitiate? He had not the passage money himself; that was sure.

One of the first canal boats to reach Buffalo, just after Easter, brought a large wooden box from Prague for Father Neumann. Dr. Anton Rost, of the Seminary, had answered his appeal for books and religious articles. He had sent no monstrance; but thoughtfully, he had packed the books with many Catholic papers of Budweis and Prague and Vienna, back issues of the past six months. Neumann was hungry for news of Europe and home. But what caught his eye was an item from Rome, an account of the canonization ceremonies of May, the previous year.

"So Blessed Liguori is a saint, at last! I wonder if that holy old Redemptorist in Vienna is a prophet? I must write to Father Prost."

One morning in early October Father Neumann stood a moment in his doorway, looking at church and school. The woods were turning to color. High overhead, rode long V's of birds, mallard and teal, and great-winged swans, flying south in answer to a secret call.

"I'll follow you in a few weeks. *Spanem Bohem!* God be with you."

Wenzl Neumann shook his brother's hand.

Snowball, tethered to an elm rope, tossed his mane and whinnied expectantly. Neumann patted the horse's nose. But he set off on foot toward Main Street, along the trail through the woods.

III

11. TRIAL BY TRAVEL

The fall of 1840 rang with oratory through every town of the twenty-six United States. An election year, Democrat Martin Van Buren running for President against the Whig candidate, Benjamin Harrison. Young men swapped their gray beavers for store-bought coonskin caps, to parade the city streets chanting: "Van, Van is a used-up man!"

A coonskin and a frontier log cabin were the campaign symbols of Benjamin Harrison. The hero of Tippecanoe was a man of the people, shouted the Whig politicos—not a wine-sipping *La-dee-la* like Van Buren. Old Tip Harrison drank hard cider like any good frontiersman!

Log cabins cropped up that October in the unlikeliest places, on Boston's Beacon Hill, south of Market Street in Philadelphia, outside the Astor House on Broadway, and in every small town too. Inside the make-believe cabins, free for the sampling, were kegs of genuine hard cider. A clever gambit it was. Cider and log cabins caught the popular fancy and swept Benjamin Harrison into office as ninth President of the United States.

Father John Neumann, waiting for a lake-boat in Buffalo that October of 1840, saw many a sham log cabin on Main Street and the Terrace. He saw them again at every small hamlet and relay on the coach-route from Erie down to Pittsburgh, at Meadville, Mercer, Butler. John Neumann was not quite clear as to what the log cabins signified. They kept reminding him of the

123

rectory he had left at North Bush, the huge sprawl of parish along the Niagara frontier.

His own American citizenship was still eight years in the offing. He had never touched hard cider either. Still, if living four years in a frontier log cabin made one eligible for the White House, Neumann could have tossed a coonskin hat in the ring. In his coat pocket that October morning, however, lay something he prized more than the Presidency—a letter from Baltimore:

"You will report to our new house at Pittsburgh as soon as you have made known your decision to Bishop Hughes."

Father Prost had answered his letter. Neumann acted at once. He was on his way to join the Redemptorists as a novice.

From the coach window he saw another log cabin flash by, another reminder of the life he was abandoning.

"Vae soli," murmured Neumann. "Woe to the loner."

No. He was not the sort who could live by himself. What he most needed was a Rule to live by, vows to bind him, the comradeship of zealous, like-minded men to buoy him up, and when the road ahead grew dim, to be his spiritual guide. At Pittsburgh, so the letter from Prost had informed him, there was just the man at the moment. Father Francis Tschenhens, a devout religious of thirty-seven, was to be Neumann's novice master. He would imbue him with the spirit of St. Alphonsus.

Father Neumann was happy that Sunday morning as the stage rattled over the Mechanic Street bridge to the south bank of the Allegheny. The driver cracked his whip, slowed the coach-wheels for a right turn on Penn Avenue, on toward the Exchange Hotel near the terminus of the Canal.

"Pittsburgh!" he shouted. "Everybody off."

It had not been a pleasure jaunt, neither the two-day trip from Erie, nor the voyage from Buffalo on the crowded steamer. With lake-wind and the high seas, the ninety-mile run had taken fifty-three exhausting hours, and standing all the way!

But stagecoach and steamer were bygones now, for a while. Now in the wooden rectory on Factory Street, if all went well, Neumann would spend the coming year, as a humble novice, in seclusion and prayer preparing to make his vows. Day by day, his novice master would mould him to the inner life of the Redemptorist with instruction in asceticism and in the moral of St. Liguori. Hour by hour, he would follow the Order's holy Rule, testing himself—and being tested also—to discover if he had the stamina of soul for religious life. He knocked at the door.

"Welcome, Father Neumann." Brother Louis Kenning opened the door.

"Upstairs, we have a room all ready for you. We've been expecting you for several days."

The candidate Brother knelt to kiss his priestly hand. Then, tucking Neumann's baggage under arm, he started off down the creaky hall.

"Father Tschenhens just finished Mass. I'll tell him you've come."

A clock began striking nine o'clock.

"Welcome to Pittsburgh, Father Neumann. Hope you had a pleasant journey."

Father Tschenhens did not wait for comment on the coach trip. He got right down to business.

"You haven't said Mass yet. Be good enough to wait till ten and say it in church for us. We're a bit short-handed today. Father Czackert is up in Brownsville for the weekend. I'm all alone."

He continued quite matter-of-factly.

"It's a High Mass, Father. The Gospel is about the man who made the marriage feast for his son. Don't preach more than half an hour."

"Yes, Father." Neumann was glad to be useful. "I'll try to get something ready at once."

Forty minutes later he was on the second floor of a squat oblong building with a belfry on the roof. The bell swung to and fro, calling Bayardstown to *Hochamt*. That belfry was the structure's only semblance of a church. In all other respects it could pass for a factory. As a matter of fact, until Father Prost last year remodeled the interior and dedicated the building to Saint Philomena, it had been just that—a cotton factory. Its walls were still dotted with dozens of windows, plain squares of glass all grimy with coal dust.

On all sides lay Bayardstown, a little world of tall belching smokestacks and huddled houses, crammed between the Allegheny and the stone rampart of Quarry Hill. The "Hill" ran from east to west, parallel with the river, cutting off Bayardstown from the rest of Pittsburgh. A far cry from North Bush, not one tree in sight!

Two blocks north, along the river, stood the Juniata iron-works; Schoenberger's foundry, a little beyond that. To the east, on Adams Street, rose Marshall Kennedy's busy flour mill, busy even on Sunday. There were five breweries in the neighborhood; and for one who disliked beer, you need not see them to know. Along Penn Avenue and Liberty, parallel with the "Hill" and the river, pinned between tavern and grog shop, ranged the houses of the parishioners.

The High Mass was crowded. These Redemptorists, thought Neumann, had the knack of making people devout. He had observed the same piety last year at Rochester. It must be personal holiness, born of keeping a religious rule that somehow diffused itself among the parishioners. Anyway, compared with Neumann's North Bush congregation, the filled benches, the attentive faces as he preached, the numbers who received Communion were so many proofs that in coming to Pittsburgh as a novice, he had made the right choice.

Father Tschenhens told Neumann he liked the sermon—plain, but solid thoughts. All his days in Pittsburgh, nobody praised him again.

Brother Louis was a wellspring of the Order's lore. It was his hobby, his private apostolate, to hoard every item about the Redemptorists in America. He kept them all in a copybook. He knew them by heart. In Rochester he had worked with Father Prost back in '37; he had helped Father Tschenhens in the forests of northern Ohio. Father Czackert had worked alone for almost two years out in Illinois. Louis managed to worm many of the details from Czackert—to jot in his copybook.

"We are so happy to be living our Rule at last," Louis told Father Neumann.

Up to a year ago, they had been scattered at lonely outposts all over Michigan and Ohio. Father Saender was now in Rochester; Father Prost, with Brother Aloys, in Baltimore at Saint John's.

"Archbishop Eccleston practically tricked us into going down to Baltimore; and once there, he gave us charge of St. John's on Saratoga Street. He's put all the German Catholics in his archdiocese under our care."

Brother Louis used "we" and "ours" with possessive *esprit de corps*. He was still a postulant!

"The rest of us are here in Pittsburgh." He counted them on his fingers.

"All told, we have four foundations in America; and five Redemptorists to man them: four priests, one brother, and now you and I."

Brother Louis also gave Neumann his first intimation that life as a novice might not be precisely what he envisioned. He might have to play the role of Martha more often than that of Mary. But Louis, with the wisdom of an old hand at religious life—he had been living in the community for nine months— looked sagely at Neumann and said:

"The important thing, Father, is that we be docile to orders. If we obey, we're doing God's will."

Sound advice.

Neumann was two weeks in Pittsburgh when his novice master was borrowed for Baltimore.

"St. John's here is too much for one man. Come down at once," wrote Prost. "And tell Father Neumann I shall be up there at the end of the month to invest him in the Redemptorist habit."

That afternoon Tschenhens packed his carpetbag. Brother Louis had marketing to do. Father Czackert saddled the horse and rode north for Schaeffer's Station at Wexford. Neumann was alone in Bayardstown. But, he assured himself, once clothed in the habit, once the novitiate really began, matters would be different.

On the first Sunday of Advent, or rather, the night before, Father Prost arrived as promised, delighted at sight of his first new recruit.

"I brought you something, Father Neumann."

Out of his battered bag, he extracted a wrinkled black habit, cut and sewn by Brother Aloys in Baltimore. By trade, Aloys was a cook.

"Tomorrow at High Mass, we shall invest you with full solemnity for all Bayardstown to behold. Here, Father. Try it on you for size."

Prost had told his amateur tailor that the novice was about five feet, six inches tall. A miscalculation of four inches!

"We'll fix that; won't we, Brother Louis?"

The habit trailed like a *cappa magna* at Neumann's heels. But Louis dashed in with needle and scissors, and made the habit fit.

There was little that Louis could not do. By trade he was a cooper; but he groomed the horse for Father Czackert; he cooked the community's meals; he swept the house; acted as porter; even taught school next door in the church basement; and he was also the sacristan.

Next morning Louis was lighting the altar candles for the ten o'clock Mass, his mind aglow with the historic ceremony soon to take place. Everything was ready. Even Father Czackert had come home early from Steubenville, two days earlier than usual. Father Neumann knelt at the foot of the altar before Father Prost.

The church was filled but—here, for sure, was an item for Louis to jot down—in the front bench, knelt young Wenzl Neumann. He had brought the rest of his brother's belongings down from the Niagara frontier. He planned to stay, determined to join the Redemptorists too.

The investiture was a triumph of the impromptu. Father Prost ensconced himself in a rickety chair before Neumann, changed his mind, and first gave a stirring explanation to the people of what was transpiring before their eyes. The rubrics, however, he had to extemporize. He had no Redemptorist ritual. From a vague memory of his own investiture ten years before at Vienna, he assembled Latin psalms and German prayers, while Father Neumann exchanged the cassock of a diocesan priest of New York for the habit of St. Alphonsus Liguori.

"*Quam bonum et jucundum . . .*" intoned Father Prost in his high clear voice.

One by one, he, Father Czackert and Brother Louis clasped the novice in monastic embrace. Father Neumann looked down, toying with the loop of beads hanging from his belt.

The little six-room rectory had but the scantiest library—a book of Meditations, a dog-eared German Bible, a copy of the Visits to the Blessed Sacrament by St. Alphonsus. All else had been lost in a warehouse fire in New York. Vienna, of course, would send more. But who could say when? Lucky that Neumann had brought all his books down from North Bush.

Everything was ramshackle, makeshift, improvised—tables, beds, kitchen; the whole rickety house, the factory-church next door. It was a monastery only by good intention. The Allegheny winds whined through cracks in the wall. The ceilings dripped rain. There was chance aplenty to practice virtue, any virtue one could think of—humility, resignation, poverty, love of the cross.

By Christmas, Neumann's old Niagara complaint had recurred—chills, fever and the hacking cough. It alarmed him. Did he have the health for this Redemptorist life? If he were to be an intermittent invalid, how could he preach missions; how could he bear the share of the work? It would be an injustice to join the Order! But here it was Saturday afternoon. Father Prost had gone over the mountains, preaching a mission in Williamsport. Father Czackert was somewhere below Saw Mill Run. Sick as he was, the novice was once more holding the fort.

"I'd better get a sermon ready for tomorrow," thought Neumann.

Before Lent, when Prost left for Baltimore, he assigned the novice to Father Czackert, the only man left in the house. At morning meditation, Neumann saw him in the drafty chapel. After that, he was gone for the day. Little settlements of Germans all over the hills were in need of his care. But by evening meditation he was usually back again. If he had little time to give long conferences on the inner life to Neumann, he did manage to exercise him in virtue aplenty.

"You are much too worldly for a good religious—talking like an old Hausfrau with every passerby on Spring Alley!"

"But, Father Master. . . ."

Neumann mildly explains that the couple he spoke to had asked to be instructed in the Faith.

"Father, a good religious never makes excuse and takes reprimand humbly on his knees."

"Yes, Father Master." Quickly the novice kneels on the floor.

"Sit down there, Father, and tell us a story. It is an old novitiate custom to edify the brethren at evening recreation."

Rattled by the sudden request, Neumann mentions the first thing that comes to mind.

"I had a peculiar dream last night. . . . I was cornered in a little room with no escape . . . and someone kept trying to put a bishop's mitre on my head. I was trying to climb out the window."

"Enough, Father."

Father Czackert broke in, feigning shock.

"Better get rid of these conceited thoughts, if you ever hope to make your vows with us."

"Yes, Father Master."

Father Neumann never mentioned any such dream again.

"He's a born religious!" Czackert told the confreres in Baltimore.

He was edified no end by Neumann's punctilious observance of Rule, his abject humility, his recollection, his charming simplicity of heart. But to the novice he remarked icily:

"You'll never make a Redemptorist! Why don't you pack up and go back to western New York?"

There were times—as spring came over the Alleghenies, the spring of 1841—when John Neumann yearned with all his heart for Buffalo again, for a glimpse of snow-white bloodroot or hepatica; the sound of peepers in some nearby pond; the smell of spicebush, of maple-sap boiling in the frosty Amherst woods; the smell of anything but Bayardstown with its reek of malt, its gray soot, its everlasting din. Neumann was homesick in the squalid soot and flour dust of Pittsburgh, longing for the clean air, the evergreens and melting snowdrifts of his Niagara frontier.

There were times when the temptation to leave sent him down on his knees through whole nights, pleading with our Lady for the grit to stay a while longer.

"I may not have made a genuine novitiate; but I had my share of the temptations to which every recruit of St. Alphonsus must fall heir."

So he wrote to his nephew fifteen years later.

Holy Week, with the arrival in Pittsburgh of new blood from overseas, two more priests and a student awaiting ordination, brought Neumann some respite from sick call and sermon. But quarters now were cramped. The three newcomers brought the community to seven. There were only six beds. But there was one precious compensation for Neumann, the two extra priests made it possible to spend the holy season somewhat more like a novice. More heartening still for Neumann's drooping spirit, in the middle of Easter week, Father Prost came back.

"I'm back in Pittsburgh to stay," he said.

John Neumann looked ahead to many an hour of sage counsel and direction. He all but worshipped Father Joseph Prost.

But in May, a few weeks later, Father Prost declared that Baltimore would be a better house, less crowded, more congenial for a novice. He packed him off. Up to Brownsville went Neumann and down the national pike to Baltimore, doubting if the Redemptorists really wanted him. Within a week, he had even deeper cause for misgiving. Now they were shunting him off to Rochester, where his first novice master, Father Tschenhens was working.

"Go up to Ely Street, Father Neumann, but stop off in New York on your way. Father Balleis at St. Nicholas needs help."

Grimly Neumann recalled those words of Brother Louis:

"The important thing is to obey, and you're sure it's the will of God."

For two weeks the novice was a curate again, on the east side of Manhattan, in the church where, five years ago, he had said his first Mass.

It seemed a strange way to practice the interior life, rushing here and there by rail and stage and canal-boat. The east side of New York for Ascension day, Rochester for Pentecost. No sooner did he reach the little wooden rectory on Ely Street, Tschenhens left Rochester for Ohio on urgent business. For six weeks Neumann was alone, novice master, novice, superior and pastor of all Rochester. Came July and Father Pax in Buffalo asked Rochester for help. Neumann was the only available man. So, Father Neumann went back to his old stamping grounds, the Niagara frontier, while the ailing Pax lay abed.

Would he ever be a novice, he wondered!

Now came an urgent call from the Ohio woods. Father Tschenhens needed him in Tiffin. By now, Neumann was thoroughly shaken, fearful that he had made a grave mistake! Other Orders seemed more stable; more mature; less frantic in their approach to problems.

And what was this ugly rumor about Father Prost—that he had been deposed from office as Superior of Bayardstown; that he might even be expelled? Neumann made no inquiries into matters that did not concern him. It was a misunderstanding between his old friend, Prost, and Father Alexander, the new American Superior from overseas. Still it made Neumann's soul uneasy. He discussed his uncertainties with Father Tschenhens. Father Tschenhens worried for Neumann's vocation, too.

The snow lay deep in the Ohio woods when a letter came for Father Neumann from Baltimore.

"Report here as soon as possible to continue your novitiate."

Father Neumann set out at once. At Canton, Ohio, he met up with the Bishop of Cincinnati.

"Your Redemptorists are good men, but. . . ."

The Bishop relayed a rumor prevalent in the country that, with Prost expelled and so much friction among themselves, Vienna was withdrawing the Redemptorists from America, calling them back home.

"Why not join the diocese of Cincinnati, Father Neumann? We can assure you of peace and security—and plenty of hard work. I can give you whole colonies of German Catholics who are begging for a priest of their own. Think it over, Father," said Bishop John Purcell. "I'll be leaving here in the morning."

That was the strongest temptation in John Neumann's whole year of trial.

"I've thought it over, Your Excellency. . . ."

Neumann looked haggard from the struggle of deciding.

"I am going on to Baltimore to continue my novitiate."

Arrived in Baltimore, it took a while to find Saratoga Street. But when he found what he was looking for, all he saw was a ragged excavation at the site of old St. John's. They were laying the stone foundations of a much larger building.

"The Redemptorists? They're all over in Old Town."

Someone pointed in the vague direction of Jones Falls.

"You'll see a small white church at the top of Asquith Street, near the edge of town. They're living there until *this* is ready."

This, they told him, was a new church of St. Alphonsus, Redemptorist headquarters in America.

Neumann knew little of Baltimore. Jones Falls, Asquith, Saratoga Street were just names to him. He'd know them as the years went on. He could hardly surmise the part this new church of St. Alphonsus would one day play in his career—less than eleven years away.

He found the little church of St. James without much difficulty, and behind it, the monastery of the Redemptorists, a two-story house of still unpainted wood. It was ideal for novitiate, quiet, far from the bustle of docks and market, out near the tall, thick woods at the northeast edge of Baltimore.

Here, for the rest of Advent and on through Christmastide, Neumann lived in devout seclusion under the personal guidance of Father Alexander.

For once, since receiving the religious habit, he had no parish commitments. The priests at St. James, though occupied with a dozen and one parochial chores, had orders to leave him undisturbed. The rap of the carpenter's hammer, still at work in the unfinished house, was almost sweet as plainchant to Father John Neumann's ears, so content was he to have time for his soul and God.

On the day after New Year's of 1842, he commenced the long retreat in preparation for religious profession. Finally, on Sunday, January sixteenth, at morning meditation, in the still unpainted house-chapel on Eager Street, he knelt before his religious superior, Father Alexander and "before our Blessed Lady . . . and the whole court of Heaven," he pronounced his vows according to the time-honored formula:

I, John Nepomucene Neumann, in the presence of Almighty
God . . . do vow Poverty, Chastity and Obedience, together
with the vow and oath of Perseverance in this Congregation
until death. . . . So help me God. . . .

The heart of John Neumann was at peace.

12. BALTIMORE HONEYMOON

With the holy day of the Three Kings impending, old Pokorny,
the Prachatitz postman, might well have gone home. But this
afternoon on the mail-coach from Budweis, he had found a
crumbled envelope and, sentimental old soul that he was, he decided to deliver it personally that evening at Number 129 in the
Upper Lane.

House lamps glowed on the snowdrifts along the way. The
Sagastas were seated round the supper table. John Miko, the
blacksmith (Pokorny could see him through the window), was
lighting the candles on his Christmas tree. Beyond Miko's place,
at Number 129, a group of small boys were standing in the light
of Mr. Philip Neumann's open door. *Sternsaenger* they were, choir
boys garbed in bright robes and tinsel crowns—Caspar, Melchior,
Balthassar. With them were others wearing tall paper mitres like
archbishops. One held the traditional star-shaped lantern on a
long thin pole. At sight of them Pokorny quickened his walking
pace.

Years ago he had been a "Star-singer" himself, strolling the
lanes of Prachatitz each evening of the Christmas season, singing
carols from door to door, winning coins and candy for reward.
Softly Pokorny hummed the tune of the carol, reaching Number
129 just as Balthassar, last of the group, was stepping inside.

"Psst!"

He clutched at the king's green cloak.

"Here, lad, give this to Herr Neumann. Tell him you found it in your travels this holy season."

Pokorny waited outside, blowing into his chilly fists. He chuckled as the boy presented the letter. Herr Neumann, preoccupied, paid no heed.

"Herr Neumann."

The postman poked his red face inside.

"It's a letter from Father John, I think. . . . From Vienna," he added, half to himself.

"A letter from John!" shrilled Louise, dispatching the choir boys with a quick flick of her apron.

Papa edged closer to the lamp, adjusted his spectacles, broke the seal of the letter.

"My dearest Parents and everyone. . . ."

The cat mewed for its milk. Supperware sat unwashed in the pan. The kettle cooled. A letter from John was rare at Number 129, Upper Lane. All else could wait.

The Vienna postmark did not mean what Pokorny surmised. Father John Neumann was still in America. Last October, when Father Alexander set out from Baltimore to recruit more missionaries in Europe, he had taken the letter promising to mail it for Neumann in Vienna. Alexander, being superior, had business in many places—Paris, Rome, Naples. On reaching the imperial city on the Danube, he remembered Neumann and posted the letter on the next to last day of 1842.

"My superior here in Baltimore is taking this letter overseas with him. Thus I shall be sure *that it will arrive safe,* for since your own letters never reach me here in America, I never know for sure whether mine reach Prachatitz at all."

It was this that had kept him from breaking his wonderful news to them, news now almost a full year old.

"Body and soul I now belong to the family of Saint Alphonsus," read Philip Neumann under the sputtering lamp.

"I have made my vows as a Redemptorist missionary." Louise stole a quick glance at her mother, not knowing much about St. Alphonsus or Redemptorists.

"Now, with the good example and encouragement of brother religious around me, I can be a better priest. Wearing this holy habit and living this holy Rule, dear parents, I can walk without fear even into the valley of death. . . ."

Mrs. Neumann drew a quick breath as if to make a remark, but her man was now reading about Wenzl, their other boy. The two had been together for several months in Baltimore. Wenzl, too, was now wearing the Redemptorist habit and—so John had declared—had turned out to be an excellent gardener and cook. At that, Mrs. Neumann smiled. Wenzl, at home, couldn't boil a duck egg!

The letter had been written in haste, touching on only essential news. With more time, John might have given them some inkling of how different was Baltimore from land-locked Bohemia: seagulls and the salty tang of a southeaster blowing up the Chesapeake, the ring of ship bells at night, the glorious sight of schooners and clippers and packet ships forever moving up and down the bay. What if he told them that from the garret windows of their monastery of St. James one could look downhill over the chimneys of Old Town and count the masts of two dozen packets docked at Fells Point wharves? For mountain-ringed Prachatitz, thought Neumann, that would sound like some tall tale of Baron von Munchausen.

Packet ships from Bremen, Antwerp, Havre, Trieste brought hundreds of German families up the Chesapeake to Baltimore. It was to care for these immigrants that the Redemptorists had been given St. James in Old Town, and were building the large church of Saint Alphonsus on Saratoga Street. Archbishop Eccleston had given them the care of German Catholics not only in Baltimore but throughout the entire state. So young Father Neumann's Redemptorists had their work cut out for them, a job for a good dozen able-bodied missionaries. The raw-boned fact was that in Baltimore at the moment there were but two: Father Joseph Fey and John Neumann.

Baltimore was not Bavaria. Homesick immigrants missed the wayside shrines at the turn of a road, the drowsy tune of cattlebells, the cheerful *Gruesz Gott* from every passerby. They missed the bright-hued Bible-frescoes on deepeaved houses that were generations old. Compared with home, Baltimore houses had a depressing monotony, row on row of red brick dwellings each with identical white wooden steps. But the church of St. James in Old Town was for these bewildered newcomers a blessed link with all the dear things they had left in Europe, a familiar landmark in an alien world. They climbed Asquith Street on Sunday mornings to hear their mother tongue spoken from pulpit, to sing their Old World hymns and worship in ways they had known from childhood. Saint James for them was a touch of home.

For the two Redemptorists, however, St. James was a turmoil from one end of the week to the other. Catechism, convert instruction, baptisms, endless parlor problems. Now it was a mother of five who had lost her husband to ship fever in the ocean-crossing. Or perhaps a man, who for long months could find no means of livelihood in the new land—not that he had no trade, but no one would hire a foreigner who couldn't talk English! Here was a widow whose teenage son threatened to run away to sea on a China clipper.

"What will I do, Father Neumann?"

And a whole family, newly arrived from Baden, was bilked of their savings by some smooth-talking "runner" on Platt Street.

"He promised to find us lodgings, Father, and to buy our ticket to Cumberland. We gave him what money we had. He tipped his hat politely—and disappeared."

The problems brought to St. James were not all spiritual. It did not matter. There was no place else to go.

When someone was dying, German Catholics always sent to Old Town for the priest. Maybe a stevedore knifed in a brawl on Apple Alley; a lady's German maid in staid Mount Vernon Place; maybe a Charles Street bookseller; a little novice dying in the high-walled convent on Asquith Street, a few blocks below St. James. Father Neumann seemed to go on them all. In his letter home he gave no explanation; no hint of his tacit understanding with Brother Gabriel, the porter:

"I'm a light sleeper anyway, Brother. A tap at my door and I'm up. No need to disturb Father Fey."

Fey, though older by six years than Neumann, was a priest

little more than one. Archbishop Eccleston had ordained him in June of 1841 at the cathedral on Charles Street—the first Redemptorist to be raised to the priesthood in America. Ever since, he had been stationed at Old Town. He liked the city. A peppery preacher, he had a way with people, a knack for organization, and in a busy place like St. James his mere presence seemed to make things click. He was made for city life. It took no argument at all to persuade Father Fey that Neumann's years of circuit-riding the Niagara frontier gave him a natural priority for the distant mission-stations visited by St. James.

"I'm a sturdy son of the Boehmerwald," grinned Neumann.

So, this week he was off in the Community horse-and-trap for the green tobacco fields of Ann Arundel County, a small colony of Germans at Elkridge Landing. In good weather, he often made the eight miles on foot! Another week, it might be a nine-hour train ride up into Pennsylvania. (As the crow flies, York is only forty miles from Asquith Street. But in 1842 the crow got there much quicker than the Baltimore & Susquehanna.)

There were trips into western Maryland, too. Frederick, in the Allegheny foothills, was one. It straddled the National Pike, some forty miles west of Baltimore. The B&O had a new depot there. Beyond Frederick, little colonies of German Catholics—at Harper's Ferry, Martinsburg, Cumberland—also had requested a priest from St. James.

"We'll at least pay your train fare," they pleaded.

Though these stations could be reached by horse, the B&O was rapidly building out in their direction. In fact, the tracks reached Cumberland by Christmas of 1842. But train fare paid or no, St. James would have answered their request. How could they shirk when St. Alphonsus de Liguori had purposely founded their order for priestless mountain places, for "the most abandoned souls, especially those in country districts."

There were many such priestless places round about. A colony of Alsatians lived along the Patapsco near the flour mills of Ellicott City. Up at Columbia on the Susquehanna were many Bavarian farmers and a few lumberjacks. Still others lived down Virginia way. Father Neumann visited most of them. So many things to tell them about in Prachatitz if only he had the time. . . .

At Number 129, Upper Lane, the lamp-lit kitchen was quiet as Papa read the rest of John's letter. It told of shiploads of immigrants thronging down the Pratt Street gangplanks, so numerous that no matter how big you built your church, before it was under roof the structure was already too small. (That was true of St. Alphonsus on Saratoga Street, rapidly rising thanks to a generous flow of florins from Bavaria. It already looked small for the growing population of the parish.) St. James in Old Town, wrote John, could at present accommodate but a third of the German Catholics on either side of the Falls. Each Sunday it was packed to the doors. He mentioned the converts, the mission trips all over Maryland. He concluded with greetings to the neighbors and to the parish priest.

"Is Baltimore near Niagara Falls, I wonder,"

"*Donnerwetter!* No, Mutterle. Baltimore is on the other side of the Great Lakes."

American geography was a puzzle to the townsfolk of Prachatitz. But Frau Neumann, with the accurate intuition of mothers, sensed that wherever this "Baltimore" was, her John was happy there—busy but contented. She knew from the tone of the letter.

Frau Neumann was right.

Of John's twenty-four years in America, his two years as curate at St. James in Old Town were the happiest of all—his religious honeymoon. For the first time in his life, thanks to a religious Rule, he was sure of the will of God. All he need do was the bidding of those set over him—he told himself—and he was sure it pleased God. At the moment his labors were more taxing than normal, with only two priests on hand. But any week now Father Alexander would be returning with help from Europe.

Now through the chapel windows at morning prayer came a hint of lilac. The sound of robin and oriole rang through the woods across Eager Street. April was here. Not long after Easter, Father Alexander came with half a dozen men to lighten the work in Baltimore. Things became normal at St. James. What a pleasure to hear footfalls for the first time in the upstairs rooms! Alexander had brought over a novice master, Father Glaunach, and was inaugurating a genuine novitiate at St. James.

On May seventeenth of 1843, Father Alexander invested

young Franz Seelos, making Father Neumann feel like a veteran. Seelos was twenty-five, had studied his philosophy and theology at the University of Munich, and once professed, would be ordained. Watching the ceremony, Neumann remembered his own haphazard investiture at Pittsburgh, when Father Prost extemporized the psalms and prayers. In a way, he half envied Frater Seelos his full twelve months of prayerful seclusion—a genuine novitiate.

Soon the regular order of St. James began to hum at a high speed and Neumann was in paradise. This was what he most wanted. Now he had time for all that his soul yearned for: time to pray, time to study, time to prepare catechism for school, sermons for church. With the increase in the community, his country trips had diminished. Each morning at meditation he blessed his good fortune. He had no care in the world! Cares were his superior's business. All John Neumann need ever do was obey.

His comrade of the six busy months, Father Fey, had departed Old Town before Christmas. God's will! It was as simple as that. Father Fey, poor fellow, had been named superior at Pittsburgh, had to build a new stone church there. Obedience had made it God's will.

But John Neumann's honeymoon was almost over. That vow of obedience, he would discover, meant more than the meek humility of roadside violets. God's will could sometimes rip and sting like frontier brambles. It could turn the heart topsy-turvy with momentary discord and rebellion that only heroic prayer could make subside.

On a March morning in 1844, Father Neumann found, under his door, a small slip of paper signed by Alexander.

"You will report at once to Pittsburgh as superior."

"Why me?"

Like two angry hornets the words stung at Neumann's heart all the way across Baltimore to Mount Clare depot, all the way to Frederick and beyond. Prayer, repeated acts of resignation to God's will . . . all seemed futile. If his friend Fey had only given Pittsburgh a chance! If only he had faced up to the task of building the new church! If he hadn't begged off after three brief months, Neumann still would be in Old Town. No problems, no weight of responsibility, no worries over blue print and payroll. Fey, God knows, was far better equipped than himself. Offhand, Neumann could toll off half a dozen more qualified for this job at Pittsburgh. "Why me?" he groaned, his thumb sore from fingering the beads in his pocket. "Why me?" For all his prayers, the two words nagged like toothache as the B&O coach bowled across the trestle of Harper's Ferry and up the grade to Martinsburg and the mountain terminal at Cumberland.

Alongside Cumberland's Blue Springs House, a line of stages waited for west-bound customers. Capacious "land admirals" they were, sturdy Concords from the shops of Stockton in Uniontown—best coaches in the world! Neumann was an old hand at this sort of travel. He knew the pellmell democracy of the stage coach: poker, ribald jokes, reeking stogies, politics, small talk, and—against the raw weather—a jug of Red Eye or Maryland applejack! Likely as not, there would be aboard some dour-lipped Biblethumper itching for argument. Or worse, a loud-mouthed Nativist with blind hatred of all foreigners—as though his own kin were pure-blooded Iroquois! So, before paying his fare, Neumann asked if he might sit top-side with the driver.

"I enjoy the mountain air and the scenery," he explained.

By the time the stage coach reached Brownsville—after many relays of horses, after lodging the night in a mountain roadhouse with breakfast at four in the morning, and off again—after long personal debate and longer prayer, Father Neumann had thoroughly resigned himself to destiny. Father Alexander's order was plainly God's will. He would be superior at Pittsburgh.

The thirty miles from Brownesville to the journey's end took most of another day—down the Monongahela by paddlewheeler, thumping through shell ice, past timbered slopes, past soot-encrusted towns, past mine-scarred hillsides. Finally after dark, amid the clank of hammers and the eerie glow of coke ovens, he saw what Charles Dickens had described two years before him as "Hell with the lid off"—the Land in the Fork of the Rivers. Here, in Bayardstown, Father Neumann must build a church.

13.   A CHURCH FOR BAYARDSTOWN

From the wooden canal-bridge on Liberty Avenue, Neumann could see, three blocks to the east, the unfinished sidewall of the new church, the gothic outline of its six gaping windows lurid in the glow of Schoenberger's Ironworks. Construction had stopped until spring. But in a few weeks, he knew, the ice would be gone from the Allegheny. Stonecutters would come whistling back to the job. Masons would climb the scaffolding. The derrick-pulleys would squeak again. And each Saturday night he, John Neumann, must somehow have cash to pay these workmen their hire. Bluntly, that would be his job as superior; that and, somehow, to save his soul!

Familiar landmarks on Fourteenth Street were gone; the "factory-church" at Spring Alley, the old frame rectory he had known as a novice three years before. Both had been dismantled to make room for the stone foundations of the big new church. A shapeless two-story affair, like a huge whitewashed shed, now stood at the corner of Penn Avenue—a jerrybuilt omniumgatherum: school, church, and rectory under the one shingled roof.

He knocked at the door on Fourteenth Street. No answer. On Penn Avenue, he found another door; knocked again, loud and longer. With the racket of drays and coaches, the clanking inferno of the ironworks nearby, the knock was scarcely heard. It was almost nine-thirty. The whole building was in darkness. A bolt snapped; Father Tschenhens, his old novice master, seeing who it was, hastily knelt to kiss his hand.

"Welcome, Father Superior. Welcome home."

He made to waken the community; but Neumann, already embarrassed, intervened.

"Let them sleep, Father Master. They need their rest. I'll still be here tomorrow."

Only then did he spy Father Tschenhen's pink toes peeping from under his habit. In his haste to the door, "Father Master" had forgotten his shoes.

Next morning found Father Neumann kneeling upright in

his place in the little chapel long before the others, his head bowed in prayer. St. Philomena's community would soon take for granted his presence there at almost any hour of the day. Brother porter quickly learned to save himself steps and time, should Crispin, the architect, or Bishop O'Connor ask for Father Neumann—by going straightway to the chapel to see if he were there.

That first morning, after taking the oath of office, the new superior quietly struck the keynote of his regime, commenting on the verse of the Psalmist that "unless the Lord build the house, the workmen labor in vain." He meant not only the half-finished walls on Liberty Avenue, he said, but the congregation also who, please God, would pack the new church—the souls entrusted to Redemptorist care in Bayardstown and in the country-stations round about Pittsburgh. Souls were more important than any building project.

"If we Redemptorists are to be successful in working for souls in western Pennsylvania, we must make sure first to care for our own souls by making them as holy as possible; and we can do that best by keeping our religious Rule."

Father Neumann was harping on a favorite theme of his own meditations, a principle by which he lived.

Both Fathers Tschenhens and Czackert were proud of their "little novice" of two years ago. He had learned his lesson well— that keeping one's Rule at home was the key to success outside.

Big, barrel-chested Father Joseph Mueller (he did most of the circuit-riding around western Pennsylvania), listening intently, suddenly grinned a broad Bavarian smile at Neumann's matter of fact admission that the new superior was younger by at least two years than anyone in the chapel. And shorter too! He needed their prayers, he said, and in turn promised to pray for each.

Prayers to be sure! But stone-masons could not be paid in Hail Marys; they wanted cash to buy shoes for their children, a Sunday bonnet for the wife, new tools for themselves. The need for ready cash haunted Neumann everywhere. Walking downtown to the Mercy convent on Strawberry Alley for weekly confession of the six Irish nuns, the same problem weighed on his mind. It intruded even on his prayers. Many a time he sighed at the thought of what Bayardstown could do with the ten thousand Bavarian florins that Baltimore received each summer for the building of St. Alphonsus on Saratoga Street. But the Ludwigsverein had little interest in Pittsburgh.

He could borrow, of course, at interest from the local bank. In a pinch some of the German businessmen might lend him money: Christy Zug or John Schoenberger, with their roaring foundries right in his parish. And what about Dan Herwig, who owned the Red Lion on St. Clair Street? But Neumann was hardly the hale-fellow-well-met who could beg a loan of three hundred dollars to pay off an urgent debt. Still, St. Philomena's had to be built.

Neumann's financial mainstay must be his own people, the four thousand German Catholics scattered through the triangle of Pittsburgh and its surrounding hills. Not that they had money. Many, after paying for passage over, had invested what was left in a patch of land at Pine Creek, Wexford, Butler, McKeesport. Still clearing the woods and eking meager crops from the fields, they had little ready cash. Most, however, had no property at all, living hand-to-mouth by daily labor in South-side foundry and glassworks, in tannery and warehouse up by the river, working as draymen for Bayardstown breweries, as deckhands on the Ohio riverboats. Their pay was small. In the cotton mills of Allegheny-town, women and young boys, working ten hours a day, were earning $2.50 a week.

With this in mind, one Sunday morning Father Neumann announced to his congregation the founding of the Saint Philomena Building Association. Weekly dues would be five cents, one hour's wage. All with jobs were enrolled as members. A quarter a month could surely be spared to give their own and future generations a worthy house of God.

Thrifty German immigrants had no trust in paper banknotes. Gold they wanted. They hoarded it in earthern crocks in the kitchen, in carpetbags under the bed. They had known banks to fail before and were taking no chances. But someone heard how old Tilly Mohrhaus, dressmaker for the Smart Set of Lower Penn Avenue, had taken her life savings up to Bayardstown for safekeeping, six hundred dollars—to use as Father Neumann saw fit—returnable on demand.

"It's safer there than in a bank," people said.

Farmer George Berg cantered in one afternoon from Butler with a deposit of five hundred gold dollars. A few doors up from the church lived Buerckle, the grizzled Schwartzwald watchmaker. To Father Neumann's astonishment Buerckle put in his hand a nestegg of three thousand dollars, saying he was in no hurry at all to have it back. The money came just at a time when Bobby Crispin, the architect, was dunning Neumann for almost the same amount. Crispin, a Scotch Presbyterian, had a fiery red beard and, as many a careless workman could attest, a temper to match. Many a foot of brick wall he had ordered pulled down for being poorly laid. To Father Neumann, Crispin was well worth his keep. He saved him money.

Time and again it happened. On a Thursday the wooden money-till was empty. Yet somehow—a bankdraft from Father Czackert, collecting funds in New Orleans, a new deposit by Tilly Mohrhaus, a windfall donation from some riverboat skipper lucky at cards—somehow, by Saturday night, Father Neumann had the money to meet the week's payroll. Week after week it happened, a standing wonder to his confreres. Bishop Michael O'Connor used to say that St. Philomena's was being built with nothing but Father Neumann's trust in God.

But there were moments when it was touch-and-go. For one sudden emergency Neumann had to borrow two hundred dollars from the bank. A farmer from Butler, meeting George Berg on the plank road home, casually mentioned seeing the little priest down at the bank near the "Irish church" on Penn Avenue. Berg suspected the worst. Neumann must be going bankrupt! That very afternoon he stormed into town and up to the rectory door.

Up the stairs to Father Superior scurried Brother Porter with the news. If payment were not forthcoming, Berg would create a scene. Panic would spread through Bayardstown. A ticklish predicament! But Father Rector was a match for it.

"Good afternoon, George. Brother tells me you've come for your money."

With that sober-faced glance he inquired if George wished the money in Yankee silver or in gold—and if he'd brought a bag.

"B-b-but, Father Neumann," sputtered George in amazement, "if that's how it is, you'd better hold it a while. It's safer with you."

They parted friends. On the way upstairs again, Father Neumann stopped a moment at the chapel.

Stone by stone the façade, the apse, the pointed arches of St. Philomena's rose above Bayardstown. From the taffrail of any sternwheeler threshing up the Allegheny, from the roof-deck of mule-drawn canal barge, from stagecoaches rattling southward into Pittsburgh, the clean gothic lines of the glinting redstone walls stood out against the green backdrop of Quarry Hill. The sight of a new Catholic church, the third in Pittsburgh, drew proud smiles from Irish and German alike. It was more imposing than Bishop O'Connor's clapboard cathedral at Grant's Hill. It was an ornament to the city.

But to more than a few, St. Philomena's was an eyesore, an evil omen at the Fork of the Rivers. Its solid stone was solid proof of the sly conspiracy of Rome, shipping its henchmen by the boatload to America to lay secret plans for the landing of that baleful monster, the Pope. The eighteen-forties brought an era of frantic bigotry to America. Nativism with its slanted catchphrase, *America for Americans,* was something to be roundly feared.

Western Pennsylvania had its share of the deadly plague. Distorted slanders in the public press. Open insult to the Catholic Faith. Pamphlets and leaflets peddled along the river towns, carried in saddlebags through the mountains for free dissemination among the settlers there. *Beware of Rome! Beware of its vile idolatries!* And in Pittsburgh itself, bigotry's loudest, bitterest mouthpiece, Joe Barker, was almost a next-door neighbor of Father Neumann; right on Liberty Avenue, a stone's throw from the new church.

Every Sunday the rating voice of Joe Barker, surrounded by his rowdy riff-raff, rang across Bayardstown from the canal-bridge.

"Look at it," he shakes a clenched fist at Saint Philomena's.

"That solid arsenal of Papistry! That foothold of the Austrian Kaiser in our midst! It is a blight on Bayardstown, an ugly cancer on the fair face of liberty!"

They were explosive times. Two years ago the previous May a rabble, egged on by just such rabid slander, had put several churches to the torch in Philadelphia. More than once Bayardstown had been roused by mysterious fires in the dead of night, fires on Penn Avenue in the wooden building that housed Neumann's church and school. But Father Neumann had no fears for his new church. It would take more than a smoking torch to destroy the towering red stone church of Saint Philomena.

What did cause him anxious hours was the personal safety of his priests when away from home. Father Mueller's name was often bandied by Joe Barker on Sunday afternoons. The "Bible-burner," he called him, implying that like all priests, he hated the printed word of God. The circuit-riding agents of the Tract Societies gave free German Bibles to Catholic farmers in the country —Father Mueller promptly burned the Bibles. Mueller was forever tangling with the tract-peddlers, arguing, baiting, luring them into public debate—and always besting them.

Many an evening Father Neumann knelt upright in chapel, praying for his husky Bavarian's safety, until at last he heard him coming in the door. On several occasions Joe Barker's bully boys had waylaid their "Bible-burner" on his way home. But Father Mueller was far from a "babe in the woods." Before making his vows as a Redemptorist in Baltimore he had been a priest for eight years in Bavaria. Mueller could take care of himself.

It was different with the youngest member of the community, Father Franz Seelos, who had come to Pittsburgh shortly after ordination. Seelos knew little English. He was not a carefree, two-fisted type like Mueller. He would be easy prey for Joe Barker's snickering thugs.

One evening Seelos was out on a sick call below Saw Mill Run. Hastening across town to the ferry, he was too absorbed in his prayers to notice footsteps following. He boarded the crowded raft, remaining toward the rear to be away from the crowds. He was carrying Viaticum; did not think it fitting to sit.

Instead, he knelt near the ferry rail, lost in adoration of the Blessed Sacrament. An Irish servant girl noticed him; and realized his peril. She had overheard three bullies plotting to take him by surprise and topple him into the Monongahela. Had she not warned him, Seelos would have been drowned. When he returned later that evening to Bayardstown and recounted his experience, Father Neumann redoubled his prayers.

Seelos and Mueller divided the country missions between them. They set up "schools" in nearby Birmingham, in Alleghenytown, McKeesport, conducting classes in religion for the children on weekdays. Father Neumann himself taught in the parish school under the temporary church. Since Seelos and Mueller had enough to do in the country, Neumann claimed as his own most of the work at home. He had to be on hand anyway, he said, while the church was under construction.

Yet no matter where the fathers might be each morning, as noonday neared, they came hustling along Penn Avenue to be back on time for Particular Examen and the perpetual novena prayers to St. Joseph "for the speedy completion of the church." No one without urgent reason was exempt from the community act. On that point Father Neumann was adamant and he himself was always there first.

Even in chapel, he could not escape the spectre of the church. Across his mind would flit a picture of the oaken joists of its high-peaked roof, some remark Bobby Crispin had made with the quaint Scots burr, something about the pillars in the nave; the pleading eyes of a poor immigrant, newly landed in Pittsburgh and badly in need of work. Sometimes, Neumann would reproach his own sloth; was he honestly doing enough about instructing the little ones? What use all this fuss about stone and brick, if we let the faith crumble like ill-mixed mortar? (He could see Crispin squeezing a fistful of wet cement and rejecting it in a fury for having too much sand.)

"I must prepare a Catechism," he resolved one day in the chapel, "write it in simple German words that any child can grasp. (The Faith must not be let crumble in the hearts of little ones. Souls will outlast any new church.) Cost what it may, we must have it printed . . . maybe at Scriba's, down on Try Street."

Already he could see the finished booklet in the hands of little Gretchens and Georgies. He saw Gretchen's father listening at home as she prattled the answers for mother. Good! Fathers needed catechism too. Men needed just such an antidote for those venomous leaflets that were cropping up on all sides, scattered pellmell by that Philadelphia Tract Society, mocking our Blessed Lady, Confession, and the *idolatry* of the Mass. Suddenly, aware of his wandering mind, Father Neumann recollected his soul and began to pray.

Even with the church practically finished, there still were distractions in chapel—and Father Neumann so tried to keep his mind on God. Brother Stephen hobbling into Meditation, his left leg in a cast, reminded Neumann of how blessed they had been during the long months of building. Not a serious accident among the workmen, though Stephen's forty-foot fall from the scaffold had been a narrow escape. Fortunate, that Doctor Jest had been there at the time to set the broken anklebone.

Brothers Stephen and Louis, both excellent carpenters, were now making pews and confessionals. Jerome, a master wood carver, was doing the altar. With these extra three brothers from Baltimore, the Redemptorists were cramped for space in the clapboard makeshift that still served as rectory. Small wonder that Father Neumann's thoughts were often on blueprints for a new and spacious monastery, a real religious house. The roof leaked melting snow. Soot seeped in with the wind through rifts in the window sills. Drafts everywhere, the rooms impossible to keep warm.

To John Neumann, his community was a constant source of edifying wonderment. The feeling was mutual. Had he not divided his own room with a blanket to provide the youngster, Father Seelos, with a sleeping place?

After a week, Father Seelos was convinced that his Father Superior never slept more than a hour each night. Often he could hear, behind the blanket, the whisper of Neumann's praying until he himself had fallen asleep. Or it was the scratch of pen along paper, the creak of a chair as the candle made shadows on the rainsoaked plaster. He was composing another Bible story, another catechism lesson for the children! Or perhaps, he was drawing

plans for the new house! Just as poor Seelos dropped into slumber,
a husky rasping bark would shake him awake. Painful even to
hear! Beyond the blanket, the candle was still burning. Did
Father Superior go to bed at all? He ought to see a doctor about
that cold of his.

Father Mueller had noticed the long coughing spells too.
Sometimes they left Neumann gasping for breath. He spoke to
him earnestly on the matter. But the Superior side-stepped the
issue with mention of some practical feature in the new monastery
they had begun in back of the church. He talked of the resilient
toughness of his Boehmerwald countrymen: how he had known
neighbors back in Prachatitz to live to a hundred. But Father
Mueller was not taken in.

Bishop O'Connor mentioned it too—in German with a faint
touch of the county Cork. (Like Neumann, he was both scholar
and linguist—and talked German remarkably well.)

"If you don't take better care of yourself, Father Neumann,
what will I do for a confessor? You won't even be around here
for October when we dedicate your fine stone *cathedral*."

But Father Neumann was there that first Sunday of October—
though not in the procession. (Nursing another cold he was.) It
was the Solemnity of the Holy Rosary, and Bishop O'Connor com-
mandeered all Catholic Pittsburgh for the afternoon. Father Gart-
land brought his Irishmen from St. Patrick's at the Canal. St.
Paul's came too, and every Catholic German within a radius of
forty miles.

They trooped over the bridge from Allegheny, across the
river. From the far side of the triangle they marched, up from
Birmingham and Saw Mill Run. Up from Wheeling, they came
by steamboat, in picnic mood, with hampers of lunch and a gala
German band. Many hiked the twelve miles over the hills from
McKeesport. From Summit and Butler, they came; from Pine
Creek and Brownsville and Wexford—from all the nooks in the
huddle of hills around Pittsburgh where Father Neumann's Redemptorists said Mass and baptized and taught catechism in the
course of every month.

They came, of course, to see *their* church, the largest in western Pennsylvania. But there was more to their coming than just that. It was a spontaneous tribute to the little priest who built Saint Philomena's, an act of gratitude to "the three saints" of Bayardstown.

Bishop O'Connor was astonished at the turn-out. Even the Mayor was on hand. Throwing caution to the winds, in this era of Nativist bigotry, Michael O'Connor set the tall mitre on his curly head and strode proudly out of St. Paul's at the end of the long procession, moving across town to Liberty Avenue and up to Bayardstown.

At the Canal bridge that afternoon, for the first Sunday within memory, there was no anti-Catholic harangue. Joe Barker was nowhere in evidence. But towards sundown, when Quarry Hill jubilantly crackled with salvo on salvo of rifle shots, Barker in his house down the street must have felt in his bones that the awful day had come, that the Pope himself was steaming up the Ohio with an armed flotilla and would have all Pittsburgh under his thumbscrews by dark!

"O there you are, Father Neumann."

It was Bishop O'Connor after the ceremony.

"I've been talking with this little lady here, all the way from Youngstown."

(The widow Amscheid, it was, with five of her children. How she had managed to get down to Pittsburgh, God alone knew!)

"She's been telling me how you preached a powerful Mission last month in Latrobe: you and 'little Father Seelos,' as she calls him. She says you're both *saints.*"

The Bishop was enjoying Father Neumann's embarrassment.

"I suppose, now that your church is built, you'll never be home in Bayardstown?"

"But, Your Grace. . . ."

Father Superior pointed to the partly finished building behind the sacristy, his new monastery.

"That will keep me around for a while."

But even "saints" can be mistaken. Even they must take care of their health or suffer the consequences. By Christmas Father Neumann was in bed with fevers and chills, in a state of physical exhaustion. Doctor Jest shook his head, muttering about a "change of air."

Worried, Father Mueller informed Baltimore. By return mail came a letter from Headquarters.

"You will report to Baltimore as soon as you can travel."

Once more, the will of God.

14.   PEN AND INK

Father Neumann blessed his stars as the stage crossed the half-way point of Kaiser Ridge, rattling down the Pike toward Cumberland. Off to the left, in a gap of the mountains, he caught a quick glimpse of the Dipper. A long time it had been since he had seen a winter sky. Nights in Bayardstown hunched over blueprint and galleyproof, tallying payrolls for Saturday, sketching out window and altar design—there was little time for stars. All that was past now, he felt sure.

His physical breakdown had made it evident that God never meant him for a builder with all that worrisome detail. The prompt action of Headquarters, recalling him to Baltimore, struck John Neumann as pleasant evidence of God's will, that he slip back out of the limelight once and for all, back among his brethren where he could plunge heart and soul into genuine apostolic work. No more anxious preoccupation with money matters. No more giving orders, granting permissions, presiding at community acts. For that heartening prospect he blessed his stars.

But as the stagecoach lumbered over the mountains to Frostburg and down to Cumberland, as the morning train hustled out of Cumberland depot, eastward towards Baltimore . . . westward, across the Atlantic a packetship out of Antwerp steered a slow course by the same January stars. In its hold lay an important letter.

Baltimore was mild. The crisp air of the Chesapeake agreed with Neumann. Everything did—now that he was free. The wooden house on Pleasant Alley was warmer than the old rectory at Bayardstown, few drafts, no soot at all. From his third-floor window he could see, two streets away, the spires and copper dome of the cathedral and, on Sunday mornings, hear its Old World bells.

With a somewhat professional eye he stood on Saratoga Street to admire the gothic lines of St. Alphonsus, its dark brick facade shouldering above the leafless sycamores. The builder in John Neumann unconsciously compared what he saw with Saint Philomena's. The location facing the harbor was more impressive. Once the spire was up, its gilded cross would flash a welcome to every incoming clipper and packetship. An impressive facade with its five gothic windows! Still the facade was only half as high, the center aisle not quite as long as Pittsburgh's.

"There I go," chided Neumann, *"making conceited comparisons!"*

In reparation for this upstart pride, he recited five decades of the rosary before the altar, begging the Lord for true humility of heart.

Walking back from Carmel on Asquith Street, one February morning, he saw the first robin of 1847. Now that he was doing parish work again, he was beginning to feel like a spring robin himself! His coughing spells had stopped; the blood sang in his veins; he felt wonderful—not a worry in the world!

"Benedicite, Pater."

He genuflected at the superior's door. Father Superior, busily sorting mail, glanced up.

"Someone still thinks of you, Father. A letter from the other side."

Neumann's heart leaped, expecting news from home. But this was the important letter from Belgium, informing the Reverend John Nepomucene Neumann, C.SS.R. (slowly he crossed himself at this new prank of Providence), that he was to be superior over all ten Redemptorist foundations in America!

Quietly he walked down the creaky stairs to the chapel and buried his face in his hands.

No matter how one looked at the new assignment, it could not be easy. Here he was, not five years a professed Redemptorist, suddenly set over men, some of whom had held high posts in Europe; men with broader experience; men older, better versed in tradition than he. Not only that; they had come from every quarter of Europe: thirty men and a dozen nationalities—Austrians, Luxemburgers, Frenchmen, Prussians, Hollanders, Czechs, Alsatians, Hungarians, Swiss, Belgians, Bavarians—and, to add spice to the salad, two young Irishmen had just applied to enter the novitiate at St. James.

That this was but part of his problem, he realized only too well. Unlike himself, these men had joined the Order in Europe where Redemptorists lived together in large communities, preaching Missions as their principal work. Life in America was hardly what they bargained for. Scant chance here for preaching Missions, when bishops were insisting that parishes first be organized to cope with the influx of German immigrants in Maryland, New York, Pennsylvania, Ohio and the Michigan woods. From ten such parish-centers, his thirty Redemptorists were radiating out to some seventy mission-stations every day of the week. Some of them lived alone for months on end with no set hour for prayer, no common acts, no companionship, none of the mutual encouragement and counsel so helpful to religious life. Besides, there was not a printed copy of their Rule in America. Each local superior ordered matters as he vaguely remembered they used to do it "back home."

The letter from Belgium made it pointedly clear to Neumann that Superiors there were not all pleased with the state of Redemptorists affairs in America. For the past fifteen years, since 1832, more and more recruits had been sent from Europe. With them had come generous donations of money from Austria and Bavaria to help build churches for the poor German immigrant in the wilds of America. But those pioneer churches were now too small. They must be enlarged, made more permanent. In half a dozen Redemptorist centers, at the moment, schools were under construction. Debts were mounting on all sides. The Redemptorists in America now owed practically a quarter of a million dollars

—a staggering sum when their parishioners were laboring six ten-hour days for less than $3.00 per week. Responsibility for that enormous debt was now Father Neumann's.

There were too many apostolic commitments—said the letter from Belgium—too much overzealous concern for building schools and churches, too much untethered zeal to the detriment of religious observance. It was precisely because of this that Neumann was replacing his predecessor. It must all stop. Neumann must see that it did; for, to Europe's way of thinking, this scattershot apostolate among abandoned souls was the root of Redemptorist problems in America; too many far-flung centers and the men too thinly spread.

Those were his orders. Following them would hardly win him ardent friends. Bishops were importuning that he establish Redemptorist centers in New Orleans, Milwaukee, Detroit, Washington, D. C., Lower Manhattan. Badin of Vincennes could use, he said, not one but two such foundations. Indiana was a big place. There were tentative requests from Texas and the wagon-train country of Oregon. If he turned down these requests, he would be branded short-sighted. If he curtailed loans for land for the construction of needed buildings, he would be called panicky, tight-fisted, without imagination. And if at home he insisted on more punctilious observance of the Rule, there would be heated reference to his utter lack of practical realism—of zeal for abandoned souls. He could forecast the whole gamut of reaction. But he remembered the words of Passerat, Redemptorist vicar general in Vienna:

> Work in itself, even the holiest work, can neither sanctify nor save a man, if he does not increase in his heart the Love of God, by faithfully keeping his Rule. . . .

John Neumann believed those words with all his heart.

Down on Fayette Street there was a young German printer whose children Neumann had prepared for First Communion in Old Town, several years back.

"Good morning, Karl. . . ."

Neumann stopped at the print shop one day shortly after taking his oath of office.

"I have two little jobs for you. . . ."

From the Italian he had made a translation of the Redemptorist Rule—also the Common Prayers. Within the month, each man in his ten foundations had a printed copy of both.

But there was hardly need at all to print the text of the Rule with Father Neumann about. He observed it so precisely, all one need do was follow him. First in the chapel for each Common Act, first to break off a story in mid-sentence at the signal for silence, first to snuff his lamp at the final bell of the day. Never did he speak without need. The house on Pleasant Alley rapidly became the model for every Redemptorist house in America. It never mattered that several might be absent on sick calls, a conference perhaps to the Negro nuns at the orphanage, a weekend assignment at Elkridge Landing or Westminster—no matter! With only two priests in the house, Brother Franz had orders to ring the bell for Vespers in choir.

As might be expected, he had his critics. A few acid little pens were forever writing about him to Europe, informing Superiors that Father Neumann "was running St. Alphonsus as though it were a novitiate"—and in the next breath, that "he hardly had the real spirit of the Order, since he had never made a real novitiate himself." But the righteous scribes omitted mention that, with all the Regular Observance at Pleasant Alley, Neumann had St. Alphonsus High Mass with choir and sermon, evening devotions, instructions for young adults, processions, solemn First Communions; active parish societies and—facing the church on Saratoga Street—a thriving parish school, built in the summer of 1847, and taught by the School Sisters of Notre Dame. In the letters denouncing the Superior, there was no mention of the comments made by morning worshippers, walking up Park Street after attending Father Neumann's seven o'clock Mass—visitors from out of town:

"That little priest," they said, "is a living saint."

In one of his many notebooks Neumann had copied out St.

Vincent de Paul's advice to superiors. (This, his critics did not know; nor, that he was observing it to the letter.)

He is not to seem the superior and overlord. For nothing is farther from truth than to imagine that to govern well, one must "throw his weight about." Jesus taught the very opposite both by word and example. A superior ought be meek; bear with the foibles of his subjects, deeming them worthy rather of pity than pummeling.

Father Neumann never "seemed the superior." For his cell, he had chosen a room hardly bigger than a broom closet on the ground floor. His black Redemptorist habit, though neat enough, was a patchwork of dark greens and blues—an eyesore to many a motherly Hausfrau. Emmi Schnabel, the meat-cutter's wife, once proposed to make him a fine new habit for May 11, his name day. It was no use! He smiled her offer away with a phrase from Father Clement Holbauer, that a Redemptorist ashamed of a patch is a sorry one indeed.

"If I need a habit," he said, "Brother Franz will take care of me."

Franz was a handsome Bavarian, straight as a steeple and almost as tall, an awesome figure when he opened the rectory door or accompanied Father Neumann along Saratoga Street. It was a standing joke that strangers, looking for the superior, often bypassed Neumann to state their business to Brother Franz. Neumann never seemed the superior even to the school children across the street. For them, he was the priest who told stories, the one with candy in his pocket for the best catechism answer, the priest "with the big dark eyes that looked right into your soul."

One morning during the second week of the parish Mission, Emmi Schnabel met Brother Franz at Lexington Market and promptly gave him a piece of her mind. Why was it, she'd like to know, that little Father Rector's only role was to say the beads in the pulpit before the Missionary started preaching? Why didn't Father Neumann orate on Death and Judgment? Franz could have told Emmi Schnabel that, during those high voltage themes, her "little Father Rector" was on his knees in the sacristy praying for the man in the pulpit. But he said:

"Father Neumann has more than just Baltimore on his mind. You should see the bundles of mail I bring him each day from the post office."

Emmi Schnabel was not impressed.

"But I saw him going into his box after the sermon," she countered. "With my very own eyes I saw him."

So had Brother Franz. During that parish mission, Father Neumann had spent as much as ten hours each day in the confessional. He never seemed the superior at all.

Still, Franz had not lied. Neumann did have many things on his mind besides Baltimore. One of them was New York. Early one April morning, while it was still dark, he arrived unannounced at the little clapboard rectory of Holy Redeemer on East Third Street. Wagons were bumping along the cobbles of Boston Post Road from farms in the Bronx and Westchester, hauling milk for Manhattan's breakfast. Three times Neumann pounded on the door, before a sleepy-eyed candidate Brother drew the bolt.

"Well! State your business, sir."

Brother-porter instantly tagged the seedy looking caller for the sexton from Bloomingdale come to borrow Mass wine or candlesticks.

"May I speak with Father Rector, Brother?"

Neumann made to enter; but brother-porter, hands on hips, stolidly blocked the narrow doorway.

"Wait here, Mister; we don't allow people inside."

Chuckling, Neumann waited on the sidewalk while the young postulant fetched the rector from Meditation. It took some time.

The horrified porter's eyes widened in panic to see Father Rector suddenly kneel to kiss the "sexton from Bloomingdale's" hand.

"Tut, Brother," smiled Neumann. "You only obeyed orders not to allow strangers in the house. Didn't he, Father Rector?"

Neumann's piercing eyes had fastened on Father Gabriel Rumpler who was now doing rapid mental tabulations of his own. (He had borrowed eight thousand dollars to purchase land on the lower west side of Manhattan. In fact, he had already begun a second church there, at the suggestion of Bishop Hughes—but with no permission from Baltimore.)

"One should always obey orders. Isn't that right, Father Rector? And never presume exceptions."

"Yes, Father."

Gabriel Rumpler agreed, not quite sure how much Father Neumann knew. He might not seem Superior, but he was.

Back in Baltimore flagmakers added the twenty-ninth, the thirtieth star to the flag for Iowa and then Wisconsin. Newsboys on Calvert, on Eutaw, on Mulberry Streets were piping news of the War: General Winfield Scott at Buena Vista, at Molino del Rey, Chapultepec.

At Pleasant Alley, although there were no newspapers, Brother Franz, on his daily stroll to the post office, managed to glean this and that. With Father Neumann now a full-fledged American citizen, Franz briefed him daily on the Mexican war. But there were other tidbits he thought it best to withhold. Fells Point was atitter with gossip about King Ludwig of Bavaria, something about a Spanish dancer called Lola Montez. Father Neuman would hardly be interested. Anyway, Franz had enough mail in his coat pocket to keep the good man occupied for the rest of the day.

His little room on Pleasant Alley was the nerve center of Redemptorist activities in America. Letters came each morning filled with heartbreak, complaint, impractical dreams. Now it was a request for Missions through all the little towns of northern Ohio, Bishop Rappe writing from Cleveland. Here was a note from Pittsburgh, Father Seelos yearning for a translation of the Rule for novices.

("My two wild Irishmen are now talking German almost as well as myself!")

News from the Michigan woods—spotted fever there. Father Poilvache had succumbed to the "black tongue" at Monroe. From Rochester, a desperately urgent plea for cash, the new church of St. Joseph on Franklin Street threatened with foreclosure.

With the March revolution of 1848, disheartening news

trickled in from Europe. In Vienna, his Redemptorists were parodied in vaudeville shows, lampooned in tavern ditties, slandered in cheap leaflets all over town. Their oldest monastery, Maria Stiegen, hallowed by the memory of Clement Hofbauer, had been confiscated, its occupants expelled at gunpoint from the city. The Order was in grave peril of losing all its houses in Europe.

But September of that year brought a bit of sunshine from smoky Bayardstown. Father Seelos wrote that "my two Irishmen, Duffy and McGrane, will make their profession as Redemptorists on the twenty fourth." Prospects for the future were rosy. Several Yankee converts had already made their vows, some studying at the moment in Belgium. Out in the Cumberland mountains people were asking for a resident priest—an ideal spot for a House of Studies.

Among the maps that littered his desk, the galley proofs of catechisms, the heaps of unanswered mail, was a battered green covered book that Father Neumann had purchased at Murphy's on Fayette Street. In a letter home he made mention of the book.

"Since we now have a house in New Orleans, I've been studying Spanish. Imagine, at thirty-six, I'm a small boy again, puzzling out rules of syntax. . . ."

He mentioned the busy church on Saratoga Street where he lived. He asked for news of mother and all his dear ones.

But to mention that he was now in charge of all the Redemptorists in the New World, that never seemed to cross his mind. In one letter, however, to his higher superiors overseas, he did mention "that." He asked to be relieved of his post.

Neumann, of course, blamed himself for the disharmony in the ranks of his brethren. He knew nothing of the dribbling quills of his few critics, the letters sent monthly to Europe, dismissing him as totally incompetent for office, branding him too meek, too imperturbable, too strict, too mousey, too unconscionably shy.

"Father Neumann," one conceited little malcontent had scribbled, "may be a paragon of piety, punctual as a church bell and all that—but he lacks that *tertium quid,* that all essential quality for an American superior. He has no presence. He lacks command of a situation and, if you'll pardon the word, he lacks "guts." He never had it and never will. . . ."

Weighty diagnosis from the youngest member of the House on Pleasant Alley, a callow whippersnapper but one year ordained.

But authorities in Europe were not quite hoodwinked by these wry dispatches from Baltimore.

"Father Neumann, if I overrated the opponents of your regime, I've made a mistake," said the letter that brought news of his longed-for replacement. "Four or five disgruntled subjects out of thirty is not surprising. No man quite suits everybody."

The replacement arrived in early January of 1849 in the person of Bernard Hafken-scheid. Neumann was overjoyed at the choice. As he took the oath of office in booming Latin, Neumann, sitting in the rear of the little chapel on Pleasant Alley, breathed a new air of peace. Bernard was the right man.

Father Bernard, as they called him, had the build of a John Bunyan, was master of many tongues, doctor of theology from Rome, missionary of many roads in Europe and already well acquainted with conditions in America. He had the resonant timbre of the famous Senator from Massachusetts—Daniel Webster himself. What was more, he possessed a heart to match that Dutch physique.

Outsiders might arch an eyebrow at Neumann's abrupt removal in mid-term. Let them! The important thing was that his successor would quickly restore harmony among the disaffected few.

"He has the warmth that I lack," thought Neumann. "Father Bernard can break tension anywhere with a single good-natured laugh."

Early that afternoon someone knocked at the rectory door.

"An accident, Brother Franz! Down at the waterfront. . . ."

"I'll take it, Brother."

"But, Father Neumann, the youngster's on duty."

The youngster was the rascal who had written those letters to Europe.

"Let him rest, Brother Franz. I'll go."

15.   THE SECRET OF SARATOGA STREET

Taper in hand, Brother Franz commenced his morning rounds at
the top floor of the new rectory, knocking on door after door.
"Tu autem, Domine, miserere nobis." Outside, a March rain pelted
the windows, sloshing last Monday's snow along the cobbles of
Baltimore. There would be few worshippers at early Mass, mused
Franz; John Krems, the young tailor from Lautner's across the
street, frail Sara May with her small son, a few of the hardy
standbys. Down another flight came Brother Franz; and another.
"Tu autem, Domine. . . ."

He was on the street floor now, knocking at Father Rector's
little room by the main entrance. The door opened. Father Neumann extended his candle for a light from Brother's taper. The
door closed again.

Unchaining the front door a moment, Franz poked out his
head into the rain of Saratoga Street. He could barely see the lamp
at the Park Street corner.

"A nasty morning for the poor man appointed for Old Town,"
thought Brother Franz. "With all this fog and icy slush, he'd
better set out before Meditation!"

Early each morning, one of the Community took the twenty-
minute walk across town to say the seven o'clock Mass at St. James.

It was St. Joseph's day. On the board outside the chapel
Franz saw that Father Neumann had assigned himself to Old
Town.

"But he has the sermon at the High Mass here at home!"

Franz was puzzled, until he remembered Wednesday. On
Wednesdays, Father Rector always went to Old Town to hear the
Sisters' confessions at their convent behind St. James'. They lived
in the old Redemptorist rectory which Neumann had sold, at cost,
to the School Sisters of Notre Dame, when they first came from
Munich to Baltimore.

It was uncanny the practical information Brother Franz could
extract from the day's appointments. Today, for example, he

knew it would be quite easy to delay the trip to the post office until after the rain. Normally, Father Neumann began his work-day right after breakfast—with the day's mail. A methodical man, Father Neumann. Franz could forecast his schedule to the last detail.

"Benedicite, Father Rector."

While the Community was taking dinner, Brother Franz had gone to the post office. The rain had stopped and, with the March wind and sunshine, the streets were already dry.

"That was a touching sermon on St. Joseph, Father Rector."

Towering over Neumann, Franz sometimes sounded like a father commending a schoolboy.

"That prayer for a Happy Death you quoted . . . we'll all be reciting it from now on."

"Brother, I learned that prayer to St. Joseph from my good mother thirty-six years ago. I've said it every night since I was four years old."

A bell rang for the end of common recreation—the start of the Little Silence. Mutely, Father Rector reached for the letters in Brother's hand and left the room.

The letter postmarked Belgium was from Father Bernard. He had been Europe since August, Neumann acting as American superior in his stead. Bernard was now enroute, said the letter. He should be back any day now.

Here was a letter from Pittsburgh. He recognized the hand-writing of Father Franz Seelos. Neumann laid it aside a while, in favor of a third, postmarked "Prachatitz." He could hardly believe it! In fifteen years, this was the first letter he had received direct from home. Not that they never wrote. They faithfully had answered all his letters from America. But somehow—one of those crosses a man must bear in patience—somehow all their letters went astray. Priest-friends in Budweis, in Linz, had no trouble reaching Neumann by mail. They sometimes mentioned meeting his father, seeing his mother, his sister: how well they looked. But now to get news straight from Number 129 in the Upper Lane—St. Joseph was good on his feast day. Father Neu-mann opened the letter in his room.

It was from Louise. Rapidly he read, then turning the page, stopped short; shook his head, disbelieving; re-read the passage again:

"*. . . my letter of two years ago, telling you of mother's beautiful death. . . .*"

He read no more. The writing blurred, the page slipped to the floor.

Twenty-one months in the churchyard and he did not know; had not even said a Requiem for her soul!

"Mother," he whispered, "rest your dear, dear soul."

The words rode off on a smothered heart-racking sob. He slumped to his knees, hiding his face in the bed. Incidents, words, little memories out of the past flickered through his mind:

"I must have the nuns pray for her," he murmured.

At several convents around Baltimore, Father Neumann was confessor and spiritual director: the Carmelites, the School Sisters of Notre Dame in Old Town; Mother Seton's Sisters of Charity out at Mount Hope; the Negro Oblates of Divine Providence at the top of Park Street. He visited them all.

On the appointment board outside the chapel, he pinned a note begging prayers for the respose of his mother's soul. Slowly, he walked down the stairs and into church, still dazed with grief; knelt before Our Lady's altar, stayed there the entire afternoon.

In the shock and distraction of that letter from home, the busy preparation of Lenten sermons, the excitement of Father Bernard's arrival the following Monday morning—somehow, Father Seelos' letter was mislaid in Neumann's room. It didn't matter. Sooner or later the news from Pittsburgh would leak out: Brother Athanasius, the sacristan—an old friend of Neumann's—was having apparitions. Or so he said.

Had anyone asked Father Neumann what sort of man was Brother Athanasius, the last thing he would have called him was a dreamer. Joseph Friedele—his name in the world—was the soul of practicality, a rock of cool common sense. A master watchmaker from Wuertemberg, he had settled in Brownsville where his business prospered. Still in his early thirties, he came down to

Pittsburgh and one morning in 1847 knocked at the wooden rectory on Penn Avenue. He asked to join the Redemptorists.

"I'm done with mending clocks. I want to mend my ways and work for Eternity."

That was how he phrased it.

Father Neumann had accepted him as a postulant, giving him Athanasius for his religious name. Father Seelos, his novice-master, had trained him in prayerful recollection. No matter what his task at St. Philomena's—filling cruets with Mass-wine, answering calls at the rectory door or mending clocks for the neighbors—the thought of Brother Athanasius dwelt in the world beyond.

Anyway, during Shrovetide of that year, 1851, tinkering one afternoon with a cheap Connecticut clock, a one-dollar gadget from the firm of Chauncey Jerome of Waterbury, he was thinking of approaching Lent. A floor-board squeaked in his room. He glanced up and, *"ewiger Gott!"* There in the doorway stood a bishop in full pontificals—cape, mitre, crozier, ring!

Quickly he ruled out Bishop O'Conner. (What would the Bishop of Pittsburgh be doing there anyway in all his robes on Shrove Tuesday afternoon?) Could it be his sainted namesake, the great fourth century Hammer of Heretics? No. It was *Father Neumann*, that's who! He had squinted his watchmaker eyes to make doubly sure but mitre, face, cope and everything slowly dissolved like . . . like coal dust in a Pittsburgh sunbeam.

So Brother Athanasius recounted his "vision" to the fathers at supper that Shrovetide evening. Everyone laughed. It was really too good a story to keep. In his letter to Baltimore, Father Seelos had mentioned it in a humorous postscript.

It was Palm Sunday before Father Neumann came across that mislaid letter from Pittsburgh. The postscript did not strike him funny at all. He did not even smile. In the back of his mind was the memory of a nightmare he had had as a novice ten years ago—someone forcing a jewelled ring on his stubby finger. A dream with all the horrified panic of "no escape." What relief it had been to waken in Bayardstown still plain Father Neumann.

"Tell good Brother Athanasius," he wrote to Seelos, "that

if he isn't already daft, he had better get down on his knees and pray. I'm afraid his brain is softening."

But as he wrote, the pen shook in Neumann's hand. That evening he got down on his own knees to pray long and earnestly by his bed.

A few days later, on Easter Tuesday, Archbishop Samuel Eccleston passed away. The cathedral bells began tolling on Charles Street. Soon, all the Catholic bells of Baltimore gave tongue. *Clang-bong! Clang-bong!* Father Neumann draped the facade of St. Alphonsus in mourning crepe. Soon the whole archdiocese was in mourning.

On Saratoga Street the sycamores were already in bud. It was the last week of April. Lilacs nodded primly along Charles Street. Tidewater orchards shimmered in a pink mist of blossom. The winds of spring came spanking up the Chesapeake, blowing the last of the China clippers back to port. April! Almost too lovely for Requiems. But that April morning, Samuel Eccleston was laid to rest alongside Bishop Carroll and Neale and Marechal in the crypt of the cathedral.

In mid-summer on a Sunday morning, Father Neumann mounted the pulpit of St. Alphonsus to bring the glad tidings to his parishioners: the See of Baltimore was widowed no longer. Francis Kenrick was coming from Philadelphia to be the new Archbishop.

That fall, Kenrick took formal possession of his cathedral of the Assumption on Charles Street. Father Bernard, the Redemptorist provincial, went up with Father Neumann to the cathedral. As yet, the See of Philadelphia was unfilled.

The Friday following, a stranger called at the rectory on Saratoga Street. A giant of a man he was, with a round pleasant face topped with a crop of thick auburn curls.

"May I see Father Rector, Brother. . . ."

The blue eyes twinkled impishly at Brother's shocked amazement to hear this Irish face talking German.

"I'm a bit of a stranger in the neighborhood. Just show me to his room."

In the slight motion of the man's hand Brother Franz caught

the glitter of an emerald. Flustered, he plumped to his knees before the new Archbishop of Baltimore. He would make no mistake next time.

Thereafter, the weekly caller became a matter of course. Punctually at four each Friday afternoon, Archbishop Kenrick strode down the slope of Charles Street, turning west on Saratoga to the red brick rectory alongside St. Alphonsus church. He had chosen Father Neumann for spiritual director.

The pair made quite a contrast, Neumann quiet and pensive, Kenrick so vitally alive. Neumann looked up to Kenrick, literally. He had to crane his neck to address the strapping six footer. But in another sense, he admired Kenrick's accomplishments in the Church—his pulpit eloquence, his cool approach to controversy, his breadth of scholarship. Had he not authored a four-volume opus of Moral, three more volumes of Dogmatic Theology and a version of the Four Gospels from the Latin Vulgate, a revision of the English of Rheims? It confused the humble Neumann no end that a man of such eminent learning should come for spiritual advice to *him,* kneel at his feet.

They were walking toward the door one Friday early in January, when Kenrick with a puckish wink turned to his confessor.

"Father Neumann, I think you'd be almost as tall as myself, if you'd go out and buy yourself a mitre."

In the soft Dublin accent, there was something more than jest. But Kenrick said no more.

Father Neumann took alarm. The daydreams of a tinkering watchmaker could be smiled away; not the pointed hint of an Archbishop. Quickly, Neumann took action, writing letters to Belgium, Vienna, Rome—to every influential person he knew. He pleaded with Kenrick, alleging a dozen sound reasons for choosing someone else. He stormed Heaven on his knees.

That very week he hurried over to Carmel on Asquith Street; he went up Park Street to his Negro nuns; to Sister Caroline in her classroom across from St. Alphonsus, to her School Sisters in Old Town. Would they please make a novena, he pleaded. Not one, several novenas? Have the little Negro orphans, have all the school children make novenas too. It was very urgent! The nuns agreed.

"But, Father, may we know the intention?"

Father Neumann reddened slightly.

"To avert impending harm to the Church in America."

Starched veil and fluted black bonnet nodded understandingly, not understanding the matter at all. Father Neumann smiled his gratitude at sister, clapped on his black hat and hurried home to Saratoga Street.

At St. Alphonsus, the Community wondered among themselves. Father Rector lately seemed so preoccupied. Thursday, he forgot to tap the bell at dinner, the bell for colloquium at table. Two evenings running, he had forgotten the *Salve Regina* at the stroke of six; Meditation had ticked anxiously on for several minutes overtime. Something was afoot. Father Neumann was not usually forgetful. Why had he asked that they recite the Seven Penitential Psalms after Night Prayer? What was the "impending harm?" Lately, when the Archbishop made his weekly visit, the hum of earnest parley could be overheard in the corridor—tones a bit too emphatic for spiritual counsel. There were rumors, of course. But only rumors.

Out in the Cumberland mountains of western Maryland at the little Redemptorist House of Studies, Father Adrian van de Braak had started the tract *De Ecclesia*. A student raised his hand.

"Father, will the students go to Baltimore for Father Neumann's consecration?"

With that uncanny clairvoyance native to all seminarians, the young Redemptorists had knitted the threads of hearsay into a sound fabric of suspicion. They had heard the story of Brother Athanasius and his vision in Pittsburgh. As usual, they were several logical laps ahead of everyone.

Rumors multiplied, spread abroad. New York, Buffalo, Detroit, New Orleans. There were those, however, who put no stock at all in such old wives tales.

"Neumann a bishop! *Gott in Himmel.* Talk sense, man."

"The day I see him in purple, I'll give up Lager for life!"

At four o'clock one March morning, the community bell at Saratoga Street rang as usual for rising. As usual, Brother Franz went knocking at door after door.

"Tu autem, Domine, miserere nobis."

As usual, on the street floor just inside the entrance, he knocked for Father Rector. The door did not open. He knocked again, louder. (Maybe Father Rector was dead!) Noiselessly he inched the door ajar and looked around. The bed was made. Brother Franz lifted the taper over his head, making something glitter like a cat's eye on the writing table. There, on his knees before the table, was Father Rector, dead asleep—looking for all the world like Christ in Gethsemane.

The glittering object? The Archbishop had called the day before. Neumann was at Fell's Point on a sick call. Francis Patrick Kenrick had left on his confessor's writing table the jeweled ring and pectoral cross that he had worn for twenty-one years as Bishop of Philadelphia. All through the night Father Neumann had been praying unto exhausted sleep.

"Tu autem, Domine, miserere nobis," boomed Brother Franz.

Father Rector stirred. *"Miserere nobis. . . .* Have mercy on us, O Lord." He groped for the candlestick; extended it quickly toward the lighted taper in Brother's hand.

At ten that morning, St. Joseph's day, the Archbishop returned to Saratoga Street. With him he brought two parchment documents. Father Rector accepted them gravely. Document the first appointed John Nepomucene Neumann, C.SS.R., under precept of formal obedience to accept the episcopal dignity. A direct command from the living Vicar of Christ! For Neumann it spelt the express will of God.

The consecration was set for Passion Sunday, just two weeks away. It would take place next door, in his own parish church of Saint Alphonsus.

On the Saturday evening before the ceremony, a group of his confreres gathered in the Saratoga Street common room. Someone leaned over to ask how he felt about it all. Neumann looked at his confrere with those honest brown eyes of his.

"Believe me, Father, if the good God gave me my choice,

I'd rather die tonight in my Redemptorist bed than wear that mitre tomorrow."

But God had not given him the choice.

On Laetare Sunday, the sonorous voice of Father Bernard rang through the high nave of St. Alphonsus. Father Provincial was explaining the significance of the rose vestments at Mass, the gladness of the Church in the midst of Lent. He paused, a twinkle in his eye.

"But we of this parish have yet another cause for gladness," and he broke the news of their pastor's elevation to the See of Philadelphia.

The congregation gasped. All save Sister Caroline who sat among the school children, smiling to herself. So *that* was the "impending harm" Father Neumann had asked her to pray against. Plump Emmi Schnabel nudged her man. "Quiet, woman!" he growled, without taking eye from Father Bernard in the pulpit. Solemnly Father Bernard lowered his pitch to a note of warning:

"After Mass, do not go looking for Father Neumann." (That was the very thought in Emmi's mind.) "Don't! At this moment, your good pastor is in his room on his knees. He is making a retreat of ten days in preparation for the new burden of next Sunday morning. If you must do something, pray for him."

Up in the deep waters of the Delaware the shad run had begun. Hucksters peddled their catch on Market Street, Spring Garden, all over Philadelphia. But when the Catholic *Herald* appeared that week, the shad run had competition. "Neumann," the name was bandied about from Moyamensing to Kensington.

"Neumann! Never heard of him. Where is he from?"

"It sounds German to me."

Catholic gentry below Market Street felt slighted that a native son had not been chosen; now particularly with these "Know-Nothings" in the saddle. The acrid stench of burning churches still prickled Philadephia's nostrils. Why tempt fate? Rome was toying with fire in sending them a foreigner as bishop. They should have someone as native as Betsy Ross, as old Ben Franklin.

The Supreme Order of the Star Spangled Banner with its

slogans of *No Popery* and *America for Americans* would hardly welcome John Neumann with open arms!

Up in her clean Connecticut kitchen Nora McGill sat peeling onions for Friday chowder. Dreaming of the sweet cove of Cork she was, her eyes misty with onion spray. Suddenly there was an uproar from the Bishop's apartment. Nora blessed herself.

"Sure it's laughing he is!"

For a split moment she thought of the Know-Nothings. But it was nothing of the sort.

Bishop O'Reilly had just found a letter from Baltimore in his mail, an invitation to attend the consecration on Passion Sunday.

"John Neumann! A grand little *maneen* for Philadelphia!"

O'Reilly remembered an evening in Rochester some sixteen years ago; and the ribbing he had given the poor young priest. Father Neumann had been ordained only nine days. O'Reilly had tried to convince the young man that his ordination was invalid!

Bishop Bernard O'Reilly of Hartford was delighted with the invitation.

"I'll be in Baltimore with bells on. So I will."

Via a friend in Rome the news reached Budweis. But when word trickled into Prachatitz, old Philip Neumann was annoyed. He took it for some crude practical joke—and to think it should be the new curate with his big brown innocent eyes.

"I ought to delate him to the Dean, for making sport of a poor old father."

But an hour later the Reverend Dean himself climbed the Upper Lane to offer congratulations to Mr. Neumann that his son John was a Bishop in America.

"Preposterous nonsense!" The old man put his face in his hand and cried.

Meanwhile in Baltimore, Passion Sunday had dawned and Father Neumann, waiting in the sacristy of St. Alphonsus, absently gazed at the bright red buttons of his cassock. Somehow, his thoughts leaped home to Prachatitz, to a morning when he stood in the doorway of Number 129 in the Upper Lane, a lump in his throat, starting off on his first trip to the local school.

He could hear it now—his mother's gentle voice (God rest her!) telling him how smart he looked in his new little suit.

"Mother Church is the same," he reflected, "when she has an unpleasant job for you, she gives you new clothes."

Two blocks up the hill, the cathedral bells were pealing. Father Bernard stormed from the rectory, along the covered passage way to the sacristy, an avalanche of muttering solicitude. Where was Brother Matthew, the sacristan? He had done wonders with the altar decoration—candles, pink dogwood, azaleas. But *Donnerwetter!* He should have wrapped the statues in purple. After all, it was Passion Sunday.

"Where's Brother Matthew?" he boomed at a quaking acolyte.

Abruptly, he poked his head through the sacristy doorway, scanning the packed church. In the choirloft, a group of Cumberland students were whispering heatedly. At sight of Father Provincial, the young Redemptorists blanched. But Bernard had much too much on his mind.

Everything must click like clockwork, every detail of the ceremony; and Bernard was there to see that it did. It wasn't every day that one of his men became a bishop. Wheeling back through the sacristy doorway, he almost collided with Neumann.

"Pardon me, Father. . . . I mean Bishop," he sputtered.

"The procession starts in four minutes. We'll all be praying with you."

John Neumann reached for the silk biretta, sheepishly put it on his head. He felt out of place in his new clothes.

Out on Saratoga Street, Herr Ferdinand Schnabel, the neighborhood butcher, solemnly idled a seven-foot staff on the cobbles in front of the church. Schnabel, by special appointment of Father Bernard, was grand marshall of the procession, and a more imposing figure Baltimore had never seen. The spring sunlight flickered on the gold piping, the intricate brocade of his fancy coat. On the creases of his boots it made small golden hatchmarks. It burnished his blond moustache.

The schoolboys of St. Alphonsus ogled him appraisingly.

"Look at old Schnabel," shrilled one of them. "You'd never guess he sold Blutwurst on weekdays!"

Bystanders smirked. Sister Caroline darted down the double file of boys, hushing further comment with a glance.

Unshaken, Schnabel rapped his marshall's staff on the cobblestones. That was the signal. At once, three thousand feet were in motion—fifteen hundred Baltimore Catholics marching in staid procession towards Charles Street and the cathedral rectory where the Archbishop of Baltimore was waiting to be escorted back to Saratoga Street for the Mass.

A dozen multi-colored banners fluttered in the March air, each with its own parish society. A contingent had come from Pittsburgh, old friends from St. Philomena days. All in all, it was an impressive procession. At the end of the long line of march walked the clergy, a generous number, considering that it was Sunday when priests were busy at home. Twenty-seven Redemptorists were there, counting the novices, the students from Cumberland. Each house in the Province—from New Orleans to Buffalo—had drawn lots for the chance to be present at their confrere's Consecration.

Father Neumann—never in his whole life had he been the center of such attention—walked along at the end of the procession, his long white cope, his new purple cassock trailing the cobbles of Charles Street. Today was his birthday, too. He was forty-one.

"Ecce Sacerdos Magnus," sang the Sulpician choir from nearby St. Mary's on Paca Street. The ceremony was starting. In the old days Bishop O'Reilly had often joked with Neumann about his size. (Did *magnus* mean that a bishop must be tall? O'Reilly would have his mite of sport with the little Bishop, when the ceremony was over.)

But the little Bishop's thoughts were in other fields just now. In the name of the Catholic Church, Archbishop Kenrick was asking:

"Will you teach the people?"

"I will," answered Neumann.

"As far as human frailty allows," continued Kenrick in his soft Dublin Latin, "wilt thou be ever given to the divine interests and shun worldly affairs?"

"I will."

During the long interrogation of the Bishop Elect, the packed church intently listened, though the Latin words made little sense. The people listened more with their eyes. Everything was so different: copes, mitres, faldstool, the surpliced clergy, the seminary choir. It hardly seemed their church of St. Alphonsus at all. But when the Archbishop commenced Mass, things seemed again familiar. Yet even here, there were strange interruptions.

It was time now to stand for the Gospel. Nobody stood. All knelt, instead, for the Litany of the Saints. Father Neumann lay prostrate on the sanctuary floor. The seminarians from Paca Street and Cumberland were calling on the citizens of Heaven to pray and intercede for him.

Silence. Now they placed the open book of the Gospels on his bowed back. The weight of the book was less than the pack he had shouldered through the swampy woods of the Niagara frontier, the pack with wine and chalice and missal, all the needs of a pioneer missionary. But Neumann knew that the book on his back weighed more, much more than it seemed. During the ten days of his retreat he had devoutly reviewed his notebook *Summa,* concerning the burden of a bishop—hand-picked thoughts on the subject by great and holy men.

He must teach the people—by example as well as sermon. He must be *the* priest of his Diocese for both layfolk and clergy. Schools, he must build schools, too, for the thousands of Catholic little ones who knew only broken English, or spoke it with a brogue—the children of immigrants in peril of losing the old faith in the new land. A Bishop ought be perfect. Now more than ever, John Neumann must become a saint.

The stately function proceeded, the book still on Neumann's back. Archbishop Kenrick presented him with the golden crozier, the jeweled ring, gifts of his St. Alphonsus parishioners. Now the book was lifted from his shoulders and Kenrick embraced him with the kiss of peace.

The Mass continued normally on to the end.

Now Archbishop Kenrick set the mitre on the new Bishop, now the white silk gloves embroidered with gold. Now they had enthroned him, crozier in hand, on the golden faldstool.

Te Deum laudamus.

A flutter of pages in the choir loft! Anxiously, Father Bernard glanced up, espied a few of his Cumberland students, leaning out over the choirloft ledge for a better glimpse of the new Bishop. Quickly he looked away. He knew how proud they felt.

The choir of Sulpicians and Redemptorists took up the canticle of thanksgiving intoned by the Archbishop. Bishop John Nepomucene Neumann walked down the center aisle, blessing the familiar faces of Pittsburgh and Buffalo and Baltimore—so many, many friends.

But the mind of a man is a strange thing. As he gripped his golden staff and walked under the high gothic arches of Saint Alphonsus, for some nameless reason there flickered through the new Bishop's mind, not a memory of home, nor the dream he had had in Pittsburgh as a novice, nor even some pregnant phrase of St. Alphonsus on the office of bishop—but the garbled words of a ditty he had once heard a rollicking Irishman singing on the Erie Towpath—something about *"a bundle on me shoulder . . . and off for Philadelphia in the mornin'."*

IV

16. LOGAN SQUARE: PHILADELPHIA

Logan Square, on the wooded fringe of Philadelphia, drowsed in the fragrant air of an early April night. Schuylkill Fifth Street glistened in the radiance of the spring moon, the gangling elms, the derricks and scaffolding of the half-built cathedral making black shadows on the silver road.

From somewhere in the heart of town, a clock mentioned the time. Logan Square listened to the twelve soft *bongs*, listened as other belfries made comment of their own. Logan Square was the quietest part of town, few homes and many trees. Still, if you cocked your ear, you could hear the giddy treble of peepers in some nearby pond, the sharp warning of a barge-bell on nearby Schuylkill, the far away halloo of one fisherman to his mate. Logan Square was so remote from the city's bustle, they called it "Texas"—Texas of Philadelphia.

Up along Sassafras Street echoed the hollow *clip-clop* of horses. Old Jim Wilcox, the paper king (his mill had a hand in the bank-notes of half the western hemisphere) came riding toward Logan Square guiding his two prancing bays, his olive-green phaeton back home from an evening of chess with Professor George Allen at the Wistar Club—home to Ivy Mills, a few miles up along the river.

"The new Bishop must still be up! Still at his prayers!"

He spied the lamplight in the window at the corner of Schuylkill Sixth. Kenrick he knew well; he wondered about the new one. Passing the dark bulk of St. Charles' on the other side of the cathedral, he glanced up at the dark windows and chuckled. His boys were all dead to the world—all forty of them and their professors.

"I wonder what Bishop Neumann will think when he hears them calling me *Pop!*"

For years, the diocesan students for the priesthood had spent their summer holidays at the Wilcox farm out in the Concord hills. They regarded *Pop* and *Ma* Wilcox as their own.

Since there was no church at Ivy Mills, James Wilcox drove the family to town each Sunday morning for Mass at St. John's.

"Maybe I'll meet the new Bishop on Easter. Kenrick thinks the world of him."

In the red brick residence on Logan Square, east of the half-built cathedral, the new bishop sat writing at his table in his room on the second floor. To all appearances he was still a Redemptorist, still wearing the same black habit, white collar, loop of fifteen decades he had worn at Saratoga Street. In the house he still followed the regular order of a Redemptorist day. He missed the bells calling to common acts, the antiphonal *Te Deum* after meals on the way to chapel, the morning knock of Brother Franz with *"Tu autem, Domine, misere nobis."*

Up at St. Peter's, the Redemptorist rectory, of course, he could feel at home. There at North Fifth Street he could retire for a monthly day of recollection. He could walk there each week to make his confession. Once in a while he could even drop in for dinner—but only once in a while. Now, he had to remind himself, he was Bishop of Philadelphia. He belonged to everyone.

Sitting in his room on Logan Square that April night, he dimly heard the clock and the passing hoof beats. He heard the bell-like tinkle of the peepers, too, and the snoring gasps of Father Waldron in the room at the end of the hall. Sounds, however, were no distraction; not when he tackled a problem. Just then he was drafting a pastoral letter for his new diocese—his first.

It was little more than a week since his arrival. With a chancery-backlog awaiting dispatch, deeds, rescripts, bills and correspondence; with people dropping in at all hours to greet him, to ask a favor; with daily trips about town to churches, convents, institutions; he had scarcely a moment to himself.

Fortunately the printer was good-natured. He had agreed that if by next morning the Bishop gave him the manuscript, one hundred and twenty-five copies of the pastoral would be ready by tomorrow night. That meant a copy for each priest in his sprawling diocese. On Easter morning they could stand before their parishioners in the far nooks of Pennsylvania, places that to Neuman still were but dots on the map, and read aloud his message for them all. Busily his pen scratched along the curling sheet of foolscap. There was so much to put into words.

Till now, English had been an auxiliary language for sick-call or backwoods fervorino. His apostolate till now had been mainly among Germans. English served to find directions, to bid the time of day, to ask for bread. He could write it well; could, if necessary, show his manuscript to Father Waldron before sending it to the printer. But speaking! Now, as head of an ultra-American diocese, in the cradle city of Yankee Independence, he, foreign accent, foreign ways and all, must mount pulpits in mitre and cope as spokesman for the Roman Catholic Church. He thought of the rankling chagrin of those in Philadelphia who were expecting one of their own. It worried John Neumann. Riding up through Maryland and Delaware that Tuesday morning, it had made him nervous.

As the coach had chugged along the tracks of the Baltimore and Wilmington, he had steeled himself with prayer against the approaching cross. He had not idly chosen the motto for his coat of arms! As the train puffed over the Schuylkill at Gray's Ferry, prayerfully he repeated the motto, *Passio Christi conforta me*— "Passion of Christ, be my strength."

"Philadelphia," the conductor had shouted as they pulled through Moyamensing, south of the city limits. The wheels then had creaked to a stop at Broad and Prime. The memory of that moment was still vivid to the Bishop sitting now in Logan Square.

How baseless had been his apprehension. Philadelphia had received him with charming kindness. He had found at the depot a welcome exactly to his liking, quiet and cordial. No foolish fuss, no crowds nor bands nor parading. A committee of five men had been there to meet him, four of them priests. Father Sourin, pastor of St. John's, had acted as spokesman, introducing the others, one by one: Moriarty, the Augustinian from Villanova, a stately looking Irishman with twinkling eyes and a ready tongue; Barbelin, from the Jesuit college at Willing's Alley, affability itself. Who else? Father Waldron, the lawyer-convert from Dartmouth, New Hampshire, snoring now down the hall, but spending his waking hours on the cathedral's construction. Last, there had been George Allen, like a pigeon among blackbirds in his light brown coat. Kenrick had often spoken of Allen, his Shakespearean library, his collection of old books on chess; Mary, his wife, and their five wonderful children. One of Kenrick's converts, George Allen was professor of classical tongues at the University of Pennsylvania.

Introductions over, they were climbing into carriages when Father Amat from St. Charles' had come running up with greetings from Neumann's forty seminarians. As the carriage had moved up Broad Street and over to St. John's, Father Sourin quietly had explained how in lieu of a noisy demonstration they had thought the Bishop would prefer this—a wallet of gold "for a new school." Neumann's eyes had lit up with mingled pleasure, gratitude, astonishment. They had touched the softest spot in his heart.

"Since we have occupied our Episcopal See," the pen traced ink across the page, "we have everywhere found tokens of kindness and respect. . . ."

Sourin was a treasure. Neumann at once had appointed him Vicar General. He had a placid, easy way that disarmed all opposition. Besides, he now had a practical grasp of diocesan affairs. Since October, when Kenrick had left for Baltimore, Sourin had been administrator of the vacant See. Neumann would have him for troubleshooter, for counselor and friend.

Punctually at ten each morning, the Vicar General arrived at Logan Square, appointment-book in hand, a carriage waiting at the door. He must give the new Bishop a rapid first-hand contact with the city proper—priests, nuns, institutions. If it could be tactfully maneuvered, he must point out a few of Philadelphia's famous landmarks—the Mint, the Liberty Bell, Franklin's witty epitaph.

And there were the trees in Fairmount Park and perhaps Pratt's Garden's at Lemon Hill, for he had learned from the fathers at St. Peter's that Neumann had a scientific interest in flowers.

"Where are you taking me today, Father Sourin?"

Off they went to the Visitation Academy, to the new hospital run by Mother Seton's Sisters of Charity, passing Girard College for orphan boys on the way. They dropped in at Father Carter's at Spring Garden, visiting his pretty gothic church of the Assumption. Next door at his parish school the Bishop asked questions, beamed at the quick intelligent answers.

"But are you a match, I wonder, for the Jesuit boys at St. Joseph's?"

Teacher grinned. The classroom rocked with exuberant challenge. Quietly, the boys knelt between the desks for the Bishop's blessing.

Not far from the pro-cathedral of St. John stood St. Joseph's orphanage for boys. Here he sat down to tell stories, very much at home. He gathered the St. Joseph Sisters for an impromptu fervorino. He promised to come back, often.

A quick visit to St. Philip Neri's in Southwark; up to Father Strobel's at St. Mary's in the shadow of Carpenter's Hall; off again in fifteen minutes, up Fifth Street past St. Peter's and out to Kensington. They would have supper at St. Patrick's before administering Confirmation.

Sourin was weary on his feet but the Bishop was still fresh. The Vicar General murmured a token protest when the curate, Father Bill O'Hara, voluntered to see the Bishop home to Logan Square. Father Edward Sourin made quickly home to bed.

"A methodical German, a time for everything and everything on the dot."

Father Sourin, the past two mornings, had found the Bishop in the chapel at Sext at precisely ten o'clock. Old Meg Bradley, housekeeper since Kenrick's time, had her own comment on the new Bishop's punctual schedule.

"It's up with the birds he is! Faith, I don't think he sleeps at all. Father Sourin," (*Sour* as in pickle, she pronounced it!) "as true as I'm standing here, his bed was unmussed this morning

—not even a wrinkle on the pillow slip! And sure, he's in chapel at all hours."

Meg described the Bishop's dry little cough in the chapel, and she still in bed on the top floor.

"At six, two of the boys from across come in to serve his Mass." (Across was St. Charles' on the other side of the cathedral.) "Then he serves Father Waldron. Then he goes out and hears confessions. Then the dear soul starts praying his Book. It's all hours before he comes to breakfast."

Old Margaret Bradley tossed her head back.

"*Breakfast,* says I. He eats no more than a wren: a cup of coffee and a crusteen of bread!"

On Friday, when Father Sourin arrived, Meg was in consternation.

"He's gone! He was reading in his Book when I peeked in the chapel. Maybe he's *across.*"

But at the Seminary, Father Amat had not seen the Bishop. Mr. Dick Phelan reported that just before serving Mass, the Bishop had asked that he pray for a special intention, "two men in jail."

The Vicar General felt like the chief of the Paris *Sûreté* on the trail of a stolen jewel. "Jail?" Last evening during supper at St. Patrick's, Father Dan Devitt had mentioned the notorious Skrupinski brothers, accused of the gruesome murder of a Jewish lad. The newpapers were full of the details.

"Moyamensing!"

Sourin's intuitions were right. At that moment, the Bishop was locked in a tight cell of Moyamensing County Jail with the two young Poles. For almost two hours, he had tried to persuade them to make their peace with God. He argued, chided, threatened to no avail. He talked Polish, reminding them of their good Catholic mother and the Black Madonna to whom she daily prayed. Slowly the hard glaze of hatred dissolved. One of them began to sob. They would make their peace with God, but not today. They needed time to remember everything. As the gates of Moyamensing clanged behind him, the Bishop felt his old self again, hunting out abandoned souls. It was almost eleven o'clock.

At the turn of the Passayunk Road, the Vicar General sat waiting in a carriage.

"They're expecting us this afternoon at Eden Hall," Sourin tactfully reminded, as the Bishop climbed in beside him.

"And tonight, you have that sermon at St. Joseph's."

The Bishop showed no surprise that Sourin had guessed where to find him. In silence they rode up Broad Street; took the road for Frankford. By noon, they were spinning up the Bristol turnpike toward Torresdale and the girls' Academy of Eden Hall, conducted by the Ladies of the Sacred Heart.

In his suite at the La Pierre House on Chestnut Street, Mr. William Makepeace Thackeray paced the carpet, rehearsing his lecture for that evening. But for three things, he liked Philadelphia —the hotel cellar had not a bottle of Madeira 1820; Antoine, the chef, had his own Gallic notion of Yorkshire pudding; and the books he had ordered from a local bookstore had not come. Now there was a fourth thing—it had begun to rain.

"Sorry, sir, I got caught in a shower."

A lanky young man stood in the doorway with an armful of rain-spattered books. Thackeray received them without comment. He dug down into his pocket.

"What's your name, boy?" He enjoyed listening to the "colonial dialect."

"Wannamaker, sir. John Wannamaker." The lad grinned brightly.

Muttering to himself, the novelist put a coin in the boy's hand. He could hear the rain bucketing down the cobbles of nearby Broad Street. His mind was on the Musical Fund Hall— on gaps of unsold seats at his lecture that evening.

In spite of the merciless downpour that Friday evening, old St. Joseph's was rapidly filling with gentry. Carriages plashed along Spruce, pranced along Walnut from Rittenhouse Square, converging in the neighborhood of Third and Fourth Street. There a dozen rain-soaked horse-boys whistled and beckoned for business, before the lighted doorway of the Jesuit church. Umbrellas abruptly blossomed and closed as elite Philadelphia scurried for shelter inside.

At seven-thirty sharp, Father James Ryder began the Stations of the Cross. (Was it because of the Bishop, non-Catholics wondered, that the altars were draped in purple?) Mr. Symington, on special assignment for the notorious Know-Nothings, sat in the choir loft, piously twiddling his thumbs, waiting. The choir sang a snatch of the *Stabat Mater*. The people genuflected, knelt again.

In a pew on the Gospel side, Professor George Allen knelt with his wife and five children. He had promised ten-year-old Mary that he would introduce her to the new Bishop. Mary was delighted. Was the new Bishop as nice as Bishop Kenrick, who had taught her Catechism? Would he believe that her great grand-uncle was John Hancock, who signed the Declaration of Independence?

"We adore Thee, O Christ, and we bless Thee. . . ."

Little Mary Allen reined in her capering mind, back to the Fourteenth Station, Jesus laid in the tomb.

Old St. Joseph's in its more than hundred years had known its share of spellbinding, silver-tongued scholars. Father Ryder himself, former president of Holy Cross at Worcester, was among the best. And John Hughes, now Bishop of New York. And, of course, Kenrick. What would the new Bishop be like? What would his theme be this evening? By now the church was packed to the doors. Apologetic ushers clustered in the puddled vestibule, politely turning away the late-comers.

Deep in prayer in a corner of the sacristy knelt Bishop Neumann. It was his practice before preaching the word of God. Only prayer could give unction to what a man spoke. He blessed himself and walked out into the sanctuary. The pews coughed. The Bishop paused for quiet. His topic would be the Christian education of youth, a theme close to his heart.

Frank and Tony Drexel were fortunate. Hurrying directly from the Bank, they had found seats, the last ones left. As the Bishop blessed himself, they looked at each other and winked. The voice, the accent, had a familiar ring. It reminded them of Papa Drexel, out West at the moment, establishing a new branch of his Bank in gold-mad California. For the Drexel boys, the Bishop's theme was full of reminiscence. Catholic education, he was saying, meant more than hearing the sermon at Sunday Mass. It must be absorbed in every phase of home-life, learned by little ones as normally as one's mother tonque.

They thought of their own happy home—of Papa Drexel blessing the family at bed time, of evening prayer before our Lady's statue, of Christmas with carol and candle and the hand-carved beautiful crib. They thought of Mama Drexel teaching them their prayers, hearing their catechism. They remembered Papa rehearsing their Latin for serving Mass at St. John's. They may not have enjoyed formal Catholic schooling, since from early teens Papa had them working in his Bank. Still, thanks to a Catholic home, they had "absorbed the faith as normally as their mother tongue."

The rain was thrumming on the roof.

By now the Bishop had warmed to his theme. The church was quietly attentive. Home was not enough. No. A Catholic child should be taught under Church supervision. Indeed, it were better never to learn to read and write than, in so doing, to poison the pure wellsprings of a child's faith.

Asa Symington perked up his ears. This foreign meddler was slyly attacking native American schools!

The Bishop went on to felicitate the fortunate who could send their boys to the Jesuits, the Christian Brothers, their girls to Visitation Academy, to Eden Hall. But what of the thousands of Catholic children who could not afford such schools? They must not be robbed of their Catholic birthright. They too must learn to know, love and serve Almighty God, "for such is the Kingdom of Heaven."

The patter of the rain had abated. The Bishop genuflected and went inside. The consuming earnestness of his thought had so arrested attention that no one paid heed either to his accent or collocation. The listeners saw only the pinched features of children, grubbing for bones in crooked alleys, hunting kindling scraps and coal along the water front, the faces of immigrant youngsters who hardly knew the Mother of God. They had been conscious, at least for a passing moment, of the aching need of Catholic schools in Philadelphia, in every corner of the diocese.

Down from his hiding spot in the choirloft hurried Mr. Asa Symington with a full report on Neumann's subversive tirade. From unimpeachable sources, he had learned that the little bishop planned to implement his mouthings on special schools for Catholic children. In two weeks, they were holding a secret meeting at his house on Logan Square, pastors and prominent laymen. This stunted Austrian upstart, this Neumann, planned to organize the Catholic schools in half of Pennsylvania into one diocesan system, an insult and a threat to native America's own public schools. Something must be done . . . and quickly. Down towards Passayunk hurried Asa Symington to the local headquarters of the Order of the Star Spangled Banner.

In the sacristy of St. Joseph's young Mary Allen solemnly knelt to kiss the new Bishop's ring. Her mother followed, and the boys.

"Mary. That's a beautiful name."

"Thank you, Bishop." The little girl made a dainty curtsey. "And my middle is *Hancock*," she volunteered.

"I made my First Communion, too. And Mummy is buying me a pretty new hat for Easter, a peek-a-boo bonnet with a lovely pink flower."

She looked up at the Bishop coyly.

"Archbishop Kenrick said I'd like you. He taught me my catechism. He said you could tell stories better than anyone. . . ."

Bishop Neumann smilingly patted little Mary Allen's blue velvet hood and spoke awhile to the rest of the family.

"You must visit us soon," said the Professor.

Neumann would visit the Allens sooner than he surmised.

Outside St. Joseph's a pair of coachmen were discussing the sermon.

"I'll bet auld Makepeace with all his airs hadn't as grand a crowd. Bad cess to him! Let him go back to London where he belongs."

John Neumann felt pleased, grateful to his listeners at St. Joseph's.

"It's the grace of the Holy Spirit. They take me for what I represent, not for what I am."

It had been a surprise nonetheless here, at Eden Hall, at the pro-cathedral on Palm Sunday, at St. Patrick's in Kensington, everywhere.

"Unequivocal tokens of attachment . . ." he wrote the words into the curling foolscap on his table in the lamp-lit room on Logan Square. The rhythmic breathing of Father Waldron mingled with the tinkling of the marsh-peepers outside. The State House clock pealed two. Already it was Holy Thursday.

Nodding deeper and deeper over his quill, John Neumann drowsed at his desk.

A few blocks to the south that night, a lamp was still burning in the Allen home, just east of Rittenhouse Square. Shadows flickered to and from against the drawn shade. Inside, a small blond head turned fitfully on the pillow.

"Is the Bishop coming to tell me stories?"

Mrs. Allen cooled the child's head with a damp cloth.

At four that Holy Thursday morning, Mr. George Allen hurried up Schuylkill Sixth towards Logan Square. He tapped the knocker gently. Once. He did not have to knock again. The Bishop himself, fully dressed in his religious habit, opened the front door.

"Something is wrong, Mr. Allen."

"Little Mary, Your Excellency. Pneumonia. She's asking for *you*."

"Wait. I'll go back with you. I shall bring Communion."

Little Mary Allen received Viaticum from the Bishop, the family kneeling round her bed. Quietly, he knelt on the floor to help the little girl make thanksgiving.

The others tiptoed from the room.

Easter morning of 1852. Easter in early April with spice-wood in blossom at Lemon Hill. The first jonquils poked pretty heads through the mulch of Fairmount Park. Sunshine danced on the Delaware at the end of Market Street. It flashed on the clock-face in the steeple of Independence Hall. It poured like music, a luminous Alleluia, through the sacristy windows of the pro-cathedral where a half-dozen students from St. Charles' were vesting to serve Pontifical Mass.

Dick Phelan, poking his carrot red head through the neck of a linen surplice, spied an old friend in the sacristy doorway.

"Happy Easter, Pop."

Old James Wilcox was all smiles at sight of six of his boys.

"Where's the new Bishop?" he whispered. "By the way, *Ma* Wilcox brought a hamper of colored eggs for the lot of you. She's outside in church.

"Your Excellency . . ."

The old gentleman knelt to kiss Bishop Neumann's ring.

"Excuse this intrusion before your Mass. I stopped by Professor Allen's a moment, on the way. Little Mary died early this morning."

For sermon that Easter morning the Bishop read his own pastoral letter, speaking of many things: the unfinished cathedral, parochial schools, the coming Plenary Council in Baltimore, his personal gratitude for the kindness of Philadelphia's welcome.

"Since we have occupied our Episcopal See, we have on all sides received unequivocal tokens of attachment and obedi-ence . . ."

The crowded church was gay with new hats. But one new hat was nowhere to be seen: a small girl's peek-a-boo bonnet with a lovely pink flower.

Later that afternoon at the Cap and Gown tavern in Passa-yunk, before a packed chapter of the Order of the Star Spangled Banner, Asa Symington expounded Neumann's "open insult to American Education," his wily scheme "to subvert the public schools of Philadelphia."

17.   KNOW-NOTHINGS

The Morse code ticked the news along the Atlantic coast, across the Alleghenies, the Mississippi and beyond. A wonderful invention! But hinterland America felt beholden to Samuel Morse for more than the telegraph. Frontiersmen had rare need for electric dots and dashes. They had greater need, they honestly imagined, for Morse's now tattered pamphlets on the perils of Popery.

Back in the mid-thirties, in the year that John Neumann arrived in New York, Morse had alerted his countrymen to the sly schemes of Rome to undermine our entire American way of life. It was he who uncovered in Austria the organization that sent financial aid to Catholic missionaries in the United States, purportedly for spiritual needs but in fact for something quite the reverse. If its purpose were truly spiritual, Morse inquired, why was the Leopold Foundation centered in imperial Vienna instead of in Rome!

Morse was not hoodwinked by the hordes of threadbare peasants from Catholic Europe, swarming like vermin from the steerage of every trans-Atlantic packet, infesting American seaports, turning cities into slums, slowly creeping westward like a plague.

"They are under the direct control of Jesuits who shrewdly arrange their settlement in strategic places. Austria need only infiltrate these Polish puppets into government and her victory is assured."

The talons of that crafty arch-fiend, the Pope, were reaching out to strangle the United States! The great immigration movement of Germans and Irish was, pure and simple, a slow-fused plot for America's destruction. When Papists had settled the Mississippi Valley in sufficient numbers, a signal would be given. They would rise up in revolt. With an Austrian army, the Pope of Rome would land at New Orleans, move up the valley and proceed to establish the sulphurous torments of the Inquisition! It was as plain as that.

Samuel Morse was not the last, nor the first, to wax lurid on the peril of Popery. One thing he did, however: he fused inseparably in the public imagination the notions of immigration and Catholicism.

For generations good Yankee mothers had shushed their children with the awful threat: "The Pope will get you!" In backwoods schoolrooms, pioneer America had learned its A-B-Cs from primers filled with crude woodcuts of martyrs bleeding for the faith at the hands of cruel Papists. Out of view of their godly parents, teen-age boys stole off behind haycock and woodshed to peruse the lewd secrets of monastery cellar and convent garret. Maria Monk's best seller was in thousands of homes. Even Ned Buntline's dime accounts of the roaring west were judiciously laced with the vile machinations of Rome. America, by mid-nineteenth century, felt that Catholics were the one imminent danger to all it held dear.

To counteract the "inroads of Popery," the Nativist movement was born. Tracts, street-corner demagogues, galloping circuit riders all dinned home the incessant slogan: *Keep America safe for Americans,* or, to phrase it more bluntly, "Keep Catholics in their place."

Small wonder that, from time to time, mob violence erupted. The times were overcharged with a lethal bigotry that needed but a spark of innuendo to work havoc anywhere. Thus, for building a parish school in Ellsworth, Maine, a priest was tarred and feathered, the school destroyed. A church was blown up with a keg of powder in Massilon, Ohio. A group of nuns were smoked from their convent in the shadow of Bunker Hill. Crosses were sometimes hacked down from steeples; tombstones defaced in Catholic churchyards. Children were taunted, badgered by bullies on their way to the parish school. Occasionally, there was murder. All in the starry name of patriotism.

A decade before Bishop John Neumann's consecration, the cobbled streets of Philadelphia rang with the catcalls of Nativist mobs. Two churches and several Catholic homes went up in flames, the local Fire Companies standing by. The riots of 1844 were not a pretty memory.

Once each summer, while the boys from St. Charles relaxed

at Ivy Mills, someone coaxed Pop Wilcox to tell of the night in '44 when he was roused from bed by a pounding on his back door.

"I opened the upper window and looked out to see who it was. There were three men, Quakers from the looks of them. Could they please have lodging for the night? they asked."

And so, on went the story. . . .

The three "Quakers" turned out to be Bishop Francis Patrick Kenrick with two of his priests. During the tumult, the Bishop of Philadelphia, taking the Blessed Sacrament for safe keeping, had hurried incognito from the city.

"And for several nights thereafter, we had to post guards to be sure no torch-happy bigots burned down Ivy Mills for harboring a Popish priest."

Pop Wilcox held his listeners spellbound every time.

In Pastoral Theology class at St. Charles' one afternoon, someone asked Bishop Neumann if he had ever heard the story. He had. His face grew very serious.

"Now we have the Know-Nothings," he said.

For the first Tuesday of June in 1852, Mr. Asa Symington had summoned a special gathering of the Order of the Star Spangled Banner at the usual place, the Cap and Gown in Passayunk. The Cap and Gown was a deserted tavern on the Greenwich Point Road not far from Hollander's Creek.

"Have you seen Sam?"

"Have you?"

That was the password. Everything about this Nativist business was secret. Ask a member the most innocuous trifle, automatically, he shrugged his shoulders.

"I don't know."

People dubbed them the Know-Nothings. They had chapters in every big city and in many small towns of the United States. Their power was growing politically, too.

At the Cap and Gown that June evening, Asa Symington had several things on the agenda. For one, there was the matter of the Washington Monument. Pius IX had sent a block of white marble from some ancient Roman temple, a gift from the Eternal City to the American People.

"A crafty gesture, so typical of Vatican trickery."

Symington knew nobody remembered that thirty-seven years ago, when the first stone of the monument was laid, the Catholic Archbishop of Baltimore had by special invitation of the President presided at the ceremony. Asa Symington's aim was to whip up a "spontaneous" protest outside the State House, noisy remonstrances at "this new Popish outrage, this bare-face insult to American liberty."

"We must go up and demand that the marble block be shipped back where it came from. Ship it to Hell and gone!"

Item the second on Asa Symington's agenda was the matter of Trinity church, the German parish battling with Bishop Neumann. For decades it had been a sore-spot. Each year at the annual election of lay trustees, there had been trouble. The Bishop had suggested to Holy Trinity that a petition be sent to the Legislature to have the power of appointing trustees put in the hands of the bishop. The solution seemed satisfactory. Several of the parish officials, however, opposed it and took the case to court. On May 29, 1852, the court handed down its verdict against Bishop Neumann.

Here was a prime chance to drub the threat of Popery again!

"We must give that verdict loud and wide publicity," said Asa Symington. "Call it a ringing victory for American democracy over the greedy autocratic scheming of Rome! Neumann the little Austrian puppet, like Kenrick his Irish predecessor, is running true to the pattern, plotting to win personal possession of every stick of church property in Pennsylvania. A meddlesome foreigner, for personal aggrandizement he is trying to destroy the corporate rights of a group of American citizens! Unmask him."

Symington ranted on.

"Unmask this Neumann for the sworn enemy of American institutions: free elections, free speech, public schools, the whole democratic process. This verdict against Bishop Neumann is a windfall for Nativism. We cannot let it pass."

Morse's dots and dashes spelled out the story for the papers of the entire United States. Neumann's name was vilified for weeks, months in the local papers. For almost two years, the smear campaign continued, for Bishop Neumann had appealed the verdict. He had now taken the case to the Superior Court of Pennsylvania. Come what may, the rights of the Church must be vindicated and upheld.

"If you want divine service in this building," Bishop Neumann told the swaggering trustees, "you will first have to cede its property rights to the head of this diocese. There is no other way. That is the decree of the Plenary Council of Baltimore, the wish of the Holy See."

Though the trustees had taken their case to court and won, all they had really won was an empty brick building and the plot of ground it stood on at Spruce and Fifth. They still had no priest, no Mass, no Sacrament or sermon. Hundreds of Catholic Germans in the heart of Philadelphia had no church to attend, except St. Peter's more than a mile uptown. The situation grieved Bishop Neumann.

"Bishop, what will you do about Trinity?"

During Pastoral Theology class at St. Charles' on Schuylkill Fifth, the students were accustomed to firing point-blank questions. His seminarians were the apple of Neumann's eye, his priests of tomorrow. With them, he freely discussed current pastoral problems. He never hedged. All his scholarship, his ascetical lore, his sixteen years of practical missionary experience—all he knew was at their disposal. They looked forward to his classes. Neumann did too. Red-headed Dick Phelan had put the question.

"About Trinity," said Neumann with a wry little smile, "we have no alternative but to go into debt. We must build a second church nearby, a church to St. Alphonsus."

The strapping red head in the third row grinned approval. Neumann knew the talents of Richard Phelan. A remarkable young man, not just in looks, in everything. He could read every language the Bishop knew, even a bit of Czech. He could speak Irish, which Neumann could not. At mathematics and the sciences, he was a wizard. He knew music, could play the organ well. The Vincentian faculty of St. Charles' could attest to the acumen of the boy's mind. Propound a problem in Scripture, in Theology, in Canon Law, in anything and before the question was fully phrased, Dick Phelan's eyes were dancing with answers.

Unfortunately for Philadelphia and Neumann, however, Phelan was already earmarked for Pittsburgh. Bishop O'Connor had brought him from Kilkenny to complete his studies in America.

"Keep an eye on this wild Irishman of mine," O'Connor had said to Kenrick when he first brought Phelan to St. Charles' on Logan Square.

"His mind may be quick, his fists are quicker. He's made for boxing!"

Kenrick had bequeathed him to Neumann, together with the unfinished cathedral of St. Peter and St. Paul, the Trinity trustees, and a few other problems. But to Neumann "Mr. Richard Phelan," as he called him, was no problem at all.

While the Bishop was answering Phelan's second question about the trustee problem in America—a topic in which Neumann had much practical experience both as a young priest in Williamsville and as a Redemptorist in Pittsburgh, Baltimore, Manhattan —the man behind whispered something in Phelan's ear.

"Bishop, they say the Council asked you to write a catechism?"

"Some of you must be Know-Nothings, with spies in every assembly. How do you find out these things?"

Neumann admitted that he was working on a catechism for German children.

"And, Mister Richard Phelan, when the galleys come from the printer, I'll have *you* do the proof-reading. Now, if you please, allow me to ask some questions."

From then on the class in Pastoral Theology went on in earnest, the last before examinations and summer vacation.

For the Bishop there was no vacation. He was teacher of Pastoral Theology only when time allowed. At the moment, he had the problem of recruiting a whole staff of seminary professors from among his own diocesan priests. The Vincentian General in Rome had withdrawn his men from St. Charles' at the close of that semester of 1852. Too many of them were being taken as bishops! Parish schools were rising within the city, separate buildings instead of the old church-basement compromises. Neumann was all about town inspecting operations. Also, there was Delaware and half of Pennsylvania that he still had to visit on confirmation tour.

That fall, he set out on his first pastoral visitation, a map and notebook in his pocket, adventure in his heart. He began with the coal regions. Leaving the city on the Belvedere & Delaware, he rode up toward Easton to the familiar tune of mule-bells on the nearby barge canal. That first week of October, the Lehigh Valley was beginning to turn gold as the train rounded the curving gorge of Mauch Chunk. Magnificent, despite the film of coal dust on everything. By Halloween when he would reach Frenchtown, up in Luzerne county, the maples would be a throbbing scarlet against the dark of Norway spruce. In Nippenose Valley he would watch a huge flock of Canada geese honking overhead on their way south. The first snowflakes would be flying on St. Martin's day when he reached Shamokin and started back for Logan Square and home.

It was to be a crowded six weeks. He wasted no time. Over a thousand confirmations administered in some twenty-six settlements and growing towns. In his little notebook, he jotted down the place names: Nesquehoning, Tamaqua, Minersville—coal towns all. There was Summit Hill where they showed him the famous Switchback, first gravity railway in the country, taking the coal down the mountain to waiting barges on the canal. There was Pittston and Wilkesbarre, where Irishmen saluted him like an emperor in the public street, tipping their caps with coal-grimy hands. And Slockum Hollow where he arrived at dusk, the miners escorting him to St. Vincent's by torchlight; and just let any sniffing Know-Nothing dispute their passage! (Slockum Hollow— they would call it "Scranton" later; and St. Vincent's would cradle a cathedral under another name.)

Nail-smiths, lumbermen, miners, barge-tenders, farmers—he heard their confessions, taught their children catechism, gratefully sampled the cooking of their wives. He chatted about their jobs, their hopes of improvement, their faith, their distant homelands so like his own. In Carbondale and Archbold he met slate-pickers— mere boys who ought to be hunched over school books learning to write and read instead of sorting anthracite, bent double from early morn till suppertime. One night he watched the constellation

Taurus rising over the Kittatinny mountains off to the northeast. He had not seen so glorious a sight since Williamsville—since Budweis, with telescope pointed over the Boehmerwald.

Rockport, in Carbon County, October 15, St. Teresa's day. He would remember the little wooden church of St. Joseph, because of an old, old woman whose married daughter came there to fetch him to hear the mother's confession.

"She has only Irish," the girl explained.

The Bishop was sad. Irish was one tongue he did not know. He went along anyway after the confirmations to please the old lady with the blessing of a bishop. She kissed his ring and, in the Gaelic way, blessed his coming and his going, and the rise of every road he traveled. It was a grander blessing than his own but he understood not a word she spoke.

"I must learn Irish," he resolved on the way back.

In Hawley, there was a little shop that had candy. He stopped and bought five pounds, an enormous bag. Thereafter, how surprised, how utterly delighted the children looked when he reached down into his cassock pocket and promised candy to any who could name him the Seven Sacraments, the Ten Commandments of God or recite the *Hail, Holy Queen.* They were worth the extra weight in his bag, those five pounds of molasses drops.

At Honesdale, on October 24, he confirmed in the stone church of St. John. During supper a sick call came for Father Prendergast, the pastor. The Bishop insisted on going himself. He baptized the week-old baby, calling him Raphael McGinty "in the name of the Father and of the Son and of the Holy Ghost." It was the Archangel's feastday.

The water of baptism made a clean rill on the grimy skin. Everything in sight was powdered with fine coal dust. Even the altar cloths in church. But John Neumann would have exchanged it any time for the scrubbed Belgian paving blocks of Locust and Chestnut Streets, the red brick houses with white marble steps. Here in the mountains were people he understood, abandoned souls, the sort he had worked for all his missionary life.

Mount Pleasant. Silver Lake. Towanda. Dushore. Danville. Methodically he noted them in his copybook. No more than a word or two in Latin, a date, a name, a statistic. But for Bishop Neumann each word in his copybook had its little story. He rode over Blue Mountain down through Pottsville and Hamburg and Reading. On the thirteenth day of November, he was on his way home.

Outside the Reading depot at Broad and Willow Streets, the Bishop paused, the soft black grime of the journey still powdering his seedy clothes. Should he go down to St. John's to see the Vicar General, or home? For just a moment he stood there, facing the jostle of Broad Street, his back to a week-old poster announcing the special appearance of Tom Sayres at the Chinese Museum on Saturday, November Thirteenth. Today!

"Fifty dollars! For the man who for seven rounds will trade punches with the Champion of England."

It was starting to get dark. A lamplighter passed, walking west along Willow Street, lifting his stick to the gas lamps, one by one. The Bishop picked up his battered satchel, following the lamplighter as far as Schuylkill Sixth. There he turned down in the directon of Logan Square.

At the Chinese Museum earlier that Saturday afternoon some twelve hundred men had each paid fifty cents for a glimpse of the great Tom Sayres. In training for his match with John Morissey, the American heavyweight, Sayres was touring the States for a chance at some pin money. (The seventh Marquis of Queensbury was still unknown. There were few boxing rules. You fought without gloves, fought till you knocked your man out. No set number of rounds.)

"Who's this Mickey McGraw? Ever seen him box?"

In England boxing was a gentleman's sport; thus did genteel Philadelphia salve its respectable conscience. The Chinese Museum was packed with young bloods and old from the best families —and then some. Not a one had ever before heard of "Mickey McGraw."

"Maybe he's one of the Moya-boys—from Moyamensing."

"Or a brawny dockwalloper from Kensington."

"Maybe he's a Freshman from Penn."

When Mickey McGraw climbed into the gas-lit ring, the crowds openly grumbled.

"That kid's no boxer! Sure he's trim, but look at him: not a scar."

"Let's get our money back. . . ."

Sayres was a husky boulder of a man. He stepped into the ring coolly acknowledging the cheers, a professional grin on his mouth. But on seeing McGraw, he stared as though the fellow were a ghost. There was some earnest conversation with his manager.

"Gorblimey! Where did you get him?"

"He dropped in here yesterday, said he could use the money. I told him: Five pounds, if he can hold out for five rounds with you."

The manager winked.

"Ten, I said, if he knocks you out." Smiling, he patted the Champion's knuckles.

"Now go easy, Tommy. Don't spoil his pretty face."

"Easy, my eye!" he snarled. "I know this pretty boy, saw him box the eyes out of Slasher Perry two years ago in Kilkenny!"

"Kilkenny," the manager yawped.

"He's got a left like a clawhammer! The Priest, they call him. His real name's. . . ."

The bell rang.

The champion dove for McGraw before the redhead could bless himself. Feinting with his right, he shot a sickening left at the pit of Pretty Boy's stomach. McGraw slumped to the floor.

The Chinese Museum stamped, snorted its disgust, moaned disappointment. Some started for the doors.

For eight seconds McGraw grovelled in dazed agony. Slowly he lurched to his feet. He started jigging around the Champion, sparring him off a few moments to fetch his breath. He began boxing.

It was a dazzling performance. Flying fists, dancing feet, a blur of dandelion-red, as Mickey crouched, bobbed, moved in. Within the five rounds he had knocked Sayres down twice—once, completely out of the ring. The house was in bedlam.

Into the open hand of Mickey McGraw the manager put a crisp new bill. In the ensuing uproar McGraw disappeared into the dressing room, quickly washed his face, got into street clothes and climbed through a window to Shippen Street, while the crowds were pounding on his locked door.

It was getting dark. He passed a lamplighter on the way to Logan Square. The bell of St. Charles' was ringing for Benediction.

During the study period that evening, Father O'Hara, the Rector, tapped Dick Phelan's elbow.

"The Bishop is outside. He wants to speak to you."

"The Bishop!"

Phelan's heart sank. Wasn't the Bishop still out on Visitation?

"Good evening, Mr. Richard Phelan. I have a small problem, and in a way, it concerns you."

Neumann's piercing brown eyes seemed to bore straight into Mickey McGraw! Prudently, Dick Phelan kept his tongue still, his left side averted.

"Do you think you could find the time to teach me Irish?"

Phelan's blue eyes fairly danced willingness.

"*That* I could, Bishop Neumann. In two months I'll have you talking with a brogue."

In the dim light of the hallway, the Bishop had not noticed the slash on Dick Phelan's left cheek. He said nothing, anyway.

"This Babylon of Philadelphia."

Alone in his house chapel, kneeling late at night before the altar, the thought of the city around him often intruded on the Bishop's prayers. Could he possibly do anything to remedy the evils? The brutal hurt of those placards on shop door and shipyard gate, even in the newspaper want-ads. *No Irish.* The vile poison of Nativism was at work. And the haggard victims of this taboo, worried for wife and children, drowned their hearts in drink. In Kensington taverns, there was gambling, brawling and worse.

And Germans in south Philadelphia, slipping away from all the dear customs of home. For want of a parish church where their own tongue was spoken, they were in danger of losing the faith. The stalemate of Trinity was a festering thorn in Bishop

Neumann's heart. Not to mention the open scandal of spiteful trustees, affronting the consecrated spokesman of the Church, impugning his motives, besmirching his name. The smug greed of Catholic gentlemen who spared no expense to buy gowns for their dancing daughters and let the cathedral stand there, a three-walled brownstone shell on Logan Square. The icy snobbery of who was seen and who was not, at the Annual Dancing Assembly on the first Friday night after New Year's. The endless round of theater parties, banquets, silver teas disturbed the Bishop's soul.

Late at night in his room, as he thumbed his Greek Testament, rephrased an awkward answer in his new catechism, wrestled with Irish syntax, "this Babylon on Schuylkill" needled his heart. He redoubled his personal penances: studied on his knees, fasted, scourged himself nightly, slept on the rugless floor. At every unoccupied moment he fingered his beads. But that was not enough. It did not hamper the summer revels on Buttercup Island. It did not stop the peddlers of obscenities skulking about the Delaware docks, or young patrons from buying their wares. Philadelphia is one perpetual carnival, thought John Neumann.

Carnival! St. Charles Borromeo had a remedy for his diocese of Milan. To atone for the sins of Milan during carnival-time, he had the Blessed Sacrament solemnly exposed in thirty parish churches in 1574: the Forty Hours Devotion. But in Philadelphia, at present anyway, that would be out of the question. Not with the Know-Nothings. The horror of public insult to Christ in the Sacrament of the Altar made Neumann's blood run cold.

His campaign for Catholic schools in the diocese was as salt in Know-Nothing wounds. Up out of church basement and rectory annex, parochial schools were rising like an open challenge—climbing story on story alongside the Catholic churches, St. Augustine's, St. Peter's, St. Patrick's. New churches, too. They were making excavations at Reed and Fourth Streets for the new St. Alphonsus—the only solution to the problem of Trinity.

Nativists had scrawled crude insults on the school doors, the windows of the new St. Patrick's in Kensington. At St. Malachy's, several bricklayers had almost been killed. Under cover of darkness, when the workmen had gone home, pranksters had loosened the scaffolding. The nuns at the Spruce Street orphanage were tormented with anonymous notes slipped under the back door. They showed them to the Bishop when he came with candy and toys for the children on his Christmas rounds.

No, thought the Bishop. Now is not the time. The anti-Popery of the Know-Nothings was too brazen just now to risk insult to the Blessed Sacrament. When he broached the idea of the Forty Hours Devotion to his Diocesan Council, the priests agreed that excellent as the idea was, the time was inopportune.

One evening in April, he was busy making a large parchment map of the diocese, printing in dark blue the towns that already had churches, marking in red the stage-routes, the railways and canals, the wandering shun-pikes linking one lonely mission with the next. He was a good draftsman. He sketched in the Susquehanna with its many branches, the diagonal mountain chains, the jigsaw county-lines. (Better to spend the time here at home, than waste it, lost on a visitation tour, later.) For Catholic schools he put a green dot. There should be more and, God willing, there would be! In black ink, he lettered in the owners of homes and barns where people gathered for monthly Mass, places a good day's walk from any church.

It was a painstaking task. He set his inkwell down between Gettysburg and Connewago in the south. He tipped his candle, dripping hot wax to fix the tallow stump in Tioga county up north among the copper mines, the high cold winds. The flame jiggled in the draft of the open window. He continued at his task. A board creaked in the hall. Or was it Father Waldron snoring? No. There it was again, someone knocking at the front door.

At once the Bishop dropped his crayons on the outspread map and hurried downstairs. It might be a sick call.

"Sorry to bother you so late, Bishop. . . ."

A hungry man in need of a bite to eat. The Bishop went out to the kitchen, sat the man down and raided Meg Bradley's bread-box and pantry. He'd have to tell her in the morning, or she'd blame it on the Know-Nothings. He put two coins in the man's hand and escorted him to the front door. The little act of mercy had taken him some fifteen minutes.

On the way upstairs he smelled smoke and remembered the lighted candle on his paper-strewn table. Bounding up the stairs, he hurried into the room to find the overturned candle still burning feebly—and all of Northumberland county scorched brown. It should have gone up in flame. His Hebrew Testament, too, the manuscript of his Catechism, the paper map! The wooden desk should have been a charred shambles, his whole "chancery" a smouldering ruin. But nothing was harmed.

He blew out the candle stump, sank to his knees, head in hands, to murmur a prayer of thanks.

"As the flame did no harm to that parchment, neither shall the fires of bigotry injure my glory in the Sacrament of the Altar. Make haste to carry out your plan for my Honor. I will pour out my Blessings to the ends of this map."

Instantly, Bishop Neumann made up his mind. He would inaugurate the devotion of the Forty Hours in Philadelphia. He would draw up a schedule. Week after week, it would continue in some parish church of the city; in some clapboard chapel, or brick church in the entire diocese—from Ivy Mills to Sugar Ridge, from Blossburg to Brandywine. At the Synod that May of 1853, he announced his decision to the gathering of pastors at Logan Square.

Down on Queen Street in Southwark, the St. Joseph sisters were enraptured that St. Philip Neri's had been chosen by the Bishop for the first Forty Hours devotion in the diocese, on Corpus Christi day. All through May they trained the children to sing *Pange Lingua* and many English hymns for the procession. They made sure that each little girl would have a white dress. They marshalled the smallest into church each afternoon to drill them in the slow gait, the uplifted flower, the curtsey to the Blessed Sacrament in the golden monstrance—before dropping daisy or bluebell in the aisle.

But Bishop Neumann was busier than the sisters. He compiled a book of ceremonies for the occasion, made several copies in longhand, so that all would know precisely what to do. He made lightning visits to Father Cantwell, the pastor, at all hours of the day. He wanted candles, many, many candles on the altar, the prettiest flowers. He invited all the priests of the city to attend;

ordered his seminarians to have fresh-laundered surplices and polished shoes. Mr. Richard Phelan would play the organ. Father Ryder would be the special preacher on the first evening. Father Moriarty from St. Augustine's, on the second. The Bishop would speak on the closing night himself. He sent his own monstrance down to St. Philip's for the occasion—brand new, the gift of St. Philomena's, when he visited Pittsburgh last summer for the dedication of Bishop O'Connor's new cathedral.

The Forty Hours devotion exceeded all hopes. St. Philip's was packed. Each evening, four priests were kept busy hearing confessions. Each day at every hour, groups of parishioners were in church praying before the twinkling altar. Bishop Neumann could vouch for this. He spent most of the forty hours somewhere in the church. It was like a Mission! Penitents coming for absolution, some who for many years had been estranged. And so many received Holy Communion! Most remarkable of all, there was no malicious disturbance on the part of Know-Nothings. All through summer and fall and winter, it was the same, as the Blessed Sacrament was enthroned among flowers and candles in church after church of the diocese. The Lord was indeed pouring out his graces to the ends of the Bishop's map. John Neumann was overjoyed.

At one important dot on the map of Pennsylvania, however, a grave problem for the Bishop was rapidly coming to a head. At Superior Court in the heart of Philadelphia, after two years of nettlesome litigation, the case of the *Trustees of Trinity* vs *the Bishop of Philadelphia* had at last come up for final summation and decision. The case had been meat for Asa Symington and his Order of the Star Spangled Banner. Every paper in Pennsylvania had been kept informed, the bulletins always slanted in favor of the "poor trustees"—battling for their rights as good American citizens, against the "land-greedy, foreign-born plutocrat of Logan Square." It was rumored that even Judge Woodward was one of the Know-Nothings. The Know-Nothings gathered in the Philadelphia courtroom that March morning of 1854 to watch and listen to Bishop Neumann, and gloat at his final defeat.

"Tell me, Bishop, why do you call your church *Roman* Catholic?"

George Woodward, the presiding judge, asked the question.

For Neumann the answer almost reminded him of something in his new catechism.

"Our Church is called Roman Catholic because the Pope, who is its visible Head, resides in the city of Rome. According to the laws of the Pope, bishops administer their dioceses; according to the laws of the bishop, pastors govern their parish flocks."

Woodward, who was not even baptized, nodded understanding. He understood the "chain of command."

The Bishop continued, drawing his conclusion, like a noose.

"Anyone who wishes to be a member of the Catholic Church must be united through his pastor with the bishop, and through the bishop with the Pope. The link is one of spiritual obedience. This is the essential and unchanging constitution of the Catholic Church. To refuse obedience is to break the chain, to cut oneself off. . . ."

The Judge now turned to the trustees.

"Do you agree with this statement? Is this the nature of jurisdiction in the Catholic Church?"

"Yes. That is correct," the plaintiffs agreed.

There was something about that last admission—the spectators leaned forward instinctively—something like the click of a sprung trap.

Now it remained for George Woodward to make the admission plain. He turned to the trustees.

"You are a disgrace to Philadelphia. From time out of mind you have been bickering with your bishops. Once you had an American. Then, an Irishman. Now you have one of your own, a German. None has ever quite suited your taste. You wrangle with them all.

"If you want to be Catholics, you must abide by Pope and bishop in church affairs. You cannot expect your contumacious disobedience to be abetted by this Court."

The courtroom was deadly quiet. Asa Symington looked at the stunned trustees, took sidelong glances at his Know-Nothings.

In short order, the jury returned with a verdict. The Bishop of Philadelphia regained legal title to the property of Holy Trinity church at Spruce and Sixth.

Judge Woodward tapped his gavel.

"Case dismissed."

At home on Logan Square a letter awaited Neumann, an invitation from the Holy Father to be present in Rome on December eighth, for the proclamation of the dogma of our Lady's Immaculate Conception.

18.   DEAR TO MY HEART

"Did you hear the news?" Down the slope of the Upper Lane ran Pokorny the postman, telling anyone along the way.

"Of course it's true. Do you think I'd make up such a story? I just brought the letter to old Herr Neumann myself. His son, John, (that's the bishop!) mailed from Paris. Yes, Paris!—on his way to Rome for December eighth."

Pokorny's eyes fairly danced with excitement. "Wait till I tell Bertie."

Bertie, as all Prachatitz knew, was young Adalbert Benesh, Pokorny's only nephew, a student at the gymnasium in Budweis. Bertie was the apple of old Pokorny's eye.

"You heard the news?"

By nightfall that first Monday in Advent, there were few in Prachatitz who had not heard that Bishop John Neumann was coming to visit his hometown on the way back from Rome. All who heard—burgomaster, dean, aldermen, commander of the imperial garrison, even Aloys Messner, the local atheist—agreed that so historic an occasion should not pass unnoticed. After all, it was not every day a native son came back from the New World, a bishop—shepherd of a piece of America as big as all Bohemia.

"He may be here for Christmas, for all we know. Better make plans."

There were more than just plans at Number 129 in the Upper Lane. Scouring and cleaning began almost at once; and old Philip Neumann hobbling among pails of hot water and brushes and suds, muttered at all the preparations.

"Why do they have to bring bishops from America, anyway, to tell us something we know already, that our Blessed Lady was conceived without sin?"

He was past eighty, and though he could no longer read the papers from Prague and Budweis, or on stormy mornings risk walking to Mass, still, thanks to the attention of his daughter Louise (and a daily noggin of apricot brandy), he was otherwise hale as a Boehmerwald lumberjack. Louise was not taken in by his pretense at grumpiness.

"Louise, did we get any more word from John?" He asked the question several times each morning.

"Is he still in Rome?"

The whole Austrian Empire, all Christendom was talking of the great event in Rome. A month previous, the Right Reverend Dean, red pompom and all, had mounted the pulpit of St. Jakob's to read a special leter from Frederick Cardinal Schwarzenberg who was leaving Prague that very week at the invitation of Pius, the Ninth. Down in Vienna, Prince Bishop Othmar von Rauscher had done much the same, reading his own eulogy of Mary Immaculate in the cathedral of St. Stephen before setting out for Rome. The Emperor himself was going, young Franz Josef with his bride! And Ludwig of Bavaria. Every European Catholic who could afford the fare was en route, it seemed, to St. Peter's where, on Friday, December eighth, the Holy Father would proclaim the dogma of the Immaculate Conception.

"I wonder what's keeping that boy anyway!"

Then remembering that the "boy" was now a bishop, old Philip Neumann crossed himself in sputtering confusion.

"He's still in Rome, Father," patiently explained Louise. "Today is Thursday, December seventh. Tomorrow is the day. . . ."

"Eh? And is it snowing there, too?"

It was raining in Rome that Thursday morning, raining so steadily and hard that the streets were almost desolate. In Piazza

Navona, Bernini's marble fountain squandered its tinkling waters in the teeming downpour. Round about the great square, the Christmas stands were shrouded in canvas—toy-stalls, sweetmeat-booths, all boarded up in the nasty weather. And a pity, with so many tourists in town.

Not far from the square a chestnut vender tried to kindle his pan of charcoal in the shelter of Maria in Monterone.

"*Buon giorno, Padre!*" The peddler thought he knew every Redemptorist attached to the church.

. ."*Buon giorno, signore.*"

S-i-g-n-o-r-e? Emm. A stranger! That much was certain! As the little padre struggled with his umbrella, the street vendor observed the long loop of beads, the white collar under the borrowed black cloak, trailing his shoes.

"Is this the way to San Sebastiano, *signore?*"

"*Si, Padre.* You follow that street. It's less than ten minutes if you walk fast." ("Crazy tourists," sighed the *castagnaio.*) "Oh and Padre, remember me at your holy Mass."

It would be some time before the "tourist" said his Mass. St. Sebastian's was but the first of seven visits, he planned on making that rainy Thursday morning—saying five Paters, five Aves and five Glorias at each to gain the special indulgence for his mother, God rest her soul. San Sebastiano's and six more: St. Peter's across the Tiber; St. Paul's outside the walls; then, Santa Croce and San Lorenzo; next, St. John Lateran, mother-parish of the world; finally, St. Mary Major on the Esquiline, where before the Madonna of the Snows, he hoped to say Mass.

At last, more than four hours later, the stocky little pilgrim descried the clock on Santa Maria Maggiore at the crest of Via Merulana. He hurried his pace, his black boots squishing rain as he walked.

In the Capella Borghese of the great Basilica, the sacristan coldly eyed the water-logged boots. He eyed the clean red carpet at the altar of Our Lady of the Snows. He eyed the sober little pilgrim with his foreign-looking face.

"*Aspettate qui, Padre.*"

Patiently the little Padre waited while the Primate of all

Ireland, His Lordship of Armagh, read the Mass of St. Ambrose, followed in turn by an archbishop from the far side of the world.

"Pronto, Padre."

The sacristan pointed to the vestments.

"And don't forget to sign your name in the guest-book."

After Mass, folding the amice, he washed his fingers in the *lavabo,* and, under the signature of + John Polding of Sydney, Australia, he signed his own. *John N. Neumann, C.SS.R., episc. Philadelphiensis.*

The sacristan matter-of-factly scanned the guest-book, glanced out in surprise at the little Redemptorist kneeling on the marble floor. Once more he squinted at the fine handwriting—*Episcop. Philadelph.*

"Filadelfia . . . per bacco! That's where my brother is."

Later, coming down the long flight of steps from the basilica, the Bishop plucked his black Redemptorist cloak tight against the chilly drizzle—but not before a passerby had observed the familiar habit underneath. Up to the pavement drew a shiny black carriage. The door snapped ajar, Habsburg eagles enameled on its glossy panel.

"May we take you home, Padre? It's raining hard."

The words were Italian but the voice, Austrian! Ex-Emperor Ferdinand was still seeking occasion to ease his conscience, to make amends for a day in '48 when he had reluctantly signed the writ expelling the Redemptorists from Austria.

To his pleasant surprise, here was not only a Redemptorist but a former Austrian subject—now a bishop in America!

"Bishop Neumann, when you pass through Prague on the way home, you must visit us at the Hradscin. Do come. We should be pleased to help in building your cathedral in Philadelphia."

Through the fine drizzle the imperial carriage quickly splashed its way to Maria in Monterone.

"My humble gratitude, your Majesty. *Auf wieder sehen."*

Across the street, the chestnut peddler's eyes bugged wide at the glittering equipage that had brought his nondescript "tourist" back home.

Friday was glorious, miraculously clear, mild as an April morning—weather the Romans smugly called typical for the season, though obviously it was something tailor-made for one morning in centuries. The sky was a color only Giotto could have remembered. Even the tawny Tiber, churning under rain-scourged bridges, ran blue. The fountains of Rome went about their melodious business, flinging tiny diamonds by the handful into the sunlight. Everything seemed brand new. At Piazza San Pietro, the colonnades, the square-cut cobbles glinted, as though by some Bernini miracle the whole square had been remade overnight. And, looming over the majestic square, looming over all Rome, hovered that cream-white wonder of Michelangelo, St. Peter's dome.

At the moment, St. Peter's was intensely quiet. Under the great dome, the lilting invocations of the choir, the booming responses of cardinals and clergy, the *vivas,* the feathery trumpet notes—all had long since hushed away. A few moments earlier the whole basilica had suddenly taken up the Hymn to the Holy Spirit: mitred hierarchy, bemedalled ambassadors, Noble Guard under white horsetailed helmets, jostling faithful from Rome, from everywhere all singing together—engulfing in their earnest roar the silvery sopranos of the Sistine choir. Now, except for the sputter of candle-flames high in the arches, the only sound was one human voice reading in the singsong Latin. While Pio Nono read, the basilica listened with a rapt excitement, waiting to hear expressed what all Christendom in its heart believed: that the Mother of the Redeemer had, by unique exception, entered time unbesmirched by Original Fault.

Not since Trent had so many mitres assembled under one roof. Under the great cupola, two hundred members of the hierarchy clustered about Pio Nono. And still they came! Even as His Holiness read, decrepit Cardinal Bianchi tottered across the aisle to his place under the great dome. It had been many years since Bianchi had been able to attend a papal function, but *this* he must not miss—even if he should die in the trying. There were more bishops present than had assembled at Ephesus for the Council in the year 431.

The voice had now trailed off to almost a whisper. Even the

little prelate, holding the open book before the Pontiff's gaze, could hardly catch the words. Was Pio Nono so overcome with joy, the book-bearer wondered, that he could not read on to the end? But gathering new strength, the feeble voice now rang clear again, reaching to the far ends of the great church, soaring up into the very dome.

> "We declare, we pronounce, we define
> that the doctrine that blessed Mary
> was, in the first instant of her Conception
> preserved . . . from all stain of original guilt
> has been revealed by God
> and therefore,
> must be firmly and constantly believed
> by all the faithful. . . ."

There. It had been infallibly spoken!

Boom! Underfoot the travertine paving of St. Peter's trembled with the far-off rumble of cannon, Castel Sant'Angelo giving Rome the signal. Now, from all points of the city, the bells were in full cry. Three hundred bell-tongues cheering our Lady's Immaculate Conception. By the clock tower of Maria Maggiore, it was almost noon.

Through one of the round windows high in Michelangelo's dome, a long shaft of sunlight had found the precious mitre, the tear-wet face of the Pope, flooding the ornately lettered document held open by one whose task that morning any cardinal present would gladly have performed. For this, Pio Nono had chosen not the oldest of his bishops, nor even the youngest but—and who could say why—the smallest. The five-foot-two Bishop of America's largest see, John Neumann of Philadelphia.

A week later, in private audience at the Vatican, Bishop Neumann made his *ad limina* report on the diocese of Philadelphia. Rather, he sat there in the papal chamber, dumbfounded by Pio Nono's knowledge of Pennsylvania—its farmlands, its coal towns and lumber camps, and the impossible distances a bishop must cover to reach the outposts of a visitation tour. His Holiness expressed delight at the thirty-four school-bells in the diocese, calling some nine thousand children to their lessons.

"You will build still more," said the Pope.

He knew all about Neumann's valiant effort to complete the huge cathedral on Logan Square. He even knew that Neumann had ordained that in every church of the diocese, the Litany of Our Lady be sung before Sunday High Mass in honor of Mary Immaculate; that, ineffectually, he had proposed at the Council in Baltimore, that December eighth be made a holy day of obligation for the whole United States.

But His Holiness did not do all the talking. He listened too, his large white head cocked sympathetically to the left, as Bishop Neumann described the plight of immigrants in his diocese; all the things he still hoped to do: more churches and schools; an orphanage and hospitals and a home for the aged—but for that, he would need nuns.

"Bishop Neumann," His Holiness interrupted, "you must found your own sisterhood. Yes. Give them the Rule of the gentle Saint Francis. Train them yourself. Instruct them in what you need them for."

All in all, the Holy Father felt satisfied that he had chosen the right man, a shepherd after his own heart, for the See of Philadelphia.

Suddenly, recalling the frantic efforts to avoid the mitre Neumann had made two years ago, the heart-sick letter he had, later, sent to Rome, inquiring if being bishop had *ipso facto* cut him off forever from his Order, Pio Nono smiled.

"Bishop Neumann, now don't you truly believe that *Obedience is better than sacrifice?* Now that you wear ring and purple, I give you my assurance, you are still a Redemptorist. Were it otherwise," he added, "by the plenary powers of Sovereign Pontiff, I would arrange it so, to make you happy."

John Neumann radiated joy at hearing those words from the lips of His Holiness.

Pio Nono rose from his chair, indicating that the audience was over. The Bishop knelt for a blessing on his sprawling diocese, on the Sisterhood he hoped to found, on his Order, his loved ones, himself.

"And tell your good father when you see him that Pio Nono sends a special blessing to Prachatitz, all for him."

At Maria in Monterone two days later, a letter arrived from

Philadelphia: one of his confreres telling of three devout souls in St. Peter's parish, who had hopes of establishing a sisterhood. They needed Bishop Neumann's approbation. How quickly Pio Nono's blessing bore fruit! Here was the very nucleus Neumann needed for his Third Order of St. Francis—nuns to staff his orphanage of tomorrow, to assist in half a dozen other social projects in his diocese.

That week at Piazza Navona, the children of Rome stared wide-eyed at the twinkling Christmas-booths stocked with drums and dolls and trumpets. They pointed at carved angels, at shepherds and kings from Naples. They clapped hands rapturously at a tiny music-box that tinkled *"Tu scendi dalle stelle"* concealed in the cradle of a life-size *Bambino Gesù* with blue crystal eyes.

How the Bishop's own dark-eyed *bambinos* at St. Mary Magdalene de Pazzi's in Southwark, and the tots at St. Joseph's at Spruce and Seventh, and those at the hospital up at Sixteenth and Girard, how they would enjoy this life-size Infant Jesus! He could see the smiles under the black bonnets of his Sisters of Charity, kindled by the delighted children. If only he could carry it with him! He already had so many bags and boxes crammed with relics of the Saints, medals of Mary Immaculate, Agnus Deis, holy pictures, souvenirs of Rome. Reluctantly he passed up the *Bambino Gesù* with its chiming music-box in Piazza Navona, setting out for Loreto to say there his three Christmas Masses on the journey home.

"Louise," asked old Papa Neumann for the hundredth time, "have we heard anything from John at all? Has he gone back to America? Or what?"

Christmas had come and gone. It was almost the end of January. Next Sunday would be Quinquagesima.

"There was a letter this morning, Papa."

Twice that morning Louise had read the letter to the old gentleman already. He wanted to hear it again.

"John is in Prague right now, Papa. He's had a long visit with Joan at the Motherhouse of the Nuns of St. Charles. He said Mass in the cathedral, too—before the body of his namesake, St.

John Nepomucene. Last night he was at the Hradscin, dining with Ferdinand, the ex-Emperor. . . ."

"Yes, but when is he coming home? Did he say *when?*"

Patiently, Louise explained all over again that tonight John was leaving for Budweis and tomorrow or the next day, please God, he would be *here,* sitting down to supper at Number 129 in the Upper Lane.

Now, no matter what day the Bishop came, his hometown was prepared. Every step of the civic reception had been thrashed out in council, warmly debated, cooly agreed upon. If the snow was deep, teams were detailed to plough the roads. In the pocket of his best coat, the Burgomaster had his speech of welcome. Lettered banners of greeting were all ready. Choir boys could sing the *Te Deum* in their sleep, so often had they practiced. At the local garrison of the Emperor's fourth Dragoons, everything from knee-boots to sleeve-buttons had been burnished to a fare-thee-well.

"We'll play for the Bishop," said the bandmaster, "as though he were Franz Josef himself!"

The band had two lively marches kept exclusively for visits of the Emperor. Altar boys and clergy had had many rehearsals. They knew what to do. Everything was ready. The schoolmaster, inspired by the air of preparation, wrote a special poem just before Christmas. He would have his star pupil learn it by heart—all sixteen stanzas. Everything was ready. Even Louise Neumann admitted that her house was spic and span. She had made a quick trip to Linz before Christmas and recklessly bought a dress. Prachatitz was ready, no matter when Bishop Neumann arrived.

"But what if he comes at night?" Messner, the local atheist, had also entered into the spirit of the occasion.

"He won't. We've thought of that, also."

Prachatitz made doubly sure it would not be taken unawares. On hilltops, commanding the main road from Budweis to Prachatitz, mortars had been emplaced in the snow. A cadet, at sight of the oncoming sleigh, would fire his mortar in salute, summoning the countryside down to the road for the Bishop's blessing, as he passed. No possibility was missed. Even a spy—Pokorny, the postman's young nephew—had been posted at Budweis. As soon as he learned the Bishop's plans for departure, he was to mount horse and gallop the dozen miles home with the news.

In the early morning of January thirty-first, Neumann arrived at Budweis. Waiting there to escort him home was John Berger, his sister Catherine's boy. Neumann should pay a courtesy call on Valerian Jirsik at the episcopal residence! Bishop Jirsik, delighted, insisted that Neumann stay overnight. By a hairbreadth the whole plan almost misfired. Young Adalbert Benesh was mounting for Prachatitz when Berger rushed into the livery stable.

"Wait, Berti! Not yet."

"We'll start early this afternoon," the Bishop told his nephew next morning. "Thus, we'll reach home after dark."

Solemnly young Berger nodded.

"Then we'd better hire you a sleigh at once."

At all costs the Bishop must arrive in broad daylight. Those were the Burgomaster's orders. Neumann must somehow be detained that evening at Nettolitz, half-way home. Quickly Berger conferred with his accomplice. Young Adalbert Benesh listened, nodded excitedly, put toe in stirrup and galloped off.

By afternoon the snow had begun. The hired sleigh was not the best. The trip was slow. By the time they reached the halfway point, it was long after dusk. As the sleigh started up the slope of Nettolitz, suddenly the church bells began. Suddenly torches flared up in the darkness, the narrow streets were packed with waiting people. They asked his blessing. They pleaded, cajoled. Neumann simply had to stay the night in their midst. The ruse had succeeded well.

"What sort of walker are you, John Berger?"

After Mass next morning the Bishop turned to his nephew with an idea.

"I remember a short cut home, back over the hills. We could make it in three hours! Suppose we send the sleigh back to Budweis and walk home."

Young Berger was dumbfounded. Once more it looked as though the Burgomaster's plan would be foiled. Berger knew that Nettolitz had already put Prince Schwarzenberg's sleigh at the

Bishop's disposal, a red limousine with four white horses to pull him home in style.

Coming out of church, the Bishop saw the gala sleigh. He shook his head. There was no escape. A coachman in gold-buttoned, scarlet greatcoat sat in the highseat, waiting.

"Your Excellency. . . ."

A liveried footman held open the velvet-lined sleigh door. He clicked his heels, bowed from the waist.

Behind his sober-faced uncle, young John Berger stepped into the sleigh, grinning knowingly at footman and bystanders.

They were off for home.

Boom! A puff of smoke rose into the cold blue sky from a nearby hill. In spite of the sunshine, the air was bitter cold. Another mortar-boom. The Bishop wondered to see groups of wool-bundled people standing, waving, kneeling by the roadside, for his blessing. How did they know? Now the four white horses lumbered up the last incline. On the other side of the hill, he knew, lay the shallow white saucer of his native valley. The bishop closed his eyes. They were blurring with tears.

Prachatitz! There it lay in the distance: just as he remembered it. There was the road, the orchards, the frozen river, the circle of snow-powdered hills. He could see the tower of Saint Jakob's, the chimneys, the slanted gables, the solid old walls of the city, the sturdy medieval gate. Nineteen years and not a thing was different! But the sleigh whisked past the church yard so quickly, the Bishop could hardly make a sign of the cross. Somewhere in there lay Mother.

"Wait!" (Would the coachman mind stopping a moment?)

With the high wind the coachman could not hear. But now the sleigh was stopping, anyway, for a group of prominent citizens. Just ahead, stood a double file of Dragoons, half frozen, buglers, fifers, blue-knuckled drummers, bravely playing the Emperor's special march. The City Fathers stood waiting to extend to the distinguished visitor a formal welcome home. The sleigh door opened. Out into the chill air stepped the smiling little visitor— hardly like a great bishop at all.

WELCOME BISHOP NEUMANN! shouted a huge banner over

the city gate. WELCOME HOME! On the stone battlements of the wall, the Double Eagle of Austria, the white and blue of Bohemia snapped in the chilly wind. Below, in the shelter of the gate, more officials had assembled with three-quarters of the townsfolk, all laughing, cheering, waving, stamping to keep warm.

There were more speeches. A dozen drummers beat a long tattoo. Up to the open sleigh door stepped a schoolboy, fidgeting with his cap. He quavered his way through four flowery stanzas of poetic welcome, faltered, burst into tears. In a loud whisper, the schoolmaster prompted. The boy, clenching his eyelids tight, scampered through the dozen remaining stanzas, on to a triumphant end.

Smiling, Bishop Neumann thanked the shiny-eyed lad. He thanked all the giggling, button-nosed children, their cheeks red from the wind. He thanked the whole town for its welcome.

"Quick now, put on your cap," he told the boy-orator, "or you'll catch cold."

The bells were ringing like Christmas morning as the Bishop walked up the steps of Saint Jakob's. There before the main altar attended by Dean, clergy and a small batallion of cassocked altar boys, he intoned the *Te Deum*. Choir and organ took up the hymn of thanks to God for his many blessings on John Nepomucene Neumann of Prachatitz—and for bringing him safely home.

The red and gold sleigh-coach of Prince Schwarzenberg stood at the church door, awaiting the Bishop's pleasure.

"Thank you, gentlemen; but let me go home on foot." He hoped for a private meeting with his dear old father, his sister, Louise; but that was not to be. Already half the town was lined along the Upper Lane. A squad of Dragoons preceded. Burgomaster, Dean and all the local clergy escorted the Bishop up the slope of the Upper Lane to Number 129.

"You'll catch cold, Father," warned Louise, smoothing her store-bought dress.

But admonition was useless now. At the open door stood Mr. Neumann, peering into the blur of neighbors, clergy, civic officials, bright-frocked Dragoons.

"Which of you is John?"

The Bishop hastened his pace through the murmurous crowd. "Here Papa! Here I am."

A quick hush fell over the gathering as father and son embraced. So tight was the old man's clasp, he literally lifted the little Bishop over the threshold. But nineteen years was a long time! The door closed, leaving the Neumann family some privacy at last.

"Tell us, John, about Rome. Did you really talk to the Pope? Tell us about America. You haven't grown an inch, have you? What did the Emperor want you for in Prague? Did you have breakfast yet? Did they tell you I've retired from the stocking business? Tell us, how's our Wenzel? Tell us about Niagara Falls. Will you say Mass for us tomorrow?"

So many questions the old man had, it would take seven days to answer them all.

The Dean had offered the hospitality of his rectory. The Bishop declined.

"I have but a few days. Let me sleep under the roof where I was born. My father will be happy."

Next day was Septuagesima. He agreed to pontificate at ten and to preach.

All Prachatitz turned out that Sunday for High Mass. Even old Mr. Neumann, bundled up like a small child, was trundled down to church in a sled. Saint Jakob's was packed to the doors: old ladies in black woolen shawls, cronies who had sat beside him as school boys, Pokorny the postman in Sunday best. Up in the front bench sat Philip Neumann with Louise and a dozen next of kin. The organ filled the church with exultation. The choir boys sang. It was like a First Mass. Though nineteen years late, that is precisely what it was, John Neumann's first Mass in his home town.

The gospel that morning was the parable of the laborers in the vineyard. The Bishop spoke of the Lord's great vineyard across the seas, where for nineteen years he had borne the heats of the day, where more and more laborers were needed. He told them of the Niagara frontier, of huddled immigrants in the seaport slums of Philadelphia and Baltimore, of Pittsburgh's two brawling rivers beyond the Allegheny Mountains—places he knew so well. He described mission trips into the hills of western Maryland, visitation tours among miners, farmers, lumberjacks in Pennsylvania—Catholics from so many parts of Europe. He spoke too of the hardships a priest must suffer in the vineyards of America. He did not ask for money.

"But remember me and my priests in all your prayers."

Lurking behind a pillar near the baptistry, a man blew his nose in a vain attempt to ward off tears. Messner, the village athiest.

"If we had a man of God like that around here all the time," he was heard to say, "I'd be a whole lot different myself!"

As the crowds milled out into the street, more than one woman remarked to her family:

"If the Bishop's good mother could only have been there in the front bench, how happy she'd be this morning!"

Somewhat the same thought must have crossed the Bishop's mind during Mass. From one of the priests in the rectory, he borrowed a pair of highboots.

"I'm going for a short walk," he told the Dean after coffee.

"A bit of private business. I'd prefer to go alone."

Out the city gate he walked and down the straight snow-banked road for almost a mile, up to the churchyard of SS. Peter and Paul. The snow was deep but he found the place.

Agnes Lebis Neumann
July 17, 1849
R.I.P.

She had never received his first priestly blessing; though at Chrobold once, she had heard him preach. For a long while he stayed, alone with his thoughts. *"Spanem Bohem!* God be with you, Mother."* Slowly he blessed the grave and turned away, leaving the print of his knees deep in the snow.

In no time, the seven days were over. Early on a Saturday morning, a small sleigh waited at Number 129 in the Upper Lane. In the lamplight of the open door, two men embraced a while. Impatiently the horse tossed its mane, shaking a string of sleigh bells. The door closed. Down through the town, the sleigh runners quickly skimmed, under the arch of the city gate, down the straight white canyon of the snow-banked road, up past the churchyard, past lamplit cow barn, up to the crest of the hill.

"Stop a moment."

The Bishop turned round in the sleigh for one more glimpse. Then quietly making a sign of the cross over the sleeping valley, he turned his face toward Budweis—and Logan Square.

19.   THE CATHEDRAL

The shad run had already begun. The Delaware swarmed with seiners off Tacony, off Petty's Island, off Buttercup, off Kensington, that Thursday morning as the railway steamer moved downstream to the Walnut Street dock. Philadelphia. Home at last! Gathering up his labeled bags and precious boxes, Bishop Neumann looked for a hackney coach to take him to his house at Summer and Sassafras across town. March twenty-ninth—Holy Week was three days off.

"Guess you've been gone a while, sir." The coachman helped hoist the luggage aboard.

"Since October." Where else but America would a coachman strike up conversation with a stranger, asking in one breath his recent whereabouts, briefing him, in the next, on local news since he'd last been in town.

"Lucky, you missed the long cold spell. They skated on the Schuylkill right up to Shrovetide!"

Skook'l he pronounced it.

The coach moved off under the prows of a dozen packets moored along Front Street while the coachmen commented on the newest influx from Europe. "They come here to live; and instead of moving up-country, where they could earn their keep, they stay in Southwark and Kensington where it's impossible to find work even in good times. Now, with this depression, they haven't a tinker's chance."

He mentioned how Mayor Conrad had opened soup kitchens, at city expense, to keep the jobless and their families from starvation.

"But they still keep coming from overseas. And we got to support them. It ain't fair, Mister. Them Know-Nothings are right: *Keep America for Americans.*"

The coach passed several soup-lines on the trip to Logan Square. Almost half of the city was unemployed.

Up on Apple Street, the following Monday morning, going with Father Hespelein to interview three aspirants for the Sisterhood, the Bishop noticed a group of men and teenage boys waiting at the rear of St. Peter's Rectory—waiting, so Father Rector told him, for the noon hour when Brothers Christopher and Aloysius would fill the dinner pails with hot Redemptorist soup to carry home to their families. Able-bodied men, they could find no work.

At the home of Mrs. Anna Bachmann on Apple Street, the Bishop found the two other young ladies, Anna Dorn and Barbara Boll, who were, he hoped, the answer to his prayer. Ever since the death of her husband, Mrs. Bachmann explained, this idea had kept growing in her heart—a Sisterhood devoted more to social service than teaching, boarding immigrant girls until they found suitable employment, perhaps caring for orphans, the sick, the aged, the down-and-out, whatever work the changing times required.

It astonished the Bishop how closely their dreams matched his own. It must have been a powerfully effective blessing that saintly Pio Nono had given to this new Sisterhood for Philadelphia. Talking to the three young women, the Bishop knew that here was the chosen nucleus for his Third Order of Saint Francis.

"I suppose you're acquainted with St. Peter's," he twinkled, knowing from Father Hespelein that the three ladies spent half their day there in prayer. "One week from today, Easter Monday after High Mass, I will invest you there in the religious habit."

Then he soberly suggested that the three jubilant ladies spend the remainder of Holy Week in closed retreat, preparing to start their year of novitiate.

"I hope to make a retreat of my own at St. Peter's from Holy Thursday till noon of Holy Saturday, that is, if Father Rector allows." He nodded toward Father Hespelein. "Thus I shall be able to give you several conferences on religious life."

On the walk back to St. Peter's (Father Rector had induced him to take dinner there and regale the Community with his trip to Europe), Neumann saw that the soup-line had grown to almost the length of Apple Street, some two hundred and fifty ragged people, each with battered pail or cannister in hand.

"How can you possibly buy enough food for all those people, Father Rector?"

"Special collections." Father Hespelein told of one begging trip to Lebanon a few weeks back.

"I came home empty-handed; but Brother Christopher met me at the door telling how several total strangers had come to the rectory with donations for our poor—enough soup funds for a week . . . and then some."

"Yes," said the Bishop. "Give a crust of bread to the poor and God gives you back a baker's dozen. But you must trust Him . . . blindly."

At lunch—a baker's dozen of Delaware shad fresh from the river—the Bishop showed the Redemptorists a golden medal of our Lady given him by the Holy Father, a souvenir of December eighth, 1854. Each bishop who had been at Rome that day received one. Neumann tried, but could hardly find words, to convey the electric expectancy of St. Peter's that sunlit morning as the Pope pronounced the Immaculate Conception a tenet of the Catholic faith.

"As he spoke, there were tears on his wrinkled face," said the Bishop, omitting to mention how he knew—that he had been as close to the Holy Father at that solemn moment as he now was to Father Rector at table. He went on to tell of the torches burning on the Tiber bridges, flickering on the dome of St. Peter's, outlining each fountain and public building that evening of December eighth;

and the happy people singing in the streets. He talked of Rome's many churches.

"I made a special trip to San Carlo on the Corso," he told them, explaining to young Father Hewitt, the one Yankee-born member of the Community, that San Carlo was the original on which Napoleon LeBrun had modeled Philadelphia's Cathedral of St. Peter and St. Paul.

"I suppose, Bishop, you can hardly wait to have it completed!" Young Father Hewitt spoke without thinking. He had no suspicion of how pointedly the thought of that abortive structure on Logan Square had harried the Bishop through Europe! Every new cathedral was a reminder of his own. He had stood in Stefan-platz in imperial Vienna gazing up at the gothic spire of *der alte Stefferl,* as Vienna fondly calls its old cathedral—and remembered his own three-walled heartache. Once, too, in his homeland, the heart-lifting bells of Saint Vitus boomed seven, almost loosening the snow on all the gables of Prague. Neumann that evening, invited to dine with ex-Emperor Ferdinand, was standing at a high window of the Hradscin, taking in the magnificent view below: the lamp-lit streets, the snow on the tall statues on Karl's Bridge over the frozen Moldau—and almost within reach of his arm, the fairy-like stonework of Saint Vitus cathedral. Logan Square would never look like it—but at dinner's end, His Imperial Highness had beckoned a liveried butler. Bowing, the butler retired a moment, returned with a large covered charger of Venetian crystal. Bowing again, he lifted the lid before Bishop Neumann's bewildered face.

"A gift from your homeland," said Ferdinand of Habsburg, "something for your Philadelphia cathedral." The charger was packed with American gold pieces.

Munich's twin-towered *Liebfrau-kirche* was another tart reminder. And Speyer. He had stopped there with Bishop Timon of Buffalo en route to Paris. The cathedral was old—St. Bernard seven hundred years ago had heard the *Salve Regina* sung there one evening and suddenly exclaimed, "O clement, O loving, O sweet Virgin Mary." Ever since, his words had been part of the lovely prayer. Casually, Bishop von Weis had mentioned that the cathedral had just been completely renovated through the generosity of his diocese. He was proud of the restoration. Timon and Neumann had admired it too, Neumann wryly wondering if the generosity of his Philadelphia would ever match that of the Rhineland.

But in reply to Father Hewitt's remark, Bishop Neumann only smiled. "Our cathedral must wait. After all, Father, it would not be right to ask money to raise stones when the poor are asking for bread."

The Bishop had in mind another orphanage to care for fatherless little ones—like the three small girls he had seen with their embarrassed mother on Apple Street. Too small to leave home, not big enough to run the errand themselves, the poor mother must gather them up and walk to St. Peter's kitchen door, or go supperless. The orphanage could take care of such youngsters until their mothers could manage. Roaming the streets of Philadelphia were hundreds of waifs, their parents lost to sickness or malnutrition on the trip from Europe. Somehow, they must be salvaged. Their souls were more important than brownstone blocks for a cathedral.

But now, please God, at least he had the seed of a Sisterhood! On Easter Monday, he invested the three young women in the religious habit and gave them a Rule of life, written in his own hand. In time, the seed would grow. In time, too, there would be homes for the aged, and hospitals and an orphanage—and a finished cathedral.

"Bishop Neumann's back . . ."

South and north of Market Street spread the word, all over town. Logan Square had no soup kitchen, but a line soon formed on Sassafras Street, east of the half-built cathedral. All Philadelphia knew that Bishop Neumann never locked his door. To the front door they came. It did not matter either if they came more than once. The little Bishop always had something for them, money if there was money on hand, otherwise, a pair of gloves, a woolen scarf, perhaps, a second-hand cap, a pair of shoes. This time the Bishop also gave to each a medal of Mary Immaculate from Rome, blessed by Pope Pius, the Ninth.

"Bishop, that's three times this fellow's been here today."

"What harm?" Neumann winked at his Vicar General. "I'm giving not just to him but to the Lord."

On an idle derrick pole one Sunday morning, a bobolink whistled a saucy greeting to Logan Square. April was practically over. It was Good Shepherd Sunday, the second after Easter. From his window, the Bishop watched the twitching blue tail and smiled. He should have been out on visitation, tending to his flock. "I know mine," said the Good Shepherd, "and mine know me."

Down in Gettysburg, the barley must be almost an inch above ground. The ramblers up in Lancaster would soon be red on the white fenceposts. Miners in Tremont and Slockum's Hollow were going down into the pits with sprigs of lilac in their caps. Soon the Poconos would be pink with laurel. Up Muncy way, on the roaring Susquehanna, lumberjacks were skittering on the log booms, laughing at death. Out beyond the Seven Mountains on the western fringe of his diocese, a lonely eagle was probably flying over Snowshoe. Neumann remembered the timber camp of Snowshoe. There on the little farm, he confirmed a sick boy on the last visitation tour. Four hours it had taken to get there from Bellefonte. But a bishop, like the Good Shepherd, must care for his lambs. He smiled. In another month, live spring lambs would be nibbling the lush green of the Wyoming, the Wayalusing valleys.

"I should be out there now," said the Bishop, half aloud.

There was more to Philadelphia than the tree-lined streets between Schuylkill and Delaware, a great deal more. That was the trouble. When he ought to be touring the Blue Mountains and the Lehigh Valley, moving up the Susquehanna and the Juniata, he must also be here at home on Logan Square. For three years he had mulled over the problem; had meant to broach it to the Holy Father at the *ad limina* last December, but something Pio Nono had asked him made him forget.

Early that May of 1855, however, he did bring up the matter in Baltimore at the Eighth Provincial Council. Archbishop Kenrick, shortly before, had proposed to the assembly that Philadelphia be made an archdiocese. Quickly Neumann was on his feet.

He did not agree. An archdiocesan see should at least have a cathedral and Philadelphia would not have one for at least five years or more. The argument sounded reasonable to the assembly. Kenrick's proposal was tabled for the nonce.

Now Neumann advanced his own proposal and the assembled bishops sat upright with surprise. He thought the diocese of Philadelphia was too big, that it should be divided, lopping sixteen counties off for a second diocese. Since coming as bishop three years before, he said, he had spent around fifteen months on pastoral visitation, and there still were parts of the diocese he had not touched. Humanly speaking, twenty-six thousand square miles of mountain and valley were too much for one bishop to cover. There were two hundred thousand souls for whom he was responsible to Almighty God. He called on Archbishop Kenrick and Bishop O'Connor to bear him out. A man must understand the topography of Pennsylvania to appreciate the difficulty of getting from one country parish to the next. And he had one hundred and fifty parishes. Therefore, he proposed that the diocese be split.

For the See city, Neumann suggested Pottsville. A small place, he agreed. Only forty-five hundred Catholics. Industrially, it would hardly overtake Pittsburgh. But, at least, its population was stable. Besides, it was centrally located, had road, rail and water-links with the rest of Pennsylvania. If Philadelphia should be divided, Pottsville seemed the logical spot for the See.

"Pottsvillensis"—even in Latin it sounded ludicrous! Who would want his cathedral in Pottsville? Anticipating that—and now he stunned the assembly—Neumann suggested that he take the new see himself, leaving Philadelphia and Logan Square for another. Once more he adduced reasons, personal perhaps, to explain his earnest proposal.

"Believe me, my Brothers, nothing would make me happier than an out-of-the-way little diocese where I would know my flock and call my priests by name. All my years as a diocesan priest in western New York, as a Redemptorist missionary both in Pittsburgh and here in Baltimore—fifteen of them—have been training for just such a diocese as 'Pottsville.' I have the background and the character for such a place. I'm long hardened to travel by horsecart and canal barge. All my life I've liked walking. I have hiked over mountains and down long valleys from one settlement to the next preaching the word of God. For another, 'Pottsville' would be a hardship, an unbearable cross. For me, and before God I mean this, it would be Paradise."

The color had mounted to his sallow cheek. His eyes flashed conviction. Not a bishop present but believed that John Neumann of Philadelphia meant what he said.

Before the Council concluded, the bishops agreed to petition the Holy See that the diocese of Philadelphia be divided. Neumann was happy. His problem was now in the hands of Rome and whatever Rome decided would be the will of God for him. Meanwhile, back to Logan Square and the unfinished cathedral.

Bishop Neumann did not quite speak his mind in Baltimore. There were things that a man, even among his fellow bishops, keeps to himself. He could not well describe how the sham etiquette of Chestnut Street revolted him, how the taffeta hoopskirts, the pearl-buttoned vests, the whole exclusive ritual of the Assembly Ball, held on the first January Friday of every year, struck him as extravagant nonsense. That fashionable enclave of Catholics "below Market Street," with their artificial taboos, their thoughtless frivolities, their lack of concern for the real things of God, was for Neumann a mystery of iniquity. Give him the slag-boys of Wilkes-Barre or Trevorton any day, with soot in the lines of their knuckles, but with the grace of God in their souls. Neumann was Old World and old-fashioned enough to think that a well-thumbed prayerbook counted more on a Sunday morning than a lace-trimmed parasol. He could never see eye to eye with Rittenhouse Square. But those were things one did not talk about —even at an Eighth Provincial Council at Baltimore.

Turning the corner of Eighteenth and Chestnut one Sunday evening, a gentleman looked again, smiled surprise, then tipped his hat.

"Good evening, Bishop."

He seemed lost for appropriate comment.

"Pardon my saying so, but I mistook you for a lamplighter in that woe-begone coat."

It seemed only proper that the Bishop of Philadelphia should be seen in a decent coat on his way to the pro-cathedral for vespers. And why didn't he use a carriage?

Instinctively, Neumann fingered the buttons on his chestfront.

"This, sir," he smiled, "is the only coat to my name; I must get a new one soon."

Early next morning, a fine black broadcloth from Spruce Street arrived at Logan Square, an anonymous gift. But later that very morning a squat little fellow from Clare knocked at the Bishop's front door, the elbows out of his frieze coat. He left wearing broadcloth.

Genteel Philadelphia warmly approved civic soup kitchens for the jobless immigrant, but looked askance at giving the coat off your back. "One just doesn't do those things south of Market Street." On "those things," Philadelphia and John Neumann could never quite agree.

By Neumann's standards, a church was more important than a music hall. Philadelphia's Academy of Music was to be built at the corner of Broad near Locust Street. Already the great names of the city—among them many wealthy Catholics—were vying for the claim of making the largest donation. But on Logan Square, for lack of funds, the cathedral had no roof or dome or facade— just three stark brownstone walls, that looked, said some local wag, like an oversize handball court. By John Neumann's standards this did not make sense.

Special church collections for the cathedral had not been successful. In June, the bishop convoked a select gathering of the well-to-do, fifty gentlemen who guaranteed to collect five hundred dollars each, before December. With twenty thousand dollars, Neumann could proceed with the building operations. He had laid down the prudent policy once more that, until the funds were on hand, no stone should be cut or put in place. There must be no debts.

Later that same month, President Franklin Pierce rode up from Washington to preside at the corner-stone laying of the new Academy of Music. The next day, and for almost two years without interruption, the lot at Broad and Locust was busy with workmen. But at Logan Square—lack of funds, again—there were long months of inactivity. Work had commenced on the three main arches of the cathedral facade. But during 1855, the fifty gentlemen had collected only nine thousand five hundred dollars—less than half the estimated goal. Construction stopped.

A new scheme was launched the following year. Instead of fifty, seven hundred interested laymen were enlisted in a four-year plan, each member to raise a specified sum by the end of each year, making an annual total of forty thousand dollars. If successful, the cathedral could be built and paid for by 1860.

For almost a year now, four monster plinths of brownstone, quarried for the pillars of the cathedral facade, had lain in Logan Square. Before they were dressed and ready for placement, the Academy of Music, the night of January 27, 1857, opened its doors to a glittering throng. The Music Hall had cost more than four and a half million dollars, according to Napoleon Lebrun who had drawn the plans. In the eighteen months of construction, the total cost had been contributed. But the seven hundred Catholic businessmen had not been too successful with their own campaign.

The Bishop said nothing, but the *Herald* made wry sport of the situation, calling it a disgrace to Philadelphia that with one hundred and twenty-five thousand Catholics in the city, such meager funds could be collected for the cathedral of St. Peter and St. Paul. Week after week the paper kept needling.

The Bishop took a broader, kinder view. There had been special collections for St. Joseph's hospital, the home for widows, the three orphanages, and the new one, now under construction, at Tacony. Not only that, but in the midst of the campaign, a priest from Ireland had knocked at the Bishop's door requesting permission to gather funds in the diocese for the cathedral of Armagh. Bishop Neumann had even made a personal donation. Father McMahon's collection for the Primate of all Ireland had almost matched the year's donation for Philadelphia's own cathedral.

Besides, in Neumann's dream "diocese of Pottsville" (nineteen months had gone by and still no word from Rome!) up in Haycock, Hazelton, Doylestown, Lykens, Tremont, Parkersburg, parish churches had been built during these past two years. Two days after Christmas, Neumann had gone up to Bethlehem to dedicate the twelfth new church—in honor of the Nativity.

Setting the four Corinthian columns on the cathedral facade was a tedious business. Each was sixty feet long and six feet in diameter—the largest quarried in Pennsylvania. One false move could spell disaster. When the operation began in early April of 1857, Neumann went out on Sassafras Street and watched.

"Pray thee, good sir. . . ."

Neumann did not hear, so intent was he on the squeaking derricks, hoisting the first column into place.

"Pray thee, good sir. Might it not be more pleasing to God, if thee gave thy money to the poor instead of spending it on all this vain display?"

The Bishop turned to the elderly Quaker beside him. "But sir, I *am* giving all this money to the poor—in exchange for their labor and time."

He pointed to the dozens of workmen on the scaffolding.

"Thus we give double, gold to our neighbor and glory to God."

For that, the Quaker had no answer. Politely tipping his hat, he politely strolled off in the direction of Broad Street.

John Mahoney, assistant architect, had stopped a moment to consult with Neumann about future work on the cathedral.

"I see by the morning papers, Bishop, that we're getting a second bishop. There aren't many places in America with two bishops in the same place! And a native son, at that."

News travels fast! Only that morning Neumann had received word from Kenrick in Baltimore. Apparently there was to be no "diocese of Pottsville." A coadjutor had been appointed to the See of Philadelphia, James Frederick Wood. After twenty-one months of wating, Rome had spoken at last. John Neumann must stay where he was. It was the will of God.

"Yes, John," said Neumann, "I know. Father Wood is a skilled businessman. I am told he held a high banking post in Cincinnati before studying for the priesthood. With him about, our cathedral should soon be completed."

"We were hoping he'd be consecrated here," added John Mahoney, "but according to the papers it's taking place the twenty-sixth in Cincinnati."

That Neumann had not heard.

"His friends and relatives are all in Cincinnati," Neumann lamely explained.

He let it go at that. But he made up his mind to attend. It would give him the chance to visit dear old Saint Philomena's in Pittsburgh. And Cumberland had asked that he ordain their large class of young Redemptorists that year! God was good. On the way there and back he could accomplish many things.

Before leaving for Cincinnati, solicitously he arranged for the new bishop's lodgings—the best room on the second floor.

"Take the carpet from my room," he told the housekeeper.

"And we may as well give him the wardrobe. I never use it anyway."

Neumann's own room was austerity itself—an iron bedstead with a thin hard mattress, a coat rack, two straightback chairs and a deal table that he used as desk. On the walls hung a few paper pictures brought from Rome: Mary Immaculate, St. Alphonsus Liguori, St. John Nepomucene, and the picture of St. Joseph that had hung in Prachatitz over his mother's bed. These, and a wooden crucifix. On the wall facing his table hung a large map of the diocese that he had sketched himself.

The housekeeper, old Margaret Bradley, seldom entered the room, except to change the linens. "Though God knows, you can still see the creases of my iron on the pillow case! He never uses the bed at all."

Each morning, the Bishop made his own bed and tidied the room, as he had done years ago as a Redemptorist. Old habits were hard to break.

"I hope he likes it."

"God love you, Bishop Neumann," soothed Maggie Bradley. "His room will be the best in the house! I'll scour the place like new between now and when you bring him back to us."

Philadelphia was utterly taken with its charming new bishop. Handsome in a stately way, perfectly groomed, he was taller by a head than Neumann, and every inch a prelate, as he walked the aisle in cope and mitre for Confirmation at old St. Mary's. That faint trace of London in his voice lent added interest at a civic banquet, a nun's profession, a cathedral Forty Hours. He had a soft, engaging laugh, a ready smile, and was never at a loss for the apt phrase to cap an anecdote. Philadelphia, south of Market, was enraptured at the polished elegance of James Frederick Wood, coadjutor with the right of succession to the See of Philadelphia.

"This time," said Chestnut to Walnut Street, "Rome has sent us a gentleman."

But the quick eye of little John Neumann had already seen that in gentlemanly Bishop Wood, he had the perfect foil for *bon-ton* Philadelphia. With his elegance and charm, his taste in clothes, his precisely inflected English, his disarming affability—Wood was many things that Neumann was not. Together, they should satisfy everyone.

Yet in all honesty, Neumann could not picture his coadjutor dangling his buttoned calfskin boots from a low-slung manure cart, as he himself once had done, on a country Confirmation tour. He could hardly picture Bishop Wood in the mountains at all. The brawling lumber camps of the Susquehanna's west branch, he felt sure, would be purgatory for the good man. His faultless English would charm the city from Rittenhouse to Lemon Hill, God bless him. But up-country, at least for the present, someone was needed who could also speak German and French, even Polish, yes—and Irish.

There were old folks from the west of Ireland living in Hazelton, in Trevorton, in Slockum's Hollow, who knew not a word of English. And now they had blessed their stars and blessed John Neumann, too, because he could understand their confession and give them a word of advice.

"Molad go deo le Dia easpog Earannach ata gainn air deire!" one beshawled grandmother had declared as she came out of church.

"Faith, it's an Irish bishop they've sent us at last."

With that fact-confronting candor that is cousin to humility, John Neumann knew in his heart that he was far better equipped for the coal towns, the winding mountain roads of up-state Pennsylvania. He must claim them for himself as a kindness—a respite, too, for Bishop Wood.

A saint in stained glass is one thing. A "saint" in the room across the hall is something else again. To the well-bred Wood, there was little about Neumann that appealed. His mere presence in a room, in the house, kept Wood on edge. There were those long ear-splitting silences. What was Neumann thinking? And the way his dark eyes seemed to bore you through! The sidelong tilt of his large head as he listened to what you were telling or asking.

To Bishop Wood it was a constant embarrassment that he must so often ask Neumann to repeat himself. Not that Wood did not hear but he had missed the key word of some phrase in Neumann's guttural English. Conversation was physically exhausting, so alert one must keep to the sound of words to return a sensible answer.

At table even those colorless feints at pleasantry unmanned Bishop Wood. They seemed like concessions to his own lack of recollection. Neumann never asked for anything at table—the salt cellar, a piece of bread, a teaspoon. If you did not watch, he went without. You could not surmise if he liked or disliked anything served. He always took the same small portion. And, the way he held his work! If Rome had combed the thirty-one United States for two more incompatible bishops, it would be no easy matter to find a match for the combination of Neumann and Wood.

Still Wood was in constant admiration of his senior's deep scholarship. He knew, too, that Neumann was a very holy man. Late at night, across the hall, he could see the lamplight under Neumann's closed door. Often he heard him at his prayers, at his private acts of penance. Did the man ever go to bed? (The housekeeper claimed that he slept on the bare floor.)

But why did he have to give everything away, like a child with no sense of values? Wood did not countenance the queues of people that came to Neumann for alms. Such indiscriminate charity! He had seen him give a good black hat to an obvious faker. Coming downstairs one afternoon he stared in horror at two small girls carrying a marble statue out of the reception room. "Where are you going with *that?*" Wood had asked.

"Home," piped Margey McSheffrey. "The *Bishop* gave it to us."

The way she had said "the Bishop" riled Wood for an instant. But she was only a child! He was tempted to snap:

"Am not I a bishop too?" That was a touchy point. He had come to Philadelphia believing that Neumann was resigning, that once the legal detail of property transfer had been arranged, Neumann was going back to his Redemptorists, and he, John Frederick Wood, would be Bishop of Philadelphia.

"Bumbling little bumpkin! Giving an art treasure to a child!" Next, he would give the dinner table to some Kensington Hausfrau, and for luncheon, they'd sit on the floor! If old Neumann ran the diocese anything like his household, no wonder the cathedral was unfinished!

To Bishop Wood, Neumann seemed a doddering old veteran, though in age they were just two years apart. The hardships of frontier living, chronic illness untended, the deliberate privations of a lifetime—all have ways of aging a man beyond his years.

It came as no surprise to Bishop Wood when Neumann placed him in charge of diocesan finances, including the completion of the cathedral.

"Be not too sanguine about the cathedral," Neumann had counselled. "You may find Philadelphia a bit slow to part with money even for a good cause."

Politely Wood accepted, taking the counsel with a grain of salt. After all, he knew his Philadelphia better than Neumann—he was born here at Front and Chestnut Streets. After all, he knew more about banking and finance than gullible, guileless old Neumann. With his accustomed zeal and energy, Bishop Wood plunged into his new assignment.

No doubt he would have been eminently successful in raising record-breaking quotas for the cathedral, had not the whole country plummeted into one of the worst financial debacles in its history. And just seven weeks after Bishop Wood took charge. But thanks to his experienced hand, the diocese did not go bankrupt, as did many bigger institutions. Thanks, too, to his presence in Philadelphia, Neumann was able to continue the important work of pastoral visitations through the mountains.

Construction on the cathedral proceeded at its normal, slow pace. If the yearly quota of funds did not exceed those of previous years, at least they matched the in-take of "guileless, gullible old Neumann." By June of 1859, the cathedral roof was practically finished. Steeplejacks were erecting the scaffold round the dome.

"We must solemnize the placement of the cross," said Neumann one day at lunch.

The copper sheeting was now on roof and dome. The final touch on the exterior would be the cross, a mammoth upright of Florida pine, twice the height of Neumann in his mitre. The date was set for September, feast of the Exaltation of the Cross.

"I put all the arrangements in your capable hands, Bishop."

Wood did not ask Neumann to repeat. He had caught every word. For special preacher, Wood invited his friend Martin John Spalding of Louisville. Neumann made no objection, though personally he would have asked Archbishop Kenrick of Baltimore who had begun the cathedral in 1847. He did object, however, when Bishop Wood said:

"Of course, we'll expect you to officiate."

For the first time Neumann alluded to his health.

"No, Bishop. I would prefer if *you* would officiate. Of late I have not been feeling myself . . . dizzy spells . . . a sharp pain in the chest."

He mentioned a sick spell up in Williamsport, how Father John Bach up there had brewed a powerful broth, made him sip it piping hot, till he had emptied the bowl.

"I don't know what he put in it—rum, I suspect! But it did me a world of good."

Wood had observed how haggard he looked after the last visitation tour.

Neumann, however, made it plain that he wanted Bishop Wood to officiate at the cathedral ceremony on September fourteenth.

"If you insist, Bishop." James Frederick Wood was all smiles.

Only recently had it dawned on Neumann's uncomplicated soul that Wood had been expecting him weekly, monthly to retire. The idea had never crossed Neumann's mind. How could he retire? Had not Rome made him bishop, and that was God's will? Rome, too, must have reason for not dividing Philadelphia.

"It must be a hard cross for poor Bishop Wood, but there's nothing I can do."

Some ten thousand people gathered that September afternoon at Logan Square as the glittering cross was lifted into the sky. Bishop Wood, in full pontificals, pulled the rope that hoisted and set the cross in position. The seminarians from St. Charles' next door sang to perfection. Bishop Spalding preached eloquently on the triumph of the Cross. Even the boys from the new college at Glen Riddel, with their four professors, were on hand in cassock and surplice. Alongside young Father Jerry Shannahan, rector of Glen Riddel, stood Bishop Neumann in a plain linen surplice, happily lost in the throng.

That summer he had purchased the property at Glen Riddel. Daringly he had borrowed the money—so important it seemed to have a preparatory college for young aspirants to the priesthood. Here, in the new cathedral in years to come, these boys would be ordained for the diocese of Philadelphia! Glen Riddel was the apple of his eye.

Said Bishop Neumann to Father Jerry Shanahan:

"I shall be out to talk to the boys at their pre-Christmas retreat . . . if not before."

20. THE TWELVE DAYS OF CHRISTMAS

Christmas was twenty-three days away. The first week of Advent was almost over. Early that Friday morning, the Bishop was on his way uptown on special business.

Girard College was in darkness, its orphan boys still deep in dreams. St. Joseph's hospital at Schuylkill Eighth was astir. A bonneted Sister of Charity moved past a lighted first-floor window on her morning rounds of the beds.

This recurrent gripe in his vitals, though? Really, he should see a doctor. But not today! The brisk walk had relieved it somewhat, anyway. There. It was practically gone.

With quick, short steps, the Bishop continued east along the unpaved road, crossing Broad Street. . . .   Thirteenth . . . Tenth . . . Eighth . . . the beads in his coat pocket edging through his fingers. It ought to be pretty close to six o'clock by now.

A few blocks ahead rose the low drone of trade, the sputter of pitch-flare and lantern, farmcarts, customers, peddlers raising the usual din at the Franklin Street markets. But the markets gave little clue to the time. The meat-stalls across from the church started business at four in the morning every day of the year.

Bishop Neumann stopped short at Sixth Street to let the horsecar go clattering past him, on the early run from Southwark to Frankford. A panting boy, surplice tucked under his coat-sleeve, shot across Fifth Street.

" '*Morgen, Herr Bischof!*"

The boy ran for dear life into St. Peter's. The Bishop, passing the church door, tipped his hat and slipped out of view. He had spoken to no one. Nor did he speak to Brother Christy, when he opened the rectory door.

"Good morning, Bishop."

Neumann nodded politely. Today was his December day of recollection, the day a religious keeps for God and his soul. Each month, he tried to make his retreat as early as possible. One never knew what might turn up.

"Your room is ready."

Smiling, the Bishop climbed the stairs to the *Praelatura,* across the hall from the oratory, on the second floor.

Down the corridor hurried Father Lawrence Holzer on the way to his office.

"*Benedicite,* Father Rector."

The Bishop, looping the fifteen decade rosary in his cincture, genuflected and made the sign of the cross. On retreat day, he was simply a member of St. Peter's community. That day, as far as the diocese went, the Bishop was dead. The only John Neumann in Philadelphia was a short Redemptorist with a ring on his finger, making preparations in the oratory for a seven-thirty Mass.

The Bishop's presence caused no commotion. Everything at St. Peter's went at its normal pace. Bells rang for community acts. The Bishop obeyed them, going to choir, to Particular Examen, to meals. He was paid no attention, could browse in the library, say Stations along the corridor, undisturbed. He could kneel half the afternoon and evening in the oratory, looking out at the main altar of the church, alone with his prayers.

"Jube, Domine, benedicere."

They are assembled for luncheon in the refectory. Father Giessen, appointed reader of the week, bows, asking blessing of the Hebdomadary, whose turn it is that week to read the prayers.

"May the King of glory grant to us all a place at his heavenly table."

Young Father Heymann pronounces the blessing in Latin. But when it comes time for the blessing of the meal, the blessing of all present, Father Hebdomadary pauses.

Bishop Neumann, at the head of the table, makes the sign of the cross and says the prayer. Father Rector has abdicated his place. That is the only mark of deference accorded the Bishop all day.

"Te Deum laudamus."

Luncheon over, priests and brothers walk two by two, up to the oratory, reciting the *Te Deum* in alternate verses. A cushioned *pre-dieu* has been placed in the oratory. The Bishop passes it by, kneels on the floor behind the Brothers.

"Praised be Jesus and Mary ever Virgin," the signal for common recreation.

But the Bishop has vanished. Maybe he has gone to his room! More likely, he had already put on an apron in the kitchen, to help dry the dinner dishes with the Brothers. As rector at Pittsburgh, at Saratoga Street, he had often performed that act of humility prescribed by Redemptorist Rule. Call it an inverse status symbol—assurance that he still belonged.

"You're coming for Christmas, Bishop?"

Night Prayer was over. The Great Silence had commenced. Now divested of Redemptorist gear, the Bishop in civilian coat and tie is standing with Father Holzer at the threshold of the Fifth Street door.

"Yes, Father Rector, for Midnight Mass. But I shall be back before that. *Benedicite,* Father."

He was on his way, walking over to Broad Street and down toward home.

At the corner of Vine, a shivering newsboy held up his three last *Evening Bulletins.*

"Read all about. *John Brown hanged today in Virginia!* Extra! Paper, mister?"

Bishop Neumann hurried on toward Logan Square, his coat collar buttoned against the bitter cold. Hanged! He thought of a windy January morning, fifteen years ago, in Old Town when he stood at the gallows in the yard of the Maryland Penitentiary with a man convicted of the murder of two wives. He had absolved the man, preparing him for death. He had prayed with him, high on the scaffold platform, the noose already on the man's neck. John Neumann could readily picture the hanging of John Brown. He remembered the eerie quiet, the trap banging open, the rope squealing with strain.

He knew, too, how waiting felt, the noose about your neck. There was a wintry afternoon in March of 1837, in the lonely woods between Cayuga Creek and Williamsville, when masked men waylaid John Neumann. They had the rope on a hickory limb, the halter on his neck. He should now be dead had not a band of Tonawanda braves come padding through the woods in the nick of time.

Walking through Logan Square, the Bishop thought of Harper's Ferry, with its busy arsenal that John Brown had tried to capture. He saw in memory the high green hills where the Potomac and the Shenandoah rush together. Louden Heights he remembered well, the tilted streets he had climbed on many weekend trips from Old Town, when he was a brand-new Redemptorist —that happiest time of his life.

John Brown was tinder for the Abolitionists of Philadelphia. All that day, while Neumann had been on retreat at St. Peter's, there had been meetings of protest, with many fiery speeches. Chief of Police Ruggles, with a band of the city's finest, had had trouble keeping peace.

The following Sunday, while the Bishop pontificated at the pro-cathedral on Thirteenth Street, a pinewood box from Virginia was gently unloaded at Broad and Prime. A small crowd of Abolitionists had gathered at the depot. Actually, the coffin was half filled with sand: a ruse of Mayor Henry's to maintain order in the city. While the Bishop preached that second Sunday of Advent, the body of John Brown, in another pine box, was quietly smuggled across Philadelphia to the Walnut Street docks en route to New York.

Christmas was three weeks away. For the children, it could not come soon enough. Three weeks was a long time to be on good behavior. In the parish schools of the diocese, sisters were frantically stitching robes for Shepherds and Madonnas, pasting and curling tissue for Archangels' wings, busily coaching Nativity pageants.

For solid weeks Reed Street rang with off-key carols.

"We'll surprise Bishop Neumann when he comes to St. Alphonsus'," Sister Bernardine told her seventh-grade boys. She did not say which way she meant that word "surprise."

Down at Pine and Seventh Street, Mrs. Ward already had the Bishop's assurance that he would be there for the school play on Friday, December 23. Mrs. Ward was the lone teacher at Father Barbelin's little school for the Negro children of Southwark.

But there would be no school play at Honesdale. The combination church-school of St. Mary Magdalene, up in the coal districts, had been in use only five weeks, when it burned to the ground on the night of the second Sunday of Advent.

The choir boys of St. John's missed no rehearsals. They never did, before Christmas. This year they were to sing Mozart's

Twelfth Mass. Father Dan Kelly's altar boys at St. Michael's in Kensington stood in the sacristy as sedately quiet, for a change, as the very seraphim. Even Father Mariani's young Italians of Fitzwater Street were on time for the early Masses on week days. And there was peace on earth in the Northern Liberties: the Irish lads of St. Michael's had declared a truce with the boys of "Dutch Pete's"—no snowball battles till after Christmas morning.

On a Thursday night, with Christmas only ten days off, fire broke out in the wooden rectory at Bellefonte, up at the end of the diocese. Hurriedly, Father Vandergun, O.S.B., shipped his dented, fire-damaged chalice down to Logan Square.

"I'll need it for Christmas," he urged.

Late Saturday afternoon, the package arrived—four hours after Bishop Neumann had left for a quick visitation of Delaware. The following Wednesday, four days before Christmas, when the Bishop returned from Wilmington and New Castle, he found the package waiting in the rectory. At once, he put on his hat again and walked down to Rosebauer, the goldsmith.

"They need for Christmas up in the mountains. Pack it for shipment. Bishop Wood will see that it gets off, in case I am not around."

As previously promised, Neumann went to visit the preparatory college at Glen Riddel next day. He wanted to talk to the boys before the holidays. On Friday he attended two school pageants. He had to visit his Franciscan Sisters, too, and their pupils on Reed Street. He could not disappoint Mrs. Ward's dark angels, either.

In the flurry of coming and going, Bishop Neumann thought no more of the chalice. But Bishop Wood gave it to young Father Quinn, the secretary, who put it on the last Pennsy freight out of Callowhill Street depot on Friday afternoon.

After the two Christmas plays, Bishop Neumann set out for St. Peter's, stopping off at St. Clare's on the way. St. Clare's was motherhouse of his newly founded sisterhood. "House" was the word! It was hardly more. Its handful of tenants were literally the poor of St. Francis. At the moment, Mother Francis had nine copper pennies in her purse. And Christmas two days away.

The Bishop speedily learned of the dire straits of his brave band of sisters.

"I'm sorry but I've brought along nothing holy to give you, sisters. But the *Christkind* is good! Here are a few Yankee medals to make your Christmas happy. And," he added, "say a prayer for someone much sicker than he looks."

On the kitchen table he placed a small cloth sack with fifty gold dollars, fresh from the mint.

At St. Peter's, Brother Christopher was expecting the Bishop. He came every Thursday or Friday for confession. Afterwards, they often exchanged a few words.

"I've just put up the Crib in church, Bishop." Brother Christy was proud of his handiwork.

"Good. I'll see it when I go over to make a visit to the Blessed Sacrament."

The Bishop stopped short and looked earnestly at Christopher.

"If you had your choice, Brother, would you prefer a sudden death to a long, lingering illness?"

"I think I'd want the long illness—to get my accounts ready."

"That's the important thing, being ready; but I should not like to linger on and be a bother to others."

Neumann went up the stairs to his confessor's room.

At supper that evening the Bishop remembered the chalice.

"Yes, Bishop. It's taken care of. They'll have it at Bellefonte on time. I sent it off on the train this afternoon while you were at Reed Street."

It would be a white Christmas in Philadelphia. All Saturday afternoon and evening, as Bishop Neumann sat hearing confessions in the cathedral chapel, he heard the stamping of feet at the Race Street doors: people shaking the snow from their boots. But by eleven that evening, when he stepped outdoors and set off for St. Peter's, the sky was clear again. A full Christmas moon shone over everything.

Sleighbells jingled past him as he made his way along Spring Garden Street to the rectory of the Assumption. His Vicar General, Father Carter, accompanied him across town to St. Peter's.

Deliberately, no announcement had been made of pontifical Mass at midnight, but St. Peter's was crowded with Irish as well as Germans. It was the only midnight Mass in the city. The church smelled of evergreens. Oil lamps and tall wax candles gave a homey warmth to everything on so cold a night. When the choir, men and boys, sang *Stille Nacht* over the strains of the violins, tears welled up even in Irish eyes. One need not know the German words to sense the spirit of the lovely melody. Happily, there was no untoward disturbance from tipsy intruders during sermon or pontifical Mass.

"Sit nomen Domini benedictum."

Father Carter placed the mitre on Bishop Neumann's head. Taking the crozier, the Bishop lifted his gloved right hand for the threefold blessing at the end of Mass.

"Pater. . . ." He winced, gasped slightly. A bolt of raw pain had rammed through his ribs.

"et Filius. . . ." The cold sweat oozed in beads through his ashgray skin. The mitre seemed to tighten on his skull.

"et Spiritus Sanctus." Propping his weight on the crozier, he inched round to the altar. Then the pain ebbed away. The spell suddenly passed.

Merrily, the organ began anew, the choir broke into the recessional, Bishop and attendants moved slowly out of view.

"Merry Christmas!"

"Frohe Weihnachten," from many Germans.

"Nodlaig maith dhuit," from the occasional old Irishman to his crony.

The crowds poured out into Fifth Street and set out for home.

"I did not like the Bishop's color tonight at all. He should take better care of his health," Frederick Horstmann said to his seminarian son.

"Last Thursday, Dad, he made a strange remark at Glen Riddel."

Young Ignatius Horstmann told how the Bishop had been out to give the boys a talk during their retreat. "His first words to us were: *'This may be the last time I shall talk to you.'* "

The dry cold air of the streets made the Bishop feel better. Between the housetops, the sky jostled with stars—like his home-town of Prachatitz, thought Neumann, that last Christmas at home. Down Twelfth Street the two made their way, Bishop and Vicar General.

"Merry Christmas again, Bishop."

Father Carter left him at Spring Garden near the rectory. Neumann continued homeward, turning west on Vine Street for Logan Square.

Few Catholics had homes in this sedately residential part of Vine Street. On either side, houses were shuttered in darkness, the occupants long asleep. It was almost two in the morning. Few sleighs were abroad. Down the middle of the street went the Bishop, where walking was less treacherous than elsewhere.

Crossing Thirteenth Street, he saw to the left the pulsing bright windows of the third house from the corner—Quayne's. From Christmas eve until Twelfth Night it was the negihborhood's holiday showplace. In the wide parlor window stood a blue spruce atwinkle with lighted, finger-size candles, at least two dozen of them. Slim icicles of clear glass, peppermint canes, baubles of many colors dangled by threads from every bough of the tree. A beautiful picture.

Christy Quayne (the "Christy" stood for "Christmas," his nickname) was neither German nor Catholic. But the Bavarian custom of making a live chandelier of an evergreen caught his Dickensian fancy and, in the spirit of the merry season, he had promptly adopted it himself. He had even imported trinkets from Nuernberg to give his tree the authentic touch. There, in his parlor window, it awed the stranger, delighted the chance passerby on Vine Street, enchanted small children from all Philadelphia. And for the many guests of Cr. Christopher Quayne, between sips of sherry cobbler and nibbles of frosted mince cakes, the tree evoked endlessly gay conversation.

As the Bishop walked up the street, softly from inside the house came the tinkling notes of a spinet, playing *Greensleeves,* that haunting Old English folk tune. There was singing too, and occasional laughter. At the hitching post near the curbstone stood a vacant red sleigh and a blanketed horse, snuffing white vapor in the cold. Nearby, stood a hatless waif of a lad, minding the parked sleigh for the visitors inside.

"Aren't you cold, boy?"

The bishop stopped a moment, talking to the ten-year-old. Cold air blew through the boy's thick hair, through the thin weave of his jacket.

"Here," said the Bishop. "Wrap this around your head, so your ears won't fall off."

"Thank you, sir, and Merry Christmas."

The boy took the black woolen scarf and did as told.

Turning from Vine into Logan Square, Neumann caught a glimpse of the new cathedral, snow on roof and dome, with the moon spilling glory on everything. Almost as lovely as Prague!

"Next year, perhaps . . . or the year after, we can have midnight Mass at the new cathedral."

Meg Bradley met him at the rectory door.

"I have hot chocolate on the fire for you, Bishop. You must be faint with the hunger, and you fasting since lunch."

But Bishop Neumann was ready to say his second Mass at once in the chapel. Resignedly, Meg Bradley knelt down in the rear of the chapel, praying her rosary through the Mass of the Shepherds, and worrying about "little Bishop Neumann's" health.

He made his thanksgiving before the figure of the Infant Jesus. Then, according to his Order's Christmas custom, he renewed his Redemptorist vows. Tomorrow he could hardly go back to St. Peter's for the community ceremony. He must pontificate at the ten o'clock Mass at St. John's.

"Margaret, I shall not be home in the afternoon," he informed the housekeeper. "I'm to have Christmas dinner with the orphans out at Tacony. I'm bringing them presents too."

Meg Bradley shook her gray head. It would be at least two o'clock in the afternoon before he touched a bite. It was inhuman, all this fasting of his. And he looked so *poorly,* anyway! After that long walk through the cold night, not a morsel of color in his face. In all probability, Bishop Wood would be dining out too, with some of his west-end friends. That left young Fathers Quinn and McMonigle, the two curates, to do justice to her Christmas roast.

Newly ordained Father Quinn was serving both as curate and secretary at Logan Square. He had a good legible hand, as neat as engraving, and the bishops gave him plenty of practice. Bishop Neumann was clearing up his deskwork before the year's end. He had written to Rome, petitioning that SS. Peter and Paul be made official patrons of the diocese. He had written—and Tom Quinn had snorted with mirth as he copied the Bishop's Latin— a request for permission for two country pastors to wear toupees in church. The cold mountain air on their pink pates gave them perpetual colds each winter, they said. Father Quinn had made a note to watch for either of the pair when next they appeared at Forty Hours or a funeral.

It was the sixth day of Christmas, the last day of the old year. In the afternoon mail came word from Bellefonte that the chalice had not yet arrived.

Neumann looked at Wood. Wood, in turn, looked at the curate. Father Quinn gulped.

"It must have got lost," was his only explanation for the two bishops. "I gave it to the baggage master with my own hands. I paid the freight. Here's the receipt."

Neumann thought of two Benedictines up in Bellefonte with but one chalice between them. They had several outmissions: Snowshoe, Sinnemahoning . . . and . . . he had the other written down upstairs, in his visitation book.

"Never mind, Father." Neumann saw Father Quinn's embarrassment. "I have an old chalice upstairs somewhere. If we can get Mr. Rosenbauer to replate it for us quickly, we can have it up to Bellefonte in a few days."

Neumann looked at Father Quinn.

"You don't even know where Bellefonte is, do you, Father?"

"No, Bishop."

"I had my nephew up there two years ago, on a six-week visitation. Maybe next spring, we can take you along, Father, to see a bit of Pennsylvania."

Sitting at his desk that New Year's eve, the Bishop read a

letter from Milwaukee. Mother Caroline had been thinking of him lately, she wrote. Gratefully, she recalled the long journey she had made with him as Redemptorist superior—from Baltimore to Pittsburgh, then Milwaukee, Buffalo, Rochester, Manhattan, Philadelphia and back to Old Town. In every Redemptorist parish along that route, her Sisters now were teaching school.

"God bless your kindness, Bishop Neumann," she had written. "To the School Sisters of Notre Dame, you are our founder in America."

New Year's eve, *Sylvesterabend,* as they called it in German. After supper tonight at St. Peter's, three small boxes would be set down on the refectory table. Father Rector would invoke the Holy Spirit in the prayer that begins community acts. One by one, in order of religious profession, his confreres' names would be read from the *tabella.* For each name read, the youngest priest would dip his hand at hazard and pluck a slip of paper from each of the three boxes: a patron Saint for the new year, an intention to pray for, a special virtue to practice. The Bishop would be first. His name stood at the head of the list on St. Peter's *tabella.*

Later, Father Rector would conduct Year's End services in church: prayers, a sermon and Benediction. The sermon was traditional, ever the same theme. Neumann had preached it often as rector himself. He knew it by heart; a glance at the past, a glance into the future, with resolutions for the coming year. It was a talk on the precious gift of time.

Reminiscing, the Bishop glanced at his own past. Here he was: three months short of forty-nine years old, three months short of eight years Bishop of Philadelphia. How much time was left? He brushed the question aside. That was God's business, not his. As Dante had said: *"In sua voluntate è la nostra pace." In God's will lies our peace of heart.*

This coming year, he must go to Rome again for the *ad limina* visit to the Holy Father. His own father was now eighty-six and growing blind. He was quite feeble, Louise had written from Prachatitz. Another visit would please the old gentleman no end. But glancing at the wall map of the diocese, the Bishop thought of the time a visit to his homeland would take from his pastoral visitations. There was still so much to do: more churches, and priests to staff them; new schools, and sisters to teach in them.

If he reached Prague this new year, he must make arrangements with the Sisters of St. Charles Boromeo, for a group to come to Philadelphia. He could find a task for them: a new orphanage, a hospital, an industrial school. The New World would make their numbers grow. He thought of the little handful of School Sisters of Notre Dame that first came to Baltimore in 1847, and his own Order of St. Francis that, though not yet five years old, was increasing every year. He thought of the "Blue Nuns," the Sisters of the Immaculate Heart of Mary, at Susquehanna and Reading, the sisterhood founded in Michigan by his confrere Father Gillet.

Vocations to the Sisterhoods were bountiful. Girls at Chestnut Hill were joining the Sisters of St. Joseph. At Eden Hall, many felt inspired to spend their lives as Ladies of the Sacred Heart. The Sisters of the Good Shepherd were filling their convent down on Walnut Street near the Schuylkill. It was the sign of God's blessing on the Sisters. Their good example was attracting recruits to continue the work tomorrow. The Bishop could not count the number of Profession ceremonies he had attended in the convents of Philadelphia.

Downstairs, the hall clock ticked on toward twelve.

At his own Seminary of St. Charles, there now were some forty in preparation, and at Glen Riddel he had more than twenty-five youngsters anxious to wear the cassock and study Theology.

His Redemptorists, too, were attracting recruits. Down at Cumberland, the House of Studies was overcrowded: over fifty students. And at Annapolis, thirty-two novices. He had been invited down to Cumberland next spring to ordain three of them priests. Now that his nephew was there, John Berger, professed not quite a year, Cumberland had an added inducement. And Father Franz Seelos, he smiled, was Rector there and Prefect of students.

The wheels of the hall clock downstairs whirred noisily. *Bong!* Simultaneously, from all directions, steeples and belfries counted off midnight. Philadelphia blew fish-horns, laughed, shook straps of harness bells, shouted greetings to 1860, put fingers in mouth and whistled rowdily for joy.

Now came a humming, a high pitched whine like a giant mosquito buzzing at the Bishop's face. The whole room seemed to heave and sway as in an earthquake. It pitched to and fro like a ship's cabin in high seas. Neumann clenched the corners of the writing table, his skull throbbing as though all the bell-tongues of the world were at large in his brain. A white-hot wire drew tight around his chest, tighter.

"Passio Christi, conforta me. Passion of Christ be my strength," he whispered.

The spell lasted less than a few seconds but, for that reeling interval, John Neumann felt nauseous unto death.

"Happy New Year."

Someone shouted across Logan Square. A sleigh-load of singing merrymakers skimmed along the new snow of Schuylkill Fifth (Eighteenth Street, as they now were calling it). In the hallway the clock ticked through the first hour of the new year.

Next morning at breakfast, the seventh day of Christmas, Meg Bradley observed to young Father Quinn:

"Bishop Neumann looks as though he has seen a ghost! He doesn't look well at all, at all."

To which, the curate-secretary retorted:

"For a sick man, he's doing a lot of writing!" Father Tom Quinn had a sheaf of letters waiting to be mailed first thing on Monday morning.

The eighth day of Christmas. Bright and early, the Bishop went down to his friend Rosenbauer the goldsmith.

"George, we have a little emergency."

He produced the tarnished old chalice.

"Could you make it like new in two or three days?"

"I'll do my best, Bishop Neumann. By Wednesday night, I'll have it back to you at Logan Square."

"Vergelt's Gott—May God reward you, George." At the door the Bishop turned back, smiling. "And a Happy New Year."

The tenth day of Christmas. By nightfall, the chalice had not come from the goldsmith. But Bishop Neumann had other things on his mind. He had kept to his room, except for meals, nursing this numb ache at the base of skull, a drowsy lassitude of body that made it almost an effort to open his eyes. He had never felt this way before.

Father Sourin, his old Vicar General, turned Jesuit, dropped in for a brief social call. Shocked at Neumann's looks—the yolk-like color of his eyes, the greenish cast of his skin—he said to him:

"Would you mind, Bishop, if I called in a doctor?"

"I'll be all right again tomorrow." Neumann confessed that he had felt bad and good alternately for almost three weeks. But the headache seldom improved. Pills? Medicine? No. He had not bothered.

For lunch on Thursday, the eleventh day of Christmas, he had eaten hardly anything, just picked at the food.

The door-bell tinkled.

"That was Mr. Rosenbauer with your chalice, Bishop," said Meg.

"Thank you, Margaret."

"If you want," volunteered Tom Quinn, "I'll take it up to the depot. We could catch the 3:15." He broke into a grin. "That is, if you trust me!"

"No. I haven't been outside since Monday. The air may do me good," said Bishop Neumann. "Besides, I have a little business up near Broad Street. I'll take it myself."

Meg Bradley answered the door-bell shortly after lunch. It was a priest who told her that he was an old friend of Bishop Neumann's. He was just passing through from Pittsburgh, and he dropped in to say hello.

"Father, he's not well today. Go up, if you want."

Instead of tapping at the Bishop's door, Father Urban walked in unannounced, to surprise him.

Neumann, dressed in street clothes, was writing at his desk. He looked up blankly at the figure in the doorway. He could not bring his eyes into focus.

"Benedicite, Father! Greetings from Pittsburgh."

But the Bishop seemed neither to hear nor see. He rubbed his eyes with his hand.

"Father Urban, Bishop. Don't you know me?" said the caller.

"Yes, Father. I am glad that you came. You can save me a trip to St. Peter's for my weekly confession. I don't feel quite myself today."

"For a moment, Bishop, you had me worried," said Urban.

He told of the German Mission starting Sunday on the east side of Manhattan. Five Redemptorists were meeting in Philadelphia, leaving on Saturday for New York.

Neumann asked about Bayardstown.

"Have they finished the tower of St. Philomena's yet?"

He had been up there last November to confer Minor Orders on a young Redemptorist, stationed there for his health. The tower, when completed, was to rise two hundred and twenty-five feet from the street. It was to be capped with a spire of cast-iron filagree-work, the first in the country.

"No, Bishop. The spire isn't finished yet. But five bells have been ordered for next spring. That will be a job for you—to consecrate them for us." Father Urban took a folded sheet of paper from his pocket.

"I was at St. Peter's for dinner, Bishop. When I told them I was coming down to see you, they gave me this: your Intentions for 1860."

Slowly the Bishop opened the paper and read:

Patron: Mary Immaculate
Intention: For Catholic Schools
Virtue: Live each day as though it were your last.

Smiling, he folded the paper again and put it in his coat pocket.

"Thank them for me, Father Urban. And tell Father Rector that I hope to be at St. Peter's on Monday or Tuesday—for my retreat."

Downstairs, the hall clock struck two.

Father Urban knelt on the floor a moment. "May I have your blessing on the Mission next Sunday? Then, I must be off on a few errands downtown."

Bishop Neumann slowly made a sign of the cross over the kneeling missionary.

"Take care of your health, Bishop." Father Urban, standing now, wagged his finger. "We'll need you in Pittsburgh next April to bless the new bells."

"Father, we go when it is God's will."

Shortly afterward, Bishop Neumann gathered a few papers from the writing table and put them in his pocket. He lifted hat and overcoat from the rack and left the room. Immediately, he hurried back again to take the package: the chalice for Bellefonte. Downstairs, he stopped at the chapel to make a visit to the Blessed Sacrament. Putting on his hat, he set out for the Pennsy freight depot up at the corner of Callowhill and Broad.

"How long will it take this to get to Bellefonte?" he asked the freight agent.

"Tomorrow or the next day, sir, at latest."

He paid the shipping cost, put the change back in his pocket with the freight slip and set off east on Callowhill, continuing the rosary as he walked.

Broad Street, Thirteenth, Twelfth, Eleventh. It was a quarter after three. Down Eleventh Street he walked to the law office of Michael Ash. The business took some time. There were papers to sign and counter-sign, to stamp and emboss officially. By the wall clock in the little office, it was now three-thirty.

"Thank you, sir, and God bless you."

The Bishop closed the office door and turned west on Vine Street, heading for Logan Square.

Three-thirty in the afternoon, January 5, 1860. Up at St. Peter's on Fifth Street, Brother Christopher was busily arranging the figures of the three kings and the camel in the Christmas Crib in church. One by one, the Fathers were entering their confessionals. Many penitents were already waiting in the pews.

At Logan Square, Bishop James Wood had opened his red-bound breviary to anticipate the Matins of the Epiphany. *"Christ hath appeared to us. Come let us adore him."* He was reciting the opening verses of the Invitatory.

Three-thirty. Down in Cumberland in the hills of western Maryland, Thursday was a recreation day. Father Seelos had taken six of the Philosophers on a walk toward Frostburg. At the moment, he was describing for Frater John Berger the old days in Pittsburgh, when his uncle, the Bishop, shared his room with the "youngest man in the house."

At the same hour, the same day, a fifty-eight-year-old Redemptorist from Austria was teaching catechism to twenty-seven Negro children on the tropic island of St. Croix. He was telling them of the Christmas star and Balthassar, the black king with golden rings in his ears, who wore ermine and purple robes and brought myrrh to the Child of Bethlehem. The priest was a dear old friend of John Neumann's, Father Joseph Prost, C.SS.R.

At Maria in Monterone in Rome, the Redemptorist Postulator for the Cause of Brother Gerard Majella was hopefully gathering data for the second miracle required for his beatification. Pope Pius the Ninth was at the Vatican, reading in his room.

Three-thirty in the afternoon, January 5, 1860. In Prachatitz, Bohemia, it was already eight-thirty, and a night of stars. Up the snow-piled lane marched five small *Sternsaenger,* piping their carols from door to door: one lad holding a star-shaped paper lantern on a stick, another, the smallest, with a paper mitre, a bishop's staff in hand. The other three were the kings, with gilded cardboard crowns.

They had paused to sing their tuneful rhymes at the door of old Messner, the village atheist. Pipe in mouth, Aloys Messner folded his arms, unmoved by all the folderol. Ultimately, he had a change of heart. To the small boy-bishop with the staff and the paper mitre, he flipped a *Kreuzer.*

"I'm giving you this," said Messner, "only because you faintly remind me of someone I like."

Back in Philadelphia, it is three thirty-six by the wall clock in the office of Michael Ash. The sun slants down the north side of Vine Street, casting a rosy tint on the neat brick homes, glossing the ribboned holly on white colonial doors. The Bishop, fingering the seventh bead of the fifth Joyous Mystery, walks headlong into the glaring sunlight.

"Pray for us sinners now and. . . ."

Bell clappers of pain begin pounding again in his head and chest, pounding so, he can no longer pray.

Turning the corner of Broad Street, come two prancing sorrels, harness-bells ajingle, pulling a gentleman in an open sleigh.

(Neumann's mind plays tricks. Where is he? Across the road, he sees his mother! She is waiting in the Upper Lane, waiting to take him by the hand to Saint Jakob's for morning Mass.) At the corner of Thirteenth Street, the Bishop starts across Vine. The sleigh-driver shouts alarm, grips the reins, slewing his lurching sorrels out of the man's way. The Bishop sees neither sleigh nor horses, only his mother—but where did she go to?

(Sleigh bells. No, they are the bells of his alma mater in Budweis: time for Father Koerner's afternoon Scripture class. John Neumann must hurry or miss that wonderful lecture on Second Corinthians.)

On the shady side of Vine Street, the Bishop continues toward Broad Street, swaying past the first, the second house.

(Father Koerner is reading the inspiring tenth chapter of St. Paul's epistle, firing young Neumann's heart with a yearning to work for souls in wild America. Out of sequence, the phrases resound through the Budweis classroom. *"In journeyings often, in danger from my own people, from false brethren . . . from the Gentiles. . . ."*)

From a curtained window on Vine Street, someone notices the staggering figure, groping for purchase, weaving, half-skating across the snow-scraped walk.

"Disgraceful! People should do their drinking at home."

(*"In journeyings often . . . danger in cities . . . in the woods . . . on the seas. . . ."*)

Desperately, the Bishop clutches the hitching post at the residence of Mr. Christopher Quayne. But knees buckle under him, fingers slacken on the iron ring, he slumps inert into a bank of snow, his black hat skidding across the pavement.

(Like an incantation, the voice of Father Koerner reads on: *"In journeyings often . . . in many sleepless nights . . . in fasting often . . . and in cold."*)

Half a dozen bypassers run toward the crumpled body on the sidewalk.

"Call a policeman, someone," shouts the lady at the curtained window. "After all, this is a respectable neighborhood!"

"Lady, the man is not drunk, he's dying." The sleigh-driver, his sorrels tied, has run back.

"Quick. Get a doctor someone. You, boy. Run."

"Does anyone know him?"

"Look. He's wearing a ring. And aren't those Catholic beads in his hand?"

Another passerby glances down at the crumpled body.

"My God! It's Bishop Neumann." Blessing himself, he hurries the five blocks to Logan Square and down to the cathedral.

Mr. Christopher Quayne, curious at the gathering outside his house, opens the front door. Instantly, he acts.

"Bring the man inside," he orders.

Two men lift the inert body up the three white steps and into Quayne's holiday parlor. The spruce tree stands by the window. A log fire is burning on the hearth. Gently, the two men lay the dying man on the carpet close to the fireplace, a pillow under his head.

Down Race Street to Broad scurries young Father Quinn, oilstock and purple stole in hand. He hurries up Broad Street to Vine.

The Quayne parlor is uncomfortably quiet, the bystanders not knowing what to do for a dying Catholic. Merrily, the pine logs sputter on the hearth not far from the Bishop's head. "By this time, that priest should be here!"

A log slumps on the fireplace, sending up a shower of red sparks. John Neumann takes a quick gulp of air, another. Slowly, he exhales them both. The breathing stops.

Across the room, near the windows, the firelight shimmers gaily on the colored Nuernberg baubles, the glass icicles of the Christmas tree. Mr. Christy Quayne wonders if he should light the candles again tonight.

A hurried knock at the door brings Father Quinn, hatless and out of breath. The Bishop is dead. Nervously, the priest anoints the five senses of the corpse according to the ritual of the Church.

"*Requiem aeternam dona ei, Domine.*" Father Tom Quinn makes the sign of the cross over the man who ordained him.

After many long journeys, John Nepomucene Neumann of Prachatitz and Philadelphia takes his rest.

EPILOGUE

Abruptly, with the last breath of Blessed John Neumann, our story stops.

Beyond that point are dramatic incidents begging for attention. The temptation to pay them heed has not been easy to restrain. The women, for instance, running up North Sixth Street to St. Peter's, breaking the news in breathless gasps to Brother Christy that "the Bishop dropped dead on the street—Vine Street, I think." Less than half an hour before, Father Urban had brought word that Bishop Neumann was coming to make his retreat on Monday or Tuesday. Eventually, he did come to St. Peter's that Tuesday as promised.

We are strongly drawn to dwell on an incidental of the next day, Epiphany, when the body of the deceased was privately laid out in the rectory at Logan Square, before removal to the cathedral chapel. It is merely incidental—but there is the touch of drama: Neumann, dead in the candle-lit reception room; out in the hallway, the clock still ticking the hours; and, in the room upstairs, the Coadjutor writing a letter to inform the Holy See of Neumann's sudden death . . . signing himself for the first time as "Bishop of Philadelphia."

We are inclined to guess at what was found in the pockets of the dead man—a freight-receipt for Bellefonte, a house key, less than half a dollar in loose change, a worn black rosary, a handful of sticky peppermints, a folded paper with the man's intention for the new year of 1860: *Live each day as though it were your last.* We could spin almost a chapter from that assortment, an index of the man who wore the coat.

To describe the funeral cortege would take many pages. Contemporary newspapers touch on most of the details. Black ostrich plumes nodding at the four corners of the glass-walled hearse, drawn by four jet horses moving solemnly down Eighteenth Street to Chestnut, along Chestnut to Thirteenth and up to the pro-cathedral. To date, it was the largest funeral procession that Philadelphia had seen.

Originally, interment was to be in the churchyard at St. John's, where Bishops Egan and Conwell, his predecessors, were buried. Archbishop Kenrick of Baltimore, however, thought St. Peter's the more fitting spot. "Let him rest in death where in life his heart had always been—near his fellow religious." Thus, the body went to St. Peter's. At the pro-cathedral on Monday morning, Kenrick preached a touching eulogy on John Neumann. His fellow Redemptorist and countryman, Father George Beranek, preached in German at St. Peter's on Tuesday before the final obsequies.

It is not easy to keep from studying the throngs who came to view the body, as it lay in state amid lighted tapers, on Saturday afternoon, all day Sunday, in the cathedral-chapel; on Monday evening and all through that night at St. Peter's before the last pontifical *Libera* on January tenth.

Touches of human interest in abundance! Sisters come in their customary twos, some of whom he had clothed in the religious habit, some who settled their vocations with his wise advice; Sisters whose Order he had brought to the diocese, Sisters for whom he had written their first religious Rule.

Priests came. Priests he had ordained, as they stopped by his casket, cast a blessing on the remains. Clean-cut young men were there from Glen Riddel, remembering his softly spoken prediction at the pre-Christmas retreat: "This may be my last chance to speak to you." Older seminarians came from St. Charles' at Eighteenth and Race, alongside the cathedral.

Children came, of course, school tots in whispering wide-eyed queues. His sudden death had brought mixed emotions: his pockets would hold no more peppermints for the best answer at catechism class—but his funeral had brought a windfall of five days free from school! Orphans trooped by with attending Sisters. Mrs. Ward brought two dozen Negro tots from her school on Pine Street.

Up from dock-side slums, from all Philadelphia came the poor: German and Irish immigrants he had befriended with clothing, money, food. People, from God-knows-where, for whom he had done secret favors—they touched their beads to his folded hands. They bent down to kiss his shoes—new shoes, that for once he could not give away. They waited in long lines stretching across Logan Square, reaching the length of Fifth Street and Franklin (Girard Avenue), for a last glimpse.

We are enticed to wonder what Meg Bradley, the housekeeper, said to herself, or to anyone in range, when she first saw, under the "little Bishop's" head, a brocaded purple cushion with heavy silver tassels? And what did Brothers Joachim and Rupert and Christopher think: those with whom he had dried saucers after supper on retreat days? During the Divine Office, did Father Tom Quinn think to look for the two country pastors in their henna toupees? What parish in the diocese that Sunday to Tuesday was holding the Forty Hours devotion?

Questions linger, coaxing for plausible answers. Did Wenceslaus, his younger brother, come up from New Orleans for the funeral; or was the trip too long? The annals of St. Peter's do not tell. But Cumberland was less than a day's train ride away. Yet neither his nephew, Frater John Berger, nor his good friend, Franz Seelos, came to Philadelphia that weekend. Or did they? And what about the newly plated chalice, he had sent to Bellefonte? Did it perhaps arrive that Tuesday morning, as Bishop Neumann was being laid to rest at the foot of the high altar in the basement of St. Peter's?

Should we devote a page or chapter to chronicle his Cause? Tell how, twenty-five years after his burial, Philadelphia took Rome by surprise, petitioning the Holy See for the introduction of the Cause of its fourth Bishop, John Nepomucene Neumann, C.SS.R. No such request had ever come from the United States! The patient investigations began. Forty-six years later, in 1921, Rome declared that John Neumann had practiced virtue in heroic degree and "Venerable" became his title. Forty-two years more go by. More investigation, now the quest for two first-class miracles wrought through Venerable Neumann's intercession. Miracles found and proved beyond doubt, in October of 1963. Rome—and the world—may now call this man *Blessed John Neumann.*

These odds and ends are of interest only to the living. What happened in Philadelphia, Budweis, Rome—anywhere on earth— made small difference to John Neumann after that last slow breath in the Vine Street parlor of Mr. Quayne. Time had run out: time, that John Neumann had made a private vow never to waste. *"Christ hath appeared. Come let us adore Him."* For John Nepomucene Neumann, the Twelfth Day of Christmas was forever.

A POSTSCRIPT FOR SCHOLARS

You may or may not remember the British critic's wry comment on Alexander Pope's translation of the *Iliad:* "A pretty poem, Mr. Pope, but do not call it *Homer!"*

The practicing historian may be tempted to say much the same of this book. "A pretty story, to be sure, but hardly Bishop Neumann!" The comment might be clever, but would it be fair? Does this story give a true-to-life picture of the man Rome beatified in October of 1963? We honestly think so.

We have called it a story. Story it is, not a study nor a chronicle. Carefully, we have sought to avoid a pitfall noted by George Trevelyan in his famous essay on the *Muse of History* that "some writers would seem never to have studied the art of telling a story. There is no "flow" to their events, which stand like ponds instead of running like streams." To give lively flow to the events of Blessed John Neumann's life, we have adopted the style of the storyteller.

But is the story true? If, to your way of thinking, only that is true which can be fully documented, then parts of this story are not true. For example, Pokorny, the postman is not true; nor Meg Bradley, the housekeeper; nor is Christopher Quayne entirely true; nor the seminarian, Dick Phelan. We have given them names and character; we have used them as a device to either bind together or help advance the story. If they are not completely true, does that in any way distort the true-to-life picture of John Neumann?

It is true that someone delivered the mail in Neumann's home town. We gave that someone the name, "Pokorny." Someone, too, was the Bishop's housekeeper at Logan Square, someone beyond the reach of our research. We called her "Meg Bradley" and gave her a bit of a brogue. She helped us mention documented facts about the Bishop, for example, that he ate sparingly, seldom slept in bed, gave away his wardrobe to furnish the room of Bishop Wood.

There are documents to tell us that Bishop Neumann died on Vine Street in the parlor of a non-Catholic, a Mr. Quein. That is all we could find. We have spelled the name "Quayne." We have given him a flair for keeping Christmas until Twelfth Night.

One last instance: someone taught Bishop Neumann Irish. Research does not reveal the priest's name. For this we have used a seminarian, "Red" Phelan. As a matter of fact Richard Phelan is a real person; eventually, he became third bishop of Pittsburgh. We described him accurately in every detail, even that of the bout with Sayres, boxing champion of Great Britain; every detail but one: in the early Fifties the real Dick Phelan was not a seminarian at St. Charles' on Logan Square—but at St. Mary's in Baltimore. In truth, he may never have met Bishop Neumann in his life. There, admittedly, we have taken liberty with history, yet in doing so, we have in no way distorted the person who is our main concern, Blessed John Neumann.

Still, it would be erroneous to assume from the carefree swing of this story, that the whole thing is sheerest fiction. Far from it. Though none of the scientific apparatus of scholarship is in evidence, this book is, actually, the fruit of eight years of intermittent research into the times and background of Blessed Neumann. If the exact wording of dialogue cannot be documented, its content, when important, is drawn from the man's letters and personal diary. If, in the sequence of episode, we have taken liberty, here and there, it was done in the interest of a tighter knit story. One incident, a sick call to an old Irishman and his blind daughter in the Niagara woods, is a composite of details from several separate episodes.

One other incident demands comment, that of the toppled candle and the charred papers that led to the Bishop's establishing the cycle of the Forty Hours in 1853. Both Berger and Curley, our two chief sources for biographical detail, quote a letter from Abbot Wimmer, O.S.B., written some nineteen years after hearing the details from Neumann himself. The letter says that Neumann fell asleep at his desk; the candle tipped, charring the papers. Mulling these facts imaginatively, we found many questions hard to answer. Why should he use a candle without a candlestick? Why use a candle at all, when the cathedral rectory had gas illumination in the 1850's, or oil lamps? If he did fall asleep, and the papers smoldered, why was his hair, his cassock sleeve not singed? Why was he not wakened by the acrid stench of burning? What we did, was keep the tipped candle stub and the charred papers (a map of the diocese) but instead of his falling asleep, we had the doorbell ring, calling him downstairs for ten minutes. To us, it seemed more plausible.

We cannot conclude without a word of deep thanks to our confrere Rev. Michael J. Curley, C.SS.R., who read through the manuscript and made many worthwhile suggestions about historical details. Likewise to Rev. John V. McGuire, C.SS.R., who helped us to edit the manuscript in its final stages.

For research in the libraries of Vienna, for background color and customs of Neumann's homeland, now behind the Iron Curtain, our gratitude to Rev. Franz Huschka, C.SS.R., of Katzelsdorf a.d. Leitha.

Retracing the travels of John Neumann in America, we are indebted to the cheerful kindness of many librarians in the Local History rooms of the Rochester Historical Society, the Buffalo Historical Society, the Carnegie Free Library at Pittsburgh, the

Enoch Pratt Library at Baltimore, and the New York Public Library. Thanks to their assistance, we had old maps of their cities, coach and canal routes, directories, local newspapers and many books that supplied us with more color and detail than we could possibly make use of. We thank them one and all.

To the question, "But is it really Neumann?" it is our honest belief that anyone who knew the blessed priest and bishop, could he read this story, would say "yes, that's the man all right. That's John Neumann."

So, we give you John Neumann, called in turns Father, Bishop, Servant of God, Venerable and now Blessed. May he bless you who read, and may he bless the one who wrote it too.

JAMES GALVIN, C.SS.R.
Mt. St. Alphonsus, Esopus, N.Y.